W9-AMX-715

Dreams of Fiery Stars

Penn Studies in Contemporary American Fiction
Emory Elliot, Series Editor

A complete list of books in the series is available from the publisher.

Dreams of Fiery Stars

The Transformations of
Native American Fiction

Catherine Rainwater

PENN

University of Pennsylvania Press

Philadelphia

Copyright © 1999 University of Pennsylvania Press
All rights reserved
Printed in the United States of America on acid-free paper

10 9 8 7 6 5 4 3 2 1

Published by
University of Pennsylvania Press
Philadelphia, Pennsylvania 19104-4011

Library of Congress Cataloging-in-Publication Data
Rainwater, Catherine, 1953–
Dreams of fiery stars : the transformations of native American fiction / Catherine
Rainwater.
    p.   cm. — (Penn studies in contemporary American fiction)
    Includes bibliographical references and index.
    ISBN 0-8122-3481-2 (cloth : alk. paper). — ISBN 0-8122-1682-2 (pbk. : alk.
paper)
    1. American fiction—Indian authors—History and criticism.   2. American
fiction—20th century—History and criticism.   3. Indians in literature.   I. Title.
II. Series.
PS374.I49R35   1998
813'.540897—dc21   98-49977
                                                                                  CIP

For Bill Scheick

Contents

Prologue
A Universe Perfused with Signs

> Ruth Tate . . . had also visited Horse and said she remembered
> a dream of fiery stars that fell to earth and when they landed,
> everything burned.[1]

In Linda Hogan's novel, *Mean Spirit* (1990), a character dreams of
"fiery stars" that fall to earth and terminate more than five hundred
years of Euro-American domination. Other contemporary Indian
authors, perhaps most notably Leslie Marmon Silko in *Almanac of
the Dead* (1991), refer frequently to various tribal prophecies pre-
dicting the restoration of the "old world."[2] I borrow Hogan's phrase
for the title of this study—*Dreams of Fiery Stars: The Transformations of
Native American Fiction*—because it concerns the counter-colonial,
world-transformative efforts of writers such as Hogan. Over the
past three decades, an ever-increasing number of American Indian
authors have written themselves into the discourse of the dominant
society and encoded it with alternative notions of what it means to
inhabit the earth as human beings. These writers dream of nothing less than revision of contemporary reality, beginning with its
representation in art. I will argue that in their semiotic re-creation
of the world, Native American artists are also "reinventing" tribal
people following their long consignment to silence and stereotypical representation within mainstream culture.

According to anthropologist Michael J. Fischer, "the newer
works" of American ethnic literature lead us to see that "ethnicity
is . . . reinvented and reinterpreted in each generation by each individual."[3] Likewise, in the introduction to a collection of essays on
ethnicity and identity, Werner Sollors notes the frequent use of the

word "invention" by scholars from many disciplines: indeed, the word has apparently "become a central term for our understanding of the universe."[4] I, too, understand ethnicity to some degree as an imaginative construction subject to changes from person to person, generation to generation. Throughout most of United States history, the imaginative constructions of American Indians have been imposed from without by the mainstream society, steeped in its own mythology about indigenous peoples. Serious efforts to listen to the voices of tribal people, to learn how they "invent" themselves and the world, are a recent phenomenon.

My experience of contemporary Native American art suggests to me that semiotic analysis is best suited to study of these cross-cultural constructions. First, Native American philosophy (and the literature informed by it) conveys an inherently semiotic theory of existence. N. Scott Momaday, for example, remarks that "naming confers being," and Gerald Vizenor observes that Native Americans, like semioticians, "locate *being* in discourse."[5] I believe that semiotic analysis is, in fact, necessary to any study of the literature of marginal groups, where we must confront questions about how readers from the dominant culture gain access to the Other's meanings and, more fundamentally, questions about how these readers learn the Other's strategies for producing meaning. "Unreceptive" readers without appropriate responses to the signifying strategies of a writer are doomed to misread, even if they are equipped with historical and anthropological facts about the culture of the Other. Thus any study of the literature of the Other must suggest how readers become receptive to it and must clarify the processes of reception—in Robert Scholes's terms, the processes by which we "connect texts to our own systems."[6]

Semiotic analysis facilitates this essential critical task by attempting to operate from trans-cultural grounds. By "trans-cultural," I do not mean grounds that somehow "transcend" all difference, or grounds that are "culturally neutral" or completely "outside" of any cultural matrix. I merely argue that no matter what our cultural background, our "texts," "our own systems," and the "connections" we make are the products of universally human, sign-wielding behavior. Indeed, according to one leading semiotician, Thomas Sebeok, "There exists a vast array of universes, but, as far as we know, only one of these is inhabited by creatures endowed with the semiotic capacity, on which hinges all knowledge of existence and cosmology, and much besides. A preordained ecosystem, a world tailor-made for its denizens, has inevitably got to be a universe perfused with signs."[7]

Sebeok defines the "anthropic principle" of the universe as that means by which "creatures endowed with the semiotic capacity" affect reality. This principle uncannily recalls Native American epistemology, especially the belief that "story" shapes "reality." Elaborating on the anthropic principle, Sebeok says he is "drawn to [the physicist John] Wheeler's suggestion that the fundamental physical constants, the nuclear and cosmological parameters, and others, are constrained by the unbudging requirement that life evolve, and that these constants are altered by our consciousness of them. In brief, life modifies the universe to meet its needs, and accomplishes this by means of sign action."[8]

As an inhabitant of the western world steeped in the rationalist tradition, Sebeok is struck by the "mind-blowing" implications of Wheeler's post-Enlightenment theory of a "participatory universe."[9] Though they have not, of course, explained themselves scientifically, Native Americans have always taken for granted the idea of such a universe. Far from "mind-blowing," the idea that our words and deeds affect some larger pattern is a pan-tribal assumption. As Leslie Marmon Silko says in an interview, "I am . . . intrigued with how, in many ways, there are many similarities in the effect of the so-called post-Einsteinian view of time and space and the way the old [Indian] people looked at energy and being and space-time."[10]

Silko's allusions to her readings about quantum physics reinforce my own impression that in recent years the informational background of the contemporary reader has expanded to allow for easier access to sophisticated American Indian thought, long dismissed as "primitive" or "superstitious." I do not mean that misreading and misinterpretation no longer occur; nor do I deny that profound cultural differences frequently interfere with mainstream readers' understanding of "marginal" art.[11] The cosmologies of the Euro-American and the Native American are not the same, and the differences are not a matter of one or the other culture's lagging behind in either scientific or metaphysical sophistication. Moreover, many contemporary western scientists and intellectuals (including Wheeler, and even Sebeok) worry legitimately about simplistic notions afloat in the popularized, mystical view of current developments in science. These scientists' understanding of how "consciousness" and "sign action" affect the universe is not necessarily mystical, while tribal, theurgical views of sign action usually are so.

Still, whatever one makes of the current controversy over any alleged metaphysical implications of modern science, the contemporary, mainstream reader has certain bodies of information available (whether such information is scientifically, or only metaphorically, accurate) that facilitate the process of "connect[ing the] texts" of the Native American Other to his or her own systems.[12] From this welter of information, the widely popularized idea of a participatory universe facilitates non-Indian readers' comprehension of how contemporary Native American narrative "connects" to the mainstream semiotic system with the apparent intention of modifying the universe through sign action.

I will presently discuss in detail how, in pursuit of their regenerative, world-altering ends, contemporary American Indian writers draw heavily on oral storytelling traditions as well as on mainstream postmodern developments. Both traditional oral storytelling and postmodern literature demand active audience participation or "performance." Anthropologist Victor Turner explains that "with the postmodern dislodgement of spatialized thinking and ideal models of cognitive and social structures from their position of exegetical preeminence, there is occurring a major move towards the study of processes [such as reading and writing] . . . as performances."[13] In a subsequent chapter, we will note Louise Erdrich's trope, in *Tracks* (1988), concerning the "tribe of pressed trees" that refers subtly to the performative action of a steadily increasing "tribe" of books such as her own and those by other Native American writers; this paper "tribe" aims to revise not simply the record of the past, but the shape of the future, by reinscribing the audience with new rules for constructing self and world.

In pursuit of this and other issues, my study deals with novels written by ten Native American writers over approximately the past twenty-five years. Since 1968, the publication date of N. Scott Momaday's *House Made of Dawn*, a new generation of Native American storytellers has chosen writing over the oral storytelling tradition. While their works necessarily observe many of the conventions of the novel as developed in Anglo-European cultures, Native American written narrative is also profoundly different, even from the postmodern novel with which it has most profitably been compared.[14]

Following the appearance of Momaday's Pulitzer Prize-winning novel, works by writers such as James Welch, Leslie Marmon Silko, Louise Erdrich, Paula Gunn Allen, Gerald Vizenor, Thomas King, Anna Lee Walters, Linda Hogan, and others have proliferated in the literary marketplace and in well-known anthologies of literature.[15] Naturally, their art is by definition "cross-cultural." The very act of writing narrative imposes constraints on these authors that are foreign to Native American literary expression. Thus their works amount to a break with and a transformation of the American Indian storytelling tradition. However, perhaps far outweighing the inevitable losses that come with such change are the benefits of having these works available to the general population (including Native and non-Native Americans, alike). The messages these writers deliver, as well as their manner of delivery, have profound implications for the contemporary world.

The current generation of Native American writers, like their oral storytelling predecessors, insist that humanity makes the world through the stories we tell. The American Indian concept of "medicine" bears a notion of language as a powerful force of creation and destruction. For many tribal peoples, words are action. Their effects are strong and immediate. As we learn from Silko's *Ceremony* (1977), if we tell an "evil" story of "monstrous design," we create disaster. Like Silko's character Tayo, humanity must cure its own sickness by inventing a new story of itself. This preoccupation with individual and collective illness and death as well as with modes of personal and social transformation pervades the otherwise varied and unique narratives of Native American writers. My study focuses on how these works encode at almost every textual level an urgent agenda of regeneration through the power of sign action.

Chapter One ("Acts of Deliverance: Narration and Power") looks at the counter-colonial moves of contemporary "writing Indians" who have learned how to exploit semiotic power relations between authors and audience that are inherent in written narrative. In the process, these writers have also "invented" the "Indian author." Beginning with a discussion of Tzvetan Todorov's claims about the Europeans' semiotic conquest of Native peoples, I explain how Native American writers today employ the self-conscious language games of the colonizers in pursuit of their own ends. Moreover, they artfully manipulate power relations inherent in the semiotic practices of both dominant and marginal societies; they invent methods for opening the dominant discourse to power tactics commonly associated with nonwestern aesthetic forms such as oral storytelling, which emphasizes "paralinguistic" and "kinesic" dimensions of human communication.[16]

In this chapter, I also discuss how contemporary Native American written narrative invents itself within the weakly delineated and unstable social semiotic boundaries characterizing ethnically diverse societies such as that of the United States. This cross-coded, or cross-cultural, writing is best analyzed in terms of its semiotic resistance to the traditional "content of the [narrative] form."[17] A discursive site of ethnosemiotic conflict, contemporary Native American narrative encodes ethnic signs and nonwestern worldviews, yet achieves its full meaning under social and textual conditions defined within the dominant culture. Indeed, in carrying out complex, cross-cultural tasks, contemporary Indian writing subversively enters the dominant discourse and exposes the ways in which both Native and non-Native frames of reference constantly undergo revision. Consequently, works by these Native American authors also collectively challenge traditional assumptions about authority inscribed within written narrative. Redefining authorial power according to a nonwestern agenda, contemporary Indian writing effects social reform through relocation of non-Indian people from positions of authority to positions of listeners and receivers of knowledge.

Chapter One elaborates on these and other issues of narrative management of power with reference to some specific contemporary Indian works. Included in my discussion are Momaday's *House Made of Dawn*, the first of the current generation of Indian novels but possibly the most resistant of them all to conventional western interpretive strategies; Silko's *Ceremony* and Momaday's *The Ancient Child* (1989), two didactic novels in which such resistance is potentially instructive; works by Thomas King that contest western assumptions about the nature and power of representation; and works by Louise Erdrich that frustrate Eurocentric readerly practices and resist western notions of moral and intellectual authority.

Chapter Two ("Imagining the Stories: Narrativity and Solidarity") elucidates ways in which Native American narrative fosters solidarity with the audience and thus revises narrativity—"the process by which a perceiver actively constructs a story from the fictional data provided by any narrative medium."[18] I argue that, to achieve solidarity with an audience, more than the initial deconstructive act of frustrating narrativity must occur. Indeed, a narration merely of resistance cannot fulfill the often-stated regenerative mission of American Indian "story." Fulfillment of this regenerative purpose requires a reader's active participation in a community of semiotic agents who understand how storytelling amounts to world-making. As authors variously deconstruct conventional narrative modes and their readers' interpretive practices, they simultaneously instate and foster alternatives. When shared, these alternatives constitute solidarity bonds. Chapter Two details types of solidarity bonds and methods for achieving them exemplified in specific works by Silko, Erdrich, Momaday, Hogan, Walters, King, Vizenor, and others who play the role of the ritual artist described by Victor Turner. Their ritual art of liminality sets out to expand cultural "metapatterns."

As the title suggests ("Re-Signing the Self: Models of Identity and Community"), Chapter Three examines questions about identity as they arise in a variety of contemporary Native American narratives. Some texts imply the semiotic origins of self. Dialogically related to their western generic counterparts, contemporary Indian narratives frequently rewrite some of the rules for production of identity in texts and in the world. These narratives also interrogate the notion that any essentially "western" or "Indian" self exists independently of semiotic practice (for example, Momaday's often-cited "idea" of himself as "Indian"). This chapter refers to Sebeok's notion of the "semiotic self," and to Hodge and Kress's social semiotic concepts of "modalities" and of "definitions of the real," to elucidate the terms of the semiotic counter-conquest of American aesthetic and philosophical space that I believe Indian writers have recently undertaken. I explore the various conceptions of self and its semiotic origins with reference to particular works by Welch, Momaday, Allen and others who insist that we may *re-sign* our limited and destructive configurations of self and world.

Chapter Four ("They All Sang as One: Refiguring Space-Time") applies a Ricoeurian theoretical context to examine spatial and temporal codes inscribed within traditional narrative forms, which American Indian authors, in turn, employ and reinscribe with alternative spatio-temporal schemas. These conventional codes profoundly challenge Native American writers' imaginations to devise representations of tribal realities that do not conform to western material and mechanical notions of space and time. Their strategies range from the fairly straightforward treatment of the issue at mimetic textual levels to more structurally complex methods enabling expression of the spatio-temporal norms of the Indian "Other." I discuss the management of these issues in works by Welch, Hogan, Erdrich, Momaday, and Silko prior to a detailed examination of spatio-temporal code revision in Walters's *Ghost Singer* (1988).

Chapter Five ("All the Stories Fit Together: Intertextual Medicine Bundles and Twins") investigates forms of intertextuality that unite contemporary Native American narratives with one another as well as with non-Indian fiction and nonfiction. This chapter explores the syncretic function of intertextuality as a mode of shaping Native American as well as mainstream literature. Employing concepts from Indian cultures as metaphors for intertextual phenomena, I discuss certain texts by Momaday, Hogan, King, and others as "medicine bundles," and two sets of paired texts by Silko and Welch as "twins," in order to suggest how intertextuality serves the overall revisionary and regenerative purposes of Native American writing. I also investigate important interconnections between intertextuality and memory that are directly and indirectly implied in the literary pieces I discuss. Works by contemporary American Indian writers present us with ideas of tribal people and realities that become part of a general intertext held in memory. This intertext in turn influences the ways in which we read "textual" worlds and produce "real" ones. Examining intertexts also leads us to important questions about the narrative construction of the "real."

Finally, in the Epilogue ("All We Have Are Stories: Semiosis and Regeneration") I broaden my discussion to consider the role that Native American literature apparently plays within mainstream society today. The literature of the Other seems to respond to some collective longing in mainstream culture; various other media and disciplines besides contemporary ethnic art appear to address this felt need, as well. I conclude that some dovetailing trends in western aesthetics and science suggest an interdisciplinary context within which we may consider such "regenerative" texts as I have focused on throughout my study; within this context, we may also begin to understand the mainstream social unrest and dissatisfaction which contemporary Native American fiction addresses for Indian as well as non-Indian readers.

Chapter One
Acts of Deliverance: Narration and Power

> He was writing for those who would come later, for the next generations and the next, as if the act of writing was itself part of divination and prophecy, an act of deliverance.[1]

In his study of the European conquest of America, Tzvetan Todorov asks how we are "to account for the fact that Cortés, leading a few hundred men, managed to seize the kingdom of Montezuma, who commanded several hundred thousand."[2] According to Todorov, a sizeable European advantage lay in their ability to impose their own versions of truth on people who were epistemologically naive and who thus quickly "lost control of communication" to the invaders (61). Whereas indigenous Americans understood primarily a ritual use of language to maintain the status quo within a cyclic cosmological order, the European invaders were imperialists and millennialists, enlisting language in their own world-transformative purposes (87). European semiotic practice proved devastating to the American Indians, says Todorov. It disrupted their world view and implied godlike, prophetic powers beyond the sixteenth-century Indian's comprehension.

"Power," according to social semioticians Robert Hodge and Gunther Kress, may derive from the "non-reciprocal use of direct speech."[3] The "superiority" and preeminence of a speaker are established partly by the listener's inability to respond, usually owing to lack of access to the meanings and frames of reference of the speaker, or to an insufficient grasp of the speaker's rhetorical moves. Such a speaker makes little or no effort to "instruct" the listener, who struggles internally for semiotic bearings. Non-reciprocal, direct speech asserts and imposes the "reality" of the speaker over that of the comparatively silenced Other. Todorov suggests that Cortés exercised just this kind of power over the Aztecs through a variety of semiotic maneuvers rivaling those of Milton's Satan. For instance, Cortés quickly turned Aztec prophecy to his own advantage, encouraging the Indians to see him as Quetzalcoatl and his actions as fulfillment of prophesied events. Montezuma fell silent and even became socially withdrawn in response to rhetorical strategies that both exploited and undermined Indian reality. Likewise, in North America, the fact that tribal prophecies apparently predicted the arrival of white people had a similar paralyzing effect on Native peoples. Seeing the invaders as a part of the cosmic design amounted to an Indian "reading" of events deemphasizing the threat to Indian reality.

Todorov hardly minimizes the actual physical violence of the Europeans against the Indians, nor does he underestimate the economic and political forces empowering the conquistadors; nonetheless, he claims that the material conquest of America was predicated on a semiotic conquest. And though Todorov asserts no inherent European cultural superiority to the American Indians who fell victim to European ways with words, he explains that, in privileging very different kinds of semiotic practice, Europeans and Native Americans did not meet as equals in power.[4] The Indians had never subjected their own ontological and epistemological assumptions to the self-reflexive, critical scrutiny typical of the invaders. Because they had never justified their beliefs to themselves, they were unable to defend those beliefs when challenged. (Such "justification" and "defense" are, in the first place, basically western philosophical practices.)

Todorov's analysis of "conquest" treats only South American Indians, but his general conclusions may reasonably be applied to North American tribes. Particularly through the Christianizing efforts of missionaries, a comparable semiotic assault on North American indigenous peoples occurred (along with the obvious physical one). Roman Catholic and Protestant missionaries alike mystified the Indians with their apparently miraculous powers of divination connected with reading and writing. Though some tribes were willing to learn the strangers' ways, their acquired knowledge did not lead to equality of power between social groups. Literate, acculturated Cherokees followed the Trail of Tears, for example, and the Navajo began the Long Walk after centuries of coping more or less successfully with the presence of strangers. North and South American Indian cultures were eventually decimated both despite and partly owing to their receptivity to western ways.[5]

Profound loss was not all on the Indians' side, however, as Todorov insists. Though European rhetorical practices, including writing, mystified the Indians and militated against their ritual use of language, Native Americans eventually "learned paper."[6] They learned the language and ways of the Other and how to survive in two worlds—Euro-American and tribal—whereas very few Euro-Americans learned Indian languages. Most could not perceive the Indian's world view, and they saw only superstition in ritualistic language. Even today, as Anna Lee Walters laments in her novel *Ghost Singer*, the average American dismisses Native American ceremonial practices as "hocus pocus."[7] For such blindness, Todorov reminds us, non-Indians pay a price: "victory . . . deliver[ed] a terrible blow to [the European] capacity to feel in harmony with the world. . . . By winning on one side, the Europeans lost on the other; by imposing their superiority upon the entire country, they destroyed their own capacity to integrate themselves into the world."[8]

In today's developed countries such as the United States, the desire to recover this integrative capacity lies at the heart of "multicultural" initiatives. The desire reveals itself most troublesomely in the romantic totalization of the ethnic Other that critics such as Gayatri Spivak, Jane Gallop, and Gerald Vizenor have decried.[9] At the cusp of the twenty-first century, the moral and ethical bankruptcy of some long-cherished western ideals is apparent to many western people, alarmed by signs of social decay and environmental crisis. Thus current fascination with alternative social systems, cosmological paradigms, and communal values probably reveals at least as much about the dominant society's fears as it does about a new respect for the ethnic Other.[10] Cynically, but perhaps justifiably, many Native Americans suspect that the latest cycle of interest in things Indian amounts to yet another form of colonial appropriation, this time of Indian ideas and spirituality instead of their land.

Native Americans' opinions about such appropriation are diverse, but many agree that, no matter what the motive, deliberately cultivating a more generally "Indian" worldview could help solve some contemporary environmental and social problems. Vine Deloria has outlined an alternative environmental ethics and practice, and Eva McKay makes the dominant society this offer: "We have learned about the people in your society . . . who dress differently, who eat differently, who are spiritually different. We have learned. We are asking now that you will come and learn from us." [11] Likewise, when Silko implores her readers in the opening and final pages of *Ceremony* to "accept this offering"—a story emphasizing an Indian vision and way of living on the earth—she suggests that the capacity to "integrate [our]selves into the world" [12] is what all of us had better acquire before it is too late.

This chapter looks at narrational strategies of contemporary Native American writers who believe in the power of storytelling to "fix up the world," as some characters in Thomas King's *Green Grass, Running Water* set out to do. [13] Like King's four "old Indians" and Coyote, these writers know their limitations: " 'It's too big a job to fix it all at once. Even with all of us working together we can't do it. . . . [W]e're going to start small . . . And once we get the hang of it . . . we'll move on to bigger jobs' " (105–6). King is more optimistic than Walters in *Ghost Singer*; though endowed with impressive medicine powers, her characters Jonnie Navajo and Wilbur Snake believe it is "too late" to intervene effectively in a problem that is "bigger than anyone dreams." [14] Nevertheless, deft management of the narrative power inherent in written storytelling constitutes one "small start" for some Indian writers (including Walters) whose fiction embodies counter-colonial semiotic acts.

The Counter-Conquest of America

All discourse, including fictional narrative, contains markers of solidarity and power. "Solidarity" occurs between social entities of equal status who share knowledge and who generally understand and consent to the rules of production and reception of messages between them. By contrast, "power" marks an exchange between social entities in an unequal relationship; the privileged participant either controls knowledge (as when adults determine what children at various stages of maturity shall know), or has superior knowledge or authority with respect to an audience made up of various "unequals" (people with different or less knowledge and less actual or sanctioned authority). Moreover, the same message directed at different receivers may express solidarity with some, and power over others (as when an audience is made up of receivers with different levels or types of knowledge). Power can also shift about among participants in certain types of exchanges.[15]

To attain solidarity or power, the speaker's (or writer's) authority must be acknowledged by the addressee; that is to say, one does not have solidarity or power simply owing to requisite knowledge. Thus the knowledgeable outsider sometimes remains permanently disfranchised when the boundaries of solidarity and power are relatively stable (for example, when female professionals cannot achieve equal status with their male counterparts in a sexist milieu). However, such boundaries are rarely, if ever, thoroughly stable, and their constant renegotiation is fundamental to social semiosis, which always involves some degree of "conflict, disagreement, [and] . . . lack of clarity and consensus."[16] In ethnically diverse societies, the boundaries tend to be vaguely defined and extremely unstable.[17]

If Todorov is correct, during the first-contact years boundaries of power were relatively fixed and stable in the Europeans' favor. Whatever knowledge the Indians might have had, they were unable to maneuver the European invaders into subordinate positions in discourse. However, in the centuries since Cortés confounded Montezuma, Native Americans have grown adept at playing the self-conscious language games of the colonizers and at managing power relations inherent in the semiotic practices of both dominant and marginal societies.[18] Contemporary Native American written narrative invents itself within the weakly delineated and unstable social semiotic boundaries characterizing ethnically diverse societies. Sustained by but exhibiting "low affinity" with mainstream culture, such cross-coded, or cross-cultural, writing makes significant incursions into the dominant discourse and might, in fact, be generally defined in terms of its power negotiations.[19]

Though the semiotic practices of all cultures present both power and solidarity mechanisms, western and Native American traditional narrative forms differ in their emphasis on power versus solidarity.[20] Overall, western narrative emphasizes power, as Barthes, Foucault, and others have shown in discussions of authorship.[21] Despite modern and postmodern violations of rules (violations that have themselves become fairly conventional), western narrative rests on a ground of assumptions about authority. Among these assumptions are the originality (superiority) of the author and his or her privileged relationship to the narrative (the work is "intellectual property"); the authority, if not of the narrative voice, at least of the author "behind the scenes"; and the referential capacity of language as the tool of the author to define "reality" and dispense "truth" about the world. Moreover, western narrative observes principles of coherence and closure according to which characters, events, and details "add up" to make sense (within an assumed epistemological frame of reference). Violations of normative principles (as in modern and postmodern texts) merely testify to their normative power, for when rules are violated, the "message" of the text frequently amounts to a self-conscious critique of normative assumptions. Challenges to referentiality, for instance, take for granted the reader's assumptions about the referential use of language. Moreover, critics tend to "recuperate and naturalize" unconventional texts "by explaining their concealed unity,"[22] or at least by explaining the ultimate message that is presumably conveyed through managed, semiotic breakdown. Perversely, perhaps, we insist on making particular kinds of sense.

Therefore, even when a writer violates conventions—and even when he or she targets authorial privilege itself—a large measure of power remains with the author. If we acknowledge the limitations of authorial control (as in postmodernism and poststructuralist critique), we nevertheless realize that the author knows and expects the reader to know myriad "rules," whether these are observed or transgressed. Indeed, readers of modern literature accommodate deliberate authorial efforts to make reading difficult, and readers of postmodern literature expect to play the "victim" in a hostile, chaotic textual world.[23] Modern and postmodern texts alike thus demonstrate the power of the writer over the reader, who consents to the rules of the game. Solidarity with the audience is, by comparison, limited and derives from writer's and reader's mutual consent to play the "game"; solidarity increases slightly as the reader becomes more adept as a "player" of a text's designated reader-role.

By contrast, Native American oral storytelling has emphasized solidarity.[24] Because the origins of oral literature are communal, stories are not the intellectual property of an "author." Traditional literature, by definition, disallows such power-driven "authorship." (This fact is brilliantly treated in Silko's *Ceremony*, where the ontological status of her storyteller-narrator is held in question, causing the reader to ponder issues of "authorial origination." [25] As we shall see, Silko employs a power tactic in narrative management to effect a change in the reader that will become the groundwork for solidarity; before solidarity can be achieved with the non-Indian members of her audience, however, such power strategies are required to free them from entrenched western assumptions.) A traditional Indian storyteller does not take credit for the story or emphasize his or her own identity but, on the contrary, frequently acknowledges the story's circulation in the community where *it*, not an "author," has accumulated authority. For example, in every Native American language, words meaning "it is said" sometimes introduce statements. Such conventional expressions simultaneously proclaim the collective sanction of the remark or story and obscure any implied origins with a particular speaker. Moreover, whereas western writers are judged for their originality, Native oral storytellers are celebrated for the "linguistic," "paralinguistic," and "kinesic" qualities of their performance of communal works. [26]

Oral storytelling is performative and dramatic; it may include verbal exchanges with the audience. The present, listening audience (as opposed to the absent, solitary reader [27]) sometimes literally participates in the telling, usually already knows some version(s) of the story and, though respectful of the storyteller's status, may even interrupt the narration from time to time. Moreover, the storyteller is not necessarily responsible for bringing "closure" to the narrative, though performance includes interpretive cues, nor is the audience necessarily expected to arrive at close-consensus interpretations. On the contrary, what happens in connection with listening to the story is more important than its definitive meaning. Because "the stories [are] alive," [28] they are, like other phenomenal mysteries, not subject to definitive interpretation. Thus we observe with Victor Turner that nonwestern performative art defines aesthetic value in processual terms, whereas western, post-Renaissance, aesthetic traditions value product over process. [29]

A related value drives most of western literary criticism as well, with its demand for consensual readings of texts and for self-conscious explanations of relatively standardized interpretive methods. Turner's work reveals how such cultural predispositions have often blinded the western eye to the subtle complexities of nonwestern performative art, which seems ephemeral and utilitarian (Kantian definitions of low art) by comparison to western art, valued for its presumed "timelessness," "universality," and other culturally defined qualities. More vexing still for the western literary critic, Native American traditional literature resists most types of western literary analysis. Although contemporary Native American written literature is less resistant, it nevertheless retains sufficient traditional components to make western critical approaches problematic. Encoded in the "ceremonial" dimensions of certain texts by Silko and Momaday, for instance, are potential reader responses that Euro-American critical systems do not legitimate, as we shall see.

Reflecting the pan-Indian value of hospitality, traditional Indian storytellers are considerate of the physically present audience from whom they hope to elicit specific (and nonwestern) kinds of responses. Because storytelling helps maintain tribal identity along with social and cosmic harmony, it emphasizes solidarity over power. Naturally, just as western narrative (characterized by power) also embodies solidarity, oral literature (characterized by solidarity) also embodies power. Still, when the audience defers to the oral storyteller's authority, the storyteller, in turn, politely defrays this authority through ritualized gestures, as Andrew Wiget reveals in his performance analysis of a Hopi Coyote story. Wiget points out the astonishingly innovative, spontaneous ways in which the Indian storyteller constantly adjusts the performance to accommodate the audience, even when the audience unexpectedly includes cultural outsiders. Overall, the oral tradition demands responsible listeners as well. Stories must be presented solicitously and the audience members are obliged to listen actively—to understand, remember, and contemplate, if not necessarily to arrive at consensus interpretations.

Until late in the twentieth century, very few Native American storytellers had worked in written media. This fact, coupled with the traditional effacement of stories' origins, has meant that, strictly speaking, the Native American "author" is a recent invention of contemporary Native American writers. Many of these writers develop strategies for encoding written narrative with the exotic agenda of nonwestern oral storytelling practices based on solidarity with an audience.[30] These practices sometimes include certain ritual uses of language. Momaday, for example, begins and ends *House Made of Dawn* with the words "Dypaloh" and "Qtsedaba," conventional Pueblo acknowledgments of the audience that signal the opening and closing of a story.[31] Silko begins and ends *Ceremony* by asking the audience to "accept this offering." Such respectful attention to the audience and careful observation of ceremonial storytelling practices are evidence that Indian writers are, in general, more solicitous of particular kinds of solidarity with their traditional audiences than are their typical twentieth-century western counterparts.

Contemporary Native American writers do, however, exploit the power relations inherent in western narrative as part of their "invention" of the Indian author. Written and published works (as opposed to yesteryear's ethnographic and "as told to" accounts) give Indian people control over the knowledge they impart as well as the means for imparting it. Momaday's use of the words "Dypaloh" and "Qtsedaba," and Silko's polite entreaty at the beginnings of their respective novels distance the non-Indian reader (unacquainted with these oral storytelling practices) even as they courteously acknowledge the audience in general. Such a nuanced strategy is indeed a marker of power: the storyteller confronts the reader with "non-reciprocal" and "direct speech" that does not explain itself in deference to what the Other necessarily understands. The writer simply requires the reader as cultural outsider to find out or figure out what many Indian readers would already know.

Through written narrative, some Native American writers manage both power and solidarity in an apparent attempt to enter the dominant discursive space with a counter-colonial agenda. Though this semiotic counter-conquest resembles (in reverse) its European antecedent that Todorov describes, its aim is not domination and empire, but social reform through relocation of non-Indian people from positions of authority to positions of listeners and receivers of knowledge. As Elaine Jahner has argued, works by Native American writers often try to establish mental and emotional harmony between writer and reader through instruction in how to listen.[32] Having appropriated and revamped the narrative and rhetorical strategies of the colonizer, these writers exploit the power relations inherent in written narrative with the ultimate aim (ironically) of multiplying solidarity bonds with an audience consisting primarily of sympathetic, non-Indian outsiders. Even more ironic, their methods for building such solidarity are predicated on the exaggerated power relations encoded in modern and postmodern texts.

Signs of the Times

As a discursive site of cultural conflict, contemporary Native American narrative incorporates ethnic signs and nonwestern worldviews, yet achieves its full meaning under social and textual conditions defined within the dominant culture. (For instance, the publishing industry that governs the circulation of texts is a western "social condition" affecting Native American writing, and the western narrative tradition that puts up generic resistance to Native American expression is a "textual condition.") Despite some Indian authors' perception of Euro-American culture as "rigid,"[33] the circulation of Indian (and other ethnic) writings within the dominant society reveals that the dominant discourse contains within itself a potentiality for its own destabilization. In other words, the (social and textual) status quo is always "at risk of disruption" by the semiotic action of the Other.[34] Indeed, in carrying out complex cross-cultural tasks, contemporary Indian writing subversively enters the dominant discourse and exposes the ways in which both Native and non-Native frames of reference are constantly revised.

The remainder of this chapter focuses on such narrative management of power in some specific contemporary Indian works. In these works, the authors' semiotically disruptive or destabilizing strategies of "resistance" exploit "power" for a variety of political, philosophical, and aesthetic purposes. Included in my discussion are Momaday's *House Made of Dawn*, marked by a high level of resistance in its management of power; Silko's *Ceremony* and Momaday's *The Ancient Child*, two novels in which resistance to narrative conventions is potentially instructive; works by Thomas King that contest western assumptions about the nature and power of representation; and works by Louise Erdrich that frustrate Eurocentric readerly practices and resist western notions of moral and intellectual authority.

Chronologically the prototype for the contemporary Indian novel, Momaday's *House Made of Dawn* marks the beginning of the current era of Native American storytelling in print.[35] And, although Welch's *Winter in the Blood* followed six years later in 1974, throughout the present study I refer not to *House* or to *Winter*, but to Silko's 1977 novel *Ceremony* as the paradigmatic Indian novel for the current generation. By "paradigmatic" I do not mean that it is "superior" to the other works I discuss, or that the novel is necessarily a "model" for other Indian writers to emulate. I believe, however, that *Ceremony* might stand out in the memories of readers of many contemporary Native American narratives as the first work to address most deliberately the difficulties inherent in cross-cultural interpretation and to foreground, as a part of its actual storyline, an array of interpretive strategies. Unlike Welch and Momaday (in his first novel, at least), Silko has painstakingly made her novel accessible to the non-Indian reader. Many Indian writers (perhaps even Momaday in his second novel) have since followed her example of metatextually instructing the reader in Native American history and culture, and in how to interpret the nonwestern components of their narratives.

Similarities between *House Made of Dawn* and *Ceremony* are striking enough also to suggest Silko's indebtedness to Momaday's *House* as a model for writing a basically Indian story for a primarily non-Indian audience: both trace a central, bicultural character's healing quest through a psycho-spiritual and physical landscape; both juxtapose Euro-American and Southwestern Indian cultural frames of reference to generate a double sociolect—an expanded reservoir of information from more than one culture on which to base our interpretations of textual particulars;[36] both authors use the traditional storyteller's voice to narrate events originating within historical and mythical time; both interrupt the narrative flow with traditional chants; both texts mix types of discourse evoking disparate interpretive responses, and a significant part of the narrative force derives from the ways in which these various discourses interrelate.[37] A pervasive difference between the two texts, however, lies in their relative exploitation of the power and solidarity tactics inherent in written narrative. Momaday presents the reader of *House* with a formidably resistant narrative characterized by power.

Perhaps reflecting Momaday's Eurocentric education as a writer, as opposed to Silko's cultivated sense of herself as an Indian storyteller, *House* confronts the reader with an array of interpretive difficulties that *Ceremony* and many other post-1970s narratives—including Momaday's second novel, *The Ancient Child*—more self-consciously arbitrate. While *Ceremony* incorporates audience-accommodating, oral narrational strategies, *House* immerses the reader in a nonwestern reality while employing narrative power tactics that today, after almost thirty years of exposure to Indian writing, remain difficult even for informed readers to negotiate. Like *Ceremony, House* is biculturally encoded, but unlike Silko, Momaday leaves all except his already bicultural readers without obvious points of entry into the text. Though Momaday is certainly not obligated—by western standards, at least—to accommodate the outsiders among the audience, his power-oriented narrative tactics problematize reader-response. Audience options are narrowly defined: seek extratextual information, (mis)read within an inappropriate framework, or give up.[38]

Some of Momaday's bicultural characters very subtly endorse the first option. Father Olguin consults outside sources; he reads Fray Nicolás's journal (printed within the narrative) in an effort to understand the Indian people among whom he lives as a Christian emissary. Though the journal is by no means an ideal source of insight, it functions as a negative example of how to "read" the Indians. Fray Nicolás is the embodiment of Spanish oppression, and as Father Olguin acquaints himself with the ignoble colonial past recorded in Nicolás's hand, he develops a limited, but sympathetic cross-cultural perspective. After living among the Indians of the Southwest for several years, Father Olguin is able to say, " 'I understand, do you hear?' And he began to shout. 'I understand! *Oh God! I understand—I understand!*' "[39]

Also raising questions in *House* about interpretive frames of reference are Tosamah, Ben Benally, and Abel's grandfather, Francisco, all of whom comment on the different ways of seeing the world that apply within different cultures. However, readers unfamiliar with these "solidarity" markers in Indian narratives will probably miss such cues in *House.* (Native American novels published subsequently to *House* have sensitized readers through more overt methods than Momaday's to bicultural characters' messages about how to read, as we shall see.) Moreover, even if a reader were to comprehend Momaday's subtle, extratextual directives, he or she must know not only where to obtain the requisite contextual information, but also how to interpret that information, as critical studies by Nora Barry, Susan Scarberry-García, and others have demonstrated.[40]

By contrast with *House* and with varying degrees of success, most Native American novels written subsequently incorporate more extensive reader instruction. For example, Anna Lee Walters artfully interweaves Navajo culture and history into the conversations of tribal characters in *Ghost Singer*, while Robert Conley less successfully juxtaposes historical writing about the Cherokee with Cherokee characters' personal narratives in *Mountain Windsong* (1992). Whatever their methods, these writers remind us that reading is itself a highly politicized, culturally circumscribed act. We cannot "read" other cultures or decode their texts without first, like Momaday's Father Olguin, learning new ways of seeing, new ideas and information, and new habits of interpretation.

Silko's *Ceremony* is the first of several contemporary Indian narratives to exercise power over the reader through strategies of destabilization aimed at just such a reformation of the reader.[41] That is to say, within one text, one set of rules for accessing meaning is *extensively* violated by, or brought into *significant* opposition with another, a conflict producing an interpretive, potentially instructive crisis in the reader. Though extratextual information about the Navajo-Pueblo world represented in the novel is ultimately required, the textual dynamic of *Ceremony*, more than that of *House*, accommodates the outsider reader. Whereas *House* rather thoroughly excludes the ill-equipped reader, *Ceremony* enlists such a reader in the deconstruction of cultural frames of reference, the first step toward bicultural understanding.

Ceremony features at least three types of discourse that destabilize each other and contribute to an overall narrative episteme of instability: lyrical chantways, prose narrative, and dialogue. Each of the three types of discourse may be subcategorized according to contrary sets of culturally bounded rules governing its production and reception. For instance, even within a single cultural frame of reference, ceremonial chants are produced and received according to rules different from those governing narration and dialogue. Moreover, all three kinds of discourse are always encountered by the reader of *Ceremony* in terms of the double (western and Pueblo-Navajo) interpretive frame of reference that the novel generates. (The frame is actually more than double, for two different tribal views—Laguna and Navajo—are encoded in the text.) For example, the Pueblo-Navajo cosmological material may be judged "true" or "mythical-imaginary," depending on the reader's epistemological screen. This destabilizing force within Silko's narrative calls attention to the culturally determined boundaries of "reality."

Her narrational tactic dislodges the reader from any apparently secure epistemological ground. Indeed, reinforcing the notion of a shaky ground, the narrator reports that at Laguna people "could hear big diesel trucks rumbling down Highway 66."[42] Also in the distance lies the world's first atomic bomb crater, at Trinity Site, the central icon of Silko's episteme of instability.

Silko deliberately destabilizes a variety of semiotic boundaries. Both lyrical and narrative passages cross-code material originating in an atemporal, mythico-spiritual realm with material originating in temporal-historical experience. Especially for the Eurocentric reader, myth and history presuppose quite different logonomic systems or "set[s] of rules . . . prescribing the conditions for production and reception of meanings." Such rules "specify who can claim to initiate or know meanings about what topics under what circumstances and with what modalities."[43] (That is to say, such sets of rules specify who may with credibility say what to whom and in what form. Historians, for instance, may authoritatively relate to a western audience the "truth" about the past in the form of historical narrative. Both historian and audience presumably understand the rules governing the production and reception of historical knowledge, which differ from the rules governing the production and reception of fiction.) Silko's novel places a variety of logonomic systems in opposition; in so doing, the text exerts its potential power over the reader to effect an interpretive crisis that could ultimately expose, revise and expand the rules of text production.

Ceremony opens with a four-page lyric passage raising questions about the identity and source of authority of the speaker. The speaker declares, "Thought-Woman, the spider, / . . . is . . . thinking of a story . . . . / I'm telling you the story / she is thinking" (1). If the story told in *Ceremony* originates with Thought-Woman, then it originates in the mythico-spiritual dimension, despite its narrative concern with the temporal-historical particulars of Tayo's life. Therefore it is subject to interpretation according to logonomic rules pertaining to cosmological accounts, and the narrator is treated as a spirit being. However, the narrator, the "I" of the passage who speaks for Thought-Woman, is also the narrator of *Ceremony* (perhaps even Silko herself), who presumably inhabits the present, material world of which she speaks. Thus, from the outset, the ontological status of the narrating voice in *Ceremony* is ambiguous, as are the truth-claims of its different types of discourse (the typical western reader sees myth as "imaginary" and narrative as mimetic, if not literally true [44].

Consequently, the protocol for decoding the text—as cultural myth or as fictional narrative—is obscured, at least for the reader who accepts the conventional western boundaries between these forms. (Obviously, many Eurocentric novels are also encoded with myth; however, the protocol for reading them is different from what I am describing here. The Eurocentric text implies figurative and symbolic relationships between myth and history, whereas American Indian texts draw less absolute distinctions between imaginal and actual realms.[45]) Pointedly raising doubts in the reader about which interpretive rules or frame of reference to engage, Silko's text poses questions about origination and legitimation of knowledge. It also exposes the "constructedness" of reality by revealing its origins in imagination and semiotic practices.[46] Silko highlights the semiotic practices that govern meaning in contexts, and she challenges the authority of western assumptions before taking the next, more politically charged step of inviting the reader to help change the rules not only of storytelling, but also of world-making. Stories "aren't just entertainment," Silko reminds us; they are "all we have to fight off/ illness and death."[47]

The second type of discourse in *Ceremony*—prose narrative—encodes a secular-historical reality that, at first, seems distinct from the spiritual world described in the chantways. However, the lyrical passages expand to refer to the narrative even as the narrative begins to allude to and follow patterns established by the traditional material in the lyrical passages. Silko implies an alignment between worlds that might, initially, seem to contradict any claim about the episteme of instability encoded in the text. Ironically, however, as the two kinds of discourse apparently merge to imply a universal cosmic design, another kind of destabilization occurs owing to the role of imagination that both discourses proclaim. Imagination is a radically unstable force; like "C'ko'yo witches," it can create a deadly reality, or, like Hummingbird, it can help repair the world. Imagination lies behind the development of atomic energy—released owing to the inherent instability of the very atoms that make up the universe. Imagination also lies behind the "story" that Thought Woman "is thinking" and that the reader is asked to "accept" together with the responsibility for its message. Through deft management of the power relations inherent in narration,

Silko tells a story making the reader responsible for his or her imaginative acts and, hence, for the world. She ends the novel on a cautionary note that things are "fixed up" only "for now" (261).

The third kind of discourse in *Ceremony* is dialogue and consists of the various speeches of characters who, like the lyrical and narrative passages, do not all originate within the same "worlds." Among the many voices in *Ceremony* are Josiah, who tells Tayo and Rocky the traditional stories of the Laguna people and so provides them with an Indian world view; the white people, the doctors in particular, who insist that Tayo understand himself in terms of Western European psychology; the medicine men, Ku'oosh and Betonie; and the characters from the spiritual realm such as Hummingbird, Buzzard, and Ts'eh. Just as the lyrical chants and the narrative sections pose fundamental questions about origination and legitimation of their content, the dialogue becomes another site of instability presenting myriad world views and corresponding interpretive systems. The multitude of "voices" confronting Tayo overdetermines Silko's encoded episteme and reminds readers of how we share in Tayo's uncertainty and responsibility.

Like *Ceremony*, N. Scott Momaday's second novel, *The Ancient Child*, is constructed of competing and mutually destabilizing discourses that potentially focus our attention on authorial power. These include Grey's "dream" discourse connecting her with Billy the Kid in the 1870s and 1880s, and with her dead ancestors; traditional stories such as the Kiowa tale of the Seven Sisters and the bear-boy visitor to the Piegan camp; historical accounts of Indian people, including Set-Angya and Kope'mah; narration concerning Grey, Set, and other characters; passages narrated first-person by Set himself; dialogue; song lyrics; and epigrams preceding each of the three sections of the novel.

As in *Ceremony*, these various discourses invoke different rule-bound agendas for production and reception and imply different origins and sources of authority. Momaday's novel also generates a double—Euro-American and Native American—interpretive frame of reference. (As in Silko's novel, the "Indian" dimension consists of multiple tribal sources, including Kiowa and Navajo.[48]) Finally, like Silko, Momaday destabilizes a variety of culturally determined boundaries, including those between "dreams" and material reality and between ceremonial and historical time. As we have seen, Silko's destabilizing tactics emphasize the constructedness of reality by demonstrating its origins in semiotic practices. She emphasizes the choice we make between constructive and destructive uses of the imagination. Momaday, however, seems bent on destroying our comfortable illusions about reality in order to reveal what he sees as an essential and stable reality beyond the material realm. Momaday portrays imagination not as an unstable force of change, but as an almost divinatory power that, unresisted, reveals our destiny.

In *The Ancient Child*, Momaday sets out to disrupt and revise, in particular, our ideas about the role of art in the human search for secure ontological grounding. According to Set, art provides an opportunity and a means for questioning beliefs; such questioning directly affects a person's well-being, defined as clear progress toward his or her apparent destiny.[49] The novel implies that for society overall, the role of art is to foster this well-being by encouraging examination of beliefs. Ostensibly contradicting the idea of storytelling as resistance, Set declares that "art is not resistance" (58). In this statement, however, he rejects the specifically modernist notion of art as existential resistance in an ultimately meaningless universe. Though he believes that the final aim of art is not resistance, Set suggests that successful artistic strategies must offer great resistance, especially to habitual ways of thinking that blind people to the essential reality of an everywhere meaningful universe.[50]

Lola Bourne and Alais Sancerre, for example, detect this performative element in Set's paintings. Lola sees "Night Window Man" and Alais sees "Venture Beyond Time" as instruction about the relationship between the material realm and the eternal realm of spirit. In Momaday's novel, we see the same instructive bent in the destabilization and revision of the conventional boundaries between these realms—a narrational act which potentially provokes the reader to self-conscious examination of frames of reference underlying his or her construction of reality. Over the course of the novel, Set rejects the Eurocentric reality that rewards his material success as a painter whose works command a high price on the market, but that also defines him as mentally ill because of his hallucinations (visions) and his emotional (spiritual) disorder. Set's recovery depends upon this rejection of one "story" (the Euro-American "portrait-of-the-artist" story) in favor of another (the Kiowa Bear story) as an interpretive framework for his life's experience. Like Silko, Momaday exploits the authorial power inherent in the novel to disconnect the reader from comfortable, conventional ideas and interpretive practices.

Recalling Momaday's and Silko's works in their counter-colonial moves, Thomas King's *Green Grass, Running Water* features a near cacophony of voices boisterously competing to tell their own stories about the world, particularly creation stories. Emphasizing cultural blindness to the views of the Other, his characters engage in so-called "conversations" in which neither party listens or responds appropriately. These disjunctive conversations parallel the disjunctive stories about the world told throughout the book. Many of the stories are a mishmash of elements drawn helter-skelter from Indian lore, the Bible, Anglo-American literature, television and movies, and even advertisements. Like Silko's and Momaday's oppositional discourses, the stories in King's novel evoke contradictory interpretive frames of reference, and even promiscuously confuse semiotic categories: fictional characters from *Moby-Dick*, for example, confront actual historical figures; characters from the Bible argue with characters from Native American traditional stories. King's characters openly confront the problems that arise when different stories invoke different logonomic rules governing who may speak to whom, what may be said, and how. When "stories" collide, Noah (from the Bible) asks Coyote (a pan-tribal character) and Changing Woman (Navajo), "Why are you talking to animals? . . . This is a Christian ship. Animals don't talk. We got rules."[51] King interweaves these different kinds of discourse, with their respectively different production and reception agendas, to illustrate his point (recalling Silko's in *Ceremony*) that responsible storytelling is a prerequisite for sane habitation of an endurable world.

Like Silko, King builds his polyphonous narrative around icons of instability. One such icon and a main character in the novel, Coyote, goes about his traditional business of destabilizing nearly everything. Indeed, the novel ends with an earthquake and a flood that presumably signal the end of one round of world-shattering storytelling and the beginning of another. As an agent of narrative disruption, Coyote almost self-consciously understands instability as a semiotic concept. He realizes that repairing the world often depends on certain types of narrative revisions. Consequently, whenever one of his "dreams" (stories) starts to inflict damage, Coyote proclaims his own innocence—" 'It's not my fault . . . I believe I was in Toronto' " (56)—and asks to start the story "over again" to "get it right" (83). Other storytellers in the novel follow Coyote's lead in starting their stories over again and again in the effort to exert better control. Semiotically self-aware characters named "Hawkeye," "Robinson Crusoe," "Ishmael," and "The Lone Ranger" argue about mistakes made in the first versions of their stories, and they discuss the liabilities of narrator "omniscience" (41).

Exploiting the power over the reader's interpretive habits inherent in semiotically self-conscious postmodern narrative, King aims ultimately to sensitize his audience to the nature of the offense committed when we "read" and construct the world narrowly according to ethnocentric readerly practices. Throughout King's works, but especially in *Green Grass, Running Water* and in his shorter "Coyote" tales (such as "A Coyote Columbus Story" [1993]), Coyote epitomizes the insensitive audience, missing the points of both Native American and Eurocentric stories alike. One of King's most successful comic ploys for dislodging his readers from their comfortable interpretive vantage points involves reverse stereotyping and scenarios depicting the world as though Indian people instead of Euro-Americans were in control of representation. For example, characters in *Green Grass, Running Water* watch slightly altered, home-video versions of John Wayne and Richard Widmark films that Coyote and his cohorts have "fixed" (266) to the Indians' advantage. Both Indian and non-Indian viewer-response to such doctored videos is based on the shock of directly perceiving the world as constructed according to the rules of the Other's game. In this sense, King's "fixed up" videos recall the larger-than-life laser holograms unleashed on contemporary America in Gerald Vizenor's "Feral Lasers."[52] Indeed, King and Vizenor appear to share a conviction that trickster figures are, in general, a pan-tribal expression of Indian peoples' sophisticated awareness of the power of sign action.

King's short story, "A Seat in the Garden,"[53] likewise underscores the world-making powers that reside with those who control representation. King points to the destabilization of the world that accompanies any sudden shifts in representational power. An Indian of dubious ontological status wreaks havoc on Joe Hovaugh's "private property" (84). Apparently, the visitor is merely a semiotic phenomenon, a slightly confused trope of an Indian generated by cowboy-and-Indian films Joe has watched starring Jeff Chandler, Ed Ames, and Sal Mineo. Unlike the local Indians to whom he appeals for help, Joe never sees that the "big Indian" in the garden is merely a construction of his own cinematically bounded, and culturally impoverished, imagination. The local Indians are dismayed but hardly surprised to see that a familiar "big Indian" stereotype has become so empowered through decades of representation that it is able to escape its representational bounds. Thus, King suggests, does representation, or "story," become "history," or reality. As narratives of resistance, "A Seat in the Garden," King's other Coyote stories, and *Green Grass, Running Water* force the reader to think of "reality" as an ethno- and egocentric construction originating within and perpetuated through the dominant discourse. King's writing resembles Vizenor's in its deployment of Indian signs within the ruptured, dominant discourse it has appropriated; like the "fixed up" videos in *Green Grass, Running Water*, and recalling the various creations of Vizenor's Almost Brown, King's texts and those of other Native American writers enter the mainstream with potentially mind- and world-altering, destabilizing force.

Louise Erdrich also crafts resistant narratives designed to unmoor the complacent reader. Her works are marked by disruptive ethnic signs and thus are characterized by what Boelhower calls "ethnic deconstructive energy." Remarking the "uncontrollable" and "ubiquitous" nature of the ethnic sign throughout American literature, Boelhower contends that it is "a constant source of disturbance" even in "so-called dominant cultural texts."[54] The ethnic sign as a constant source of a particular kind of disturbance in Louise Erdrich's novels is a distinguishing "Native American" feature of her writing. Her works constitute encounters in which negotiating the ethnic sign may result in a reader's intense, self-critical awareness of his or her own role not only in text production, but also in the acts of world-making that texts imply.[55]

Tracks, for example, draws on a variety of oral storytelling strategies,[56] including the self-conscious accommodation of cultural "outsiders" in the audience, and thus converts "reader" into "listener." This "reader-as-listener" in turn confronts a variety of tropes deployed as ethnic signs with potential for renegotiating some of the terms of contact between dominant and marginal cultures. In the same way that the Anishinabe, on the literally depicted, historical frontier in *Tracks*, lose their lands in "a storm of government papers,"[57] the reader, on the semiotic frontier comprising the novel, senses an authorial assault on the conventional position that he or she occupies and must give up some ground.[58] Likewise, *The Bingo Palace* (1994) achieves similar ends, but whereas the reader is constructed as listener in *Tracks*, in *The Bingo Palace* he or she is constructed as viewer. This "reader-as-viewer," together with several characters including a collective narrator, struggles to decode "pictures" in pursuit of an elusive "larger story."[59] This "larger story" eludes efforts to grasp "the whole of it" (5), and decoding the pictures forces the reader-viewer to reassess the act of looking in which he or she is engaged. Indeed, Erdrich's "pictures" in *The Bingo Palace* might be considered semiotic equivalents of iconic gestures that are an important part of oral storytelling.[60] We might say that in *Tracks*, Erdrich stages ethnosemiotic encounters through the "mind's ear" of the reader, while in *The Bingo Palace*, she works through the "mind's eye."

Even a superficial reader of *Tracks* is likely to notice Erdrich's apparent preoccupation with listening. The word "listen" and its grammatical variants, not to mention synonyms, appear frequently throughout the novel. Moreover, Erdrich creates a gallery of listen*ers*, ranging from characters such as the eavesdropping Pauline Puyat and Boy Lazarre, to the silent (in this novel) Lulu (Nanapush's stated audience), to the novel's reading audience. Erdrich frequently prods the reader to think about the implications of listening to other people's stories, even when "listening" means "hearing" their voices in our heads as we read the words. We understand that to read is to share Pauline's ambiguous "crow" identity—in Nanapush's words, to live on the "scraps" of other people's lives.[61] Indeed, a reader-listener is a kind of eavesdropper, perched like Crow inconspicuously outside the frame of action and savoring tidbits of other people's business. Such a reader, like Pauline-as-Crow, must consider the unflattering implications of consuming the stories of others. Why *do* we read? Do our motives even slightly resemble Pauline's unsavory ones? What do we do with the stories we gather? Like Crow, readers are snoopers and potentially petty thieves.

Crow and Pauline also have the uncanny ability to be in two places at the same time: Pauline in one scene psychically appropriates Sophie's body to enjoy the effects of a love potion on Eli Kashpaw. This ability extends to the reader, who is simultaneously outside the text and "inside," imaginatively appropriating the lives and experiences of various characters. Erdrich even implies that, like Pauline and Crow, the reader is responsible for the use of such voyeuristically acquired knowledge. Pauline (and potentially any listener) can "create damage" by repeating what she hears without regard to story's power to cure or kill.[62] The reader-as-listener shares with Pauline and Crow another important trait—"invisibility." Pauline is "invisible" primarily because none of the other characters pay her serious attention. Like Crow, she learns to take advantage of her inconspicuousness. The reader, on the other hand, is literally "invisible" through absence to the storyteller. Unlike oral storytelling, written storytelling is directed to an absent audience. In her series of paradigmatic equivalents of the reader (Pauline, Boy, Crow, Lulu, etc.), Erdrich warns that such absent, "invisible" listeners can be dangerous. Characters in the text repeatedly worry about who might be listening, including spirits and people who might act maliciously or irresponsibly (as Crow might, and Pauline does). To be overheard by spirits is dangerous because a person can become the object of their unwanted attention. Listening to some spirits can drive a person "windigo"— infect him or her with the "invisible sickness" (a malady which, a reader should note, is connected in *Tracks* with listening to disembodied voices).

Clearly, the reader is urged to add him- or herself to the long list of potentially threatening and threatened listeners named in the narrative. Erdrich's implied agenda is to make such an invisible reader-listener aware of both responsibilities and liabilities incurred in hearing stories.[63] While oral storytellers develop specific, dramatic methods for instructing the listening audience and for directing the responses of cultural outsiders, the novel's absent or invisible audience is more difficult to manage and, indeed, more likely to contain "outsiders." Nevertheless, Erdrich finds ways to direct her "absent" audience; Nanapush is Erdrich's responsible storyteller and authorial ventriloquist who subtly instructs the reader in an ethics of "listening." His stories remind the reader of the power of words over a hostile or irresponsible listener.

Rife with tropes or ethnic signs interfering with the reader's usual interpretive habits and demanding adaptation to an array of new rules, Nanapush's narration frequently challenges the reader-listener to reassess his or her own relationship to the text. Nanapush uses story figuratively to "drown" the well-intentioned but meddlesome, ethnocentric Father Damien and, by implication, the reader, another outsider-listener. (For a Chippewa, drowning, along with burning, is one of the worst ways to die, as Lulu explains in *Love Medicine*.[64]) In a thinly-disguised warning to the reader, an eavesdropper on his story addressed to Lulu, Nanapush threatens: "I talked both languages in streams that ran alongside each other. . . . I kept Father Damien listening all night. . . . Occasionally, he took in air . . . but I pushed him under with my words."[65] To emphasize his point, Nanapush equates words with water many times throughout his narrated passages. (Silence was a "frozen state" [8, 31], speech a "thawing" [205]; conversational "waters were . . . muddy" with rumors and lies [61], etc.) This trope of watery submergence, or "drowning," appears throughout each of Erdrich's novels, but in *Tracks* it is especially conspicuous as an ethnic sign serving to apprise the wary reader of the dangers of irresponsible consumption of other peoples' stories.

Nanapush also lets us know that story can be used to fend off Death as well as to summon it. Nanapush defeats Death by "starting a story" and not letting Death "get a word in edgewise" (6). His words in this case imply that Death is yet another type of invisible listener—another unflattering, paradigmatic equivalent to the reader. Fortunately, Nanapush (and Erdrich) ultimately have the best interests of the reader in mind.[66] Though they suggest that a powerful storyteller poses a threat to a careless reader-as-listener, they simultaneously offer the reader a variety of opportunities to revise ethnocentric, appropriative, and other destructive types of readerly habits such as those of Pauline, who "creates damage,"[67] or of Father Damien, who would use against the Chippewa the knowledge that he had acquired in his "well-intentioned" but misguided efforts to help.

In overdetermining the equation between listening and reading, Erdrich defines at least one role of the reader in this text as that of an outsider to be either fended off altogether or, preferably, instructed in the art of listening to the Other. The "disturbing" trope or "ethnic sign" (cf. Boelhower) of "drowning" is complexly encoded by Erdrich with its Chippewa contextual meaning (drowning prevents the victim's entry into the spirit world) and with further meaning generated by the immediate narrative (verbal "drowning," perhaps, prevents the reader's entry into a Native American reality sustained by the text). "Drowning" thus becomes one of several highly charged ethnic signs in *Tracks*—part of a semiotic network of references instructing the reader to confront his or her own identity as a heedless consumer of the "scraps" of other people's lives, or as a responsible participant in storytelling. Erving Goffman, Andrew Wiget, and other scholars of oral performance remind us that audience "engrossment" includes listener accountability for yielding collaboratively to the power of the storyteller, whose many roles include being a transformer of the audience.[68] In this novel that fashions semiotic equivalents to oral performance, the trope of "drowning" thus becomes a site where authorial demands on the reader call for various types of renegotiation—renegotiation of meaning as well as of the "listener's" place in the storytelling process. Consequently, *Tracks* may be seen as a subtly reappropriative gesture: whereas history has seen repeated incursions by non-Indians upon Indian "territory," contemporary "word warriors" such as Erdrich and other current Indian writers stand fast against ill-informed, misguided cultural appropriation of Indian "stories" (including histories, art, etc.).

Erdrich deploys another major trope as ethnic sign in *Tracks* and, as we shall see, in *The Bingo Palace*. This trope of the snare likewise causes the reader to ponder his or her own role as defined by the Native American storyteller. A most memorable scene in *Tracks* finds Clarence Morrissey about to fall into a snare set by Nanapush and Eli. Moving means possible death, and not moving means straddling the pit until fatigue brings the inevitable fall. The snare "had been invisible," says Nanapush, "and yet in one foot-pedaling instant as he fell, the certain knowledge of its construction sprang into Clarence's brain" (122–23). Clarence's position is the figurative equivalent of the reader's, potentially caught in the "snare" of words set by Erdrich through her ventriloquist character Nanapush, who is thoroughly knowledgeable of the "traps" set by storytellers like himself. For instance, he remarks of Father Damien, "I had taught him well [how to set verbal traps, so] . . . I saw the snare [in his argument] . . . the invisible loop hidden in the priest's well-meaning words" (185). Also paradigmatically replicated in Clarence's "spread-eagled" stance is his own bicultural identity. The half-blood straddles the space between two cultures, always a potential victim of snares set within the double-coded semiotic system that defines a cross-cultural reality.[69] Only a small step is required to appreciate how this dilemma is, in turn, replicated in the position of the reader who must avoid a one-sided reading of a cross-coded, bicultural text such as *Tracks*. Erdrich has set a semiotic trap for her reader, for whom "the certain knowledge of its construction" should, ideally, spring clear.

In light of this implied equation between the snared Morrissey and the reader, the pattern of Clarence's and Boy Lazarre's scars— the legacy of Nanapush's trap—is itself a subtly encoded reference to storytelling. These scars lie on the mouth, neck, arm, and fingers (sources of the voice, on the one hand, and of signing and writing, on the other). "Perhaps my snare did damage, taught a temporary lesson" Nanapush says. "The drag of Clarence's mouth was permanent." Lazarre's "fingers grew weak and numb" (123). Nanapush's "lesson" ultimately warns the reader about the proper positions to assume when telling and listening to stories. Pauline's position is especially to be avoided; a counter-example of the ideal reader and straddling the bicultural gap in undesirable ways, she constructs a frightening, damaging, albeit cross-cultural reality from bizarrely interpreted "scraps" of western and Native American "stories" that she has collected.

Erdrich's implied reader is informed and instructed; her ideal reader is not drowned by the words of the text, but perhaps she is instead like Fleur Pillager, a creature at home in the water, or like Nanapush himself, who can see "invisible snares": "I saw the deadfall beneath my feet before I stepped," he pointedly tells us (185). Fleur repeatedly escapes "drowning," and Nanapush perfects the art of ethical listening and storytelling. He wields the power of words with great finesse, able to inflict measured amounts of damage, able deliberately to "cure or kill." His keen senses extend even to the "reading" of messages in the "leaves" of his beloved trees.

Nanapush's perfected art contains a further lesson for the attentive reader. At the conclusion of *Tracks*, Erdrich introduces another ethnic sign requiring sophisticated response on the reader's part. On a note of ostensible defeat, Nanapush declares that the Chippewa are no longer anything more than a "tribe of file cabinets and triplicates, a tribe of single-space documents, directives, policy. A tribe of pressed trees. A tribe of chicken-scratch that can be scattered by a wind" (225). Though these metaphors at first appear merely self-deprecating, Nanapush the trickster must certainly be aware of their double-coded message for the alert reader who knows that "pressed trees," or paper, are what books are made of, and that there is more than one way to "translate the language of . . . leaves" (210). Although the tribe may be reduced to papers made of cherished trees stripped from lost lands, Erdrich is living proof that Indians also write counter-colonial stories on paper, stories aimed at the "invisible" listener-reader in an effort to re-colonize the colonizer, if we understand colonization as involving the appropriation of mental space and the revision of interpretive frames of reference.[70] If Nanapush's literal strength ebbs with the disappearance of the actual trees, his storyteller's trickster power as Erdrich's ventriloquist increases with the use of the "pressed trees" as "leaves" of books. Erdrich's trope of the "tribe of pressed trees" refers subtly to a steadily increasing "tribe" of books such as those by Erdrich and other Native American writers that aim to re-vise not simply the record of the past, but the shape of the future. Their readers are, ideally, displaced from a position of careless-consumer-of-exotica to that of an active agent in a social semiotic revision of contemporary reality.

Like the other novels in Erdrich's "paper tribe," *The Bingo Palace* works for audience "engrossment" with an instructive, potentially world-altering purpose. Through a narrative equation between reading and looking at pictures, Erdrich shows how photographs and various other types of visual representations may be "traps," capable of ensnaring the viewer within fixed frames of reference. She shows us the power that lies in recognizing such invisible snares, in seeing "the deadfall" beneath our feet before we step.[71] Erdrich's preoccupation with looking in *The Bingo Palace* (like her preoccupation with listening in *Tracks*) appears designed to "dis-turb" the reader's conventionally stable interpretive position in relation to the narrative and, furthermore, to increase reader self-consciousness about interpretive acts. Enhancing reader awareness of visual decoding processes is a narrative equivalent of the instruc-tive and affective "iconic gestures" of oral performance. Indeed, Erdrich's "gestures" expand the projected reader's awareness of the epistemic nature of representation and broaden the base of Ameri-can Indian semiotic power through textualized, counter-colonial moves, as we shall see.

The kinesic dimension of oral storytelling involves body lan-guage that communicates to the audience a wealth of information about possible responses to the narration.[72] Through a variety of gestures, oral narrators both express and delimit their own au-thority to suggest that the story itself is greater than the storyteller, that storytellers are not the final arbiters of meaning, and that, in fact, the story as told is a variant, not a "definitive text" belonging to a particular "author."[73] In *The Bingo Palace*, Erdrich fashions a collective narrative voice composed of tribal elders who, like a traditional oral storyteller, combine authority and humility. For example, they admit that, like the audience, they cannot always "grasp the whole" (5) of the story being told. Through such proclaimed doubt, hesitancy, and overt interpretive struggles, Erdrich's collective narrator aligns itself with the audience and elicits creative audience participation in storytelling. As in oral literature, narrator and audience alike face interpretive problems and share responsibility for the story's effects.

The collective narrator in *The Bingo Palace* openly dialogues with the audience on the subject of looking at pictures; furthermore, both collectively narrated sections and those narrated by Lipsha Morrissey are rife with pictorial tropes that restate the equation between seeing and reading. Overall, the narrative insists that looking at pictures is predicated on habits of perception that determine not only how we interpret, but also how we actively respond to such pictures. Fully aware of this fact, Lulu Lamartine and Zelda Kashpaw draw suspicious and unsuspecting viewers alike into the snare that their artful designs comprise, in Erdrich's view. Lulu's and Zelda's spider-like relationship to their prey resembles that between authors and readers, or between graphic artists and viewers. Both women manage others by subtly shaping a worldview before the eyes of their unsuspecting victims. Lipsha, in particular, seems destined to fall prey to both women's traps.

The Bingo Palace opens with Lulu Lamartine's theft from the U.S. Post Office of a Wanted Poster depicting her son, Gerry Nanapush. She photocopies it, mails the copy to Lipsha Morrissey (Gerry's son), frames the original, and places it "where you couldn't help noticing it upon first entering her apartment" (5). The collective narrator informs us that a deliberate design lies behind Lulu's visual arrangement. Determined to free her son from prison and to enlist the (witting or unwitting) aid of other people in her effort, Lulu sets up a mysterious pattern of events that begins with the photograph. Not even the "elders" understand exactly how she works her ultimately successful spell: "Lulu Lamartine was sending the picture of the father to the son. . . . Surely, it meant something. There was always a reason behind the things Lulu did, although it took a while to find them, to work her ciphers out for meaning. . . . [I]n her small act there was a complicated motive and a larger story" (3). By the end of the novel, her plan has worked. When federal marshals come to arrest her for assisting a fugitive (a charge that will not stick), Lulu, dressed beautifully in ceremonial garb, cries out a "victory yell" (265). On the scene to snap pictures of her in her "planned" victory are the media: "All of the North Dakota newspapers" will unwittingly publish photos of Lulu's victory and perhaps contribute to the further advancement of her scheme (264).

Lulu's snare begins with a carefully placed picture in her apartment, along with a copy of it deliberately given to Lipsha. Despite themselves, those drawn into her design begin to fall under Lulu's control. The collective narrator's response to Lulu's plot corresponds to the model reader's response to "designs" of the sort set in motion by authors such as Erdrich herself: "Some of us tried to resist [looking at the picture of Gerry], yet were pulled in just the same. We were curious to know more, even though we'd never grasp the whole of it. The story comes around, pushing at our brains, and soon we are trying to ravel back to the beginning, trying to put families into order and make sense of things. But we start with one person, and soon another and another follows, and still another, until we are lost in the connections" (5). This passage is a metacritical statement upon the act of looking at the "designs" that artists set up, whether verbal or visual. Once a reader begins to "see" the "picture," to detect the hint of a pattern, he or she is "pulled in . . . curious to know more." The careless reader is virtually ensnared in the view or vision of the world implied in the pattern, while the careful reader sees "the snare . . . the invisible loop hidden in the . . . words" (185) and begins to develop a more epistemologically sophisticated, larger vision of "reality" as a socially constructed, malleable phenomenon.

Like Lulu, Zelda Kashpaw and Fleur "Mindemoya" Pillager are powerful old women who have learned how to entangle others in their snares. Zelda "scans" Lipsha's mind with the "sudden zero-gaze" of a "medical machine," and she "reads" the "map of [his] feelings" before she weaves her own design around him (18). Zelda means to use Lipsha to cement the relationship between Shawnee Ray and Lyman Lamartine. Knowing he has already succumbed to Lulu's power conveyed through the Wanted Poster, Lipsha now suspects he has fallen "into Zelda's range," as well: "I have to ask myself . . . am I drawn back specifically *to watch* [emphasis mine] the circle where that pretty [Shawnee Ray] Toose now appears? And Shawnee Ray herself . . . has she rolled me into each one of her snuff-can-top jingles [on her dress]? Sewed me into her dress with a fine needle?" (19).

Schemers such as Lulu and Zelda are not the only arrangers of powerful designs. Erdrich shows that the individual mind itself is "authorial" in its arrangement of mental pictures, including those we call memories. As Lipsha says, "I see [the pictures in my memory], and I am caught" (152). A victim of his own habits of mind as well as of other people's designs, Lipsha admits to "airbrushing" the past (188). When he dislikes an experience, he revises it: "I try to recast the whole scene in my thoughts" (190). This tendency to avoid "reading" the pictures before him and, instead, to see what he wants to see is largely responsible for Lipsha's fate. Though he claims a Pillager heritage, he seems to lack definitive Pillager traits, especially the ability to alter his apparent fate by straightforwardly recognizing the "traps" such as Lulu's and Zelda's that lie in his path. Whereas Fleur has eluded the Lake Man of Matchimanito for years, even sending others to drown in her place, Lipsha seems unable to extricate himself from the simplest of webs (21).

In fact, ill-fated Lipsha in *The Bingo Palace* takes the brunt of the collective narrator's criticism: "We weren't very pleased with the picture" of Lipsha's life (8). He becomes the textual equivalent of the naive reader. Lipsha does not hear (he misconstrues Gerry's telephone message because he does not understand Chippewa), nor does he see (he "airbrushes"). He is an easy victim of other people's and his own artful management of signs. Indeed, the collective narrator contemptuously reduces him to a semiotic phenomenon—the "son of a poster" (7)—a trope to be manipulated by someone more clever, such as Lulu. When he visits Fleur Pillager in her cabin, he cannot read or speak her "language" (literally, Chippewa, but also Fleur's "language" of power, not to mention fate, the writing on the wall). The visit leaves him dazed, as if under a heavy spell. "Weakening and dizzy," Lipsha says, "I look at the strange lines on her walls, between the neat stacks of letters, and pick out familiar patterns. . . . I am reading a set of words, a sentence, something that loops toward the window, which makes no sense to me and which I can't understand. . . . I [am] afraid that I have fallen under some sort of spell" (135–36).

Indeed, Lipsha is a trope (a "son of a poster") in somebody else's "sentence" (Lulu's, Fleur's, and of course, Erdrich's); he is under someone else's "spell" (as a character he is in their power, and as a trope he is a "sign" in their system, a "spelled" phenomenon). Because he is so naive, Lipsha has little hope of seeing the "design" of the verbal and visual traps "spring clear."[74] The consequence of Lipsha's naiveté is death, for (as Nanapush tells us in *Tracks*) stories, including the stories contained in pictures, can "cure or kill." Saved from drowning as a baby abandoned in a slough, Lipsha nevertheless meets his apparently fated death by water, by freezing to death at the end of his trek with Gerry, who has successfully escaped from prison with Lulu's deliberate and Lipsha's unwitting aid. Frozen within the "designs" of others, Lipsha in death reminds us of Nanapush's remarks in *Tracks* concerning Father Damien, whom Nanapush "drowns" by "push[ing] him under with . . . words."[75]

Whereas Lipsha remains naive and dies as an example of a poor "reader," the collective narrator's "gestures" to the actual audience, as we have seen, include metacritical cues that make the careful reader aware of the power of "pictures" like those of Erdrich and other authors. Moreover, Erdrich further manages her audience through skilled deployment of the counter-colonial trope, a type of "hook" that snags an attentive reader, not only while reading *The Bingo Palace*, but possibly forever after. Adept readers, unlike Lipsha in Fleur's cabin, learn with the help of narrative cues to decode the "sentence" in which they are immersed; moreover, under Erdrich's "spell," such readers are also profoundly affected by her unique management of the ethnic sign.

Implied throughout *The Bingo Palace* in the multiply nuanced trope of ensnarement (photographs, webs, nets, and sewn and beaded garments) is the notion that stories contained in verbal and visual designs can change the world, beginning with the perceptual and interpretive habits of readers. Like Lipsha, readers and viewers may become implicated or "trapped" within the "design" of an authoritative consciousness, and this design may in turn affect their actions, especially their subsequent habits of interpretation. For some contemporary American Indian writers such as Erdrich, to change a reader's habits of interpretation amounts to a

subtle, counter-colonial, and reappropriative act. Like her character Fleur Pillager, who gambles to repossess lost Chippewa lands,
Erdrich plays a textual game with the aim of appropriating the
semiotic space of the novel, previously dominated by Eurocentric
storytellers with Eurocentric frames of reference.

As we have seen, a significant portion of the narrative energy of
her novels is devoted to bringing all preconceived frames of reference into question, especially through the example of Lipsha,
the naive "airbrusher" who does not even know his own native language. Erdrich is not satisfied with raising questions, however. Her
writings marshal the deconstructive energy of the ethnic sign in
an ultimate counter-colonial move designed to change her audience's ways of seeing, hearing, and knowing. After all, the ultimate
colonial act is to appropriate the intellectual, psychological, and
emotional space of the Other—to alter his or her sense of reality.
Fleur Pillager, Lulu Lamartine, and Zelda Kashpaw each present
to the attentive reader alternative schemes for the construction of
"reality" that resist Eurocentric explanation, not the least of which
schemes assume that well-managed stories can cure or kill, and that
storytellers and listeners alike are directly responsible for the beliefs, attitudes, and actions the stories engender. As originators of
stories or as willing participants in the designs that others' stories
comprise, we conspire in the ongoing creation, or destruction, of
realities.

In *The Bingo Palace*, Erdrich's various tropes of ensnarement,
especially the trope of the picture and the accompanying act of
looking, serve as ethnic signs to "dispel" the Eurocentric "spell"
that dictates a way of seeing and interpreting the world, as well as
to introduce an alternative epistemology. The ethnic sign, with its
disruptive, deconstructive energy, is a "hook." Generating hesita-
tion and doubt, it helps to clear a space in the reader's mind for
expanded interpretive possibilities; it redefines the position of the
reader with regard to the text, now conceived as an opportunity to
participate in, or to resist, the designs of the storyteller.

One passage from *The Bingo Palace* especially emphasizes the
way in which the ethnic sign serves as a hook for the author-as-
fisherman who casts for the minds and hearts of the audience. A
consummate gambler (and fisherman—recall that in *Tracks* Fleur
"reels in" her prey in the fateful card game [23]), Fleur Pillager
appears on the reservation dressed as a warrior with a white Pierce-

Arrow and a strange, otherworldly white boy. This white boy, doubt-less Erdrich's version of the Chippewa "evil gambler," plays cards with Fleur and Tatro, the Indian Agent. Tatro, like a hooked, "gasping fish,"[76] is easy prey in Fleur's design to repossess her lands. He wants so badly to win the Pierce-Arrow that he fails to see how Fleur has set him up: "Even the boy did not deflect his attention, though if Tatro had not been preoccupied, he would have asked questions enough to form an explanation. The automobile, the clarity of his own greed, concentrated him. He looked at the car, he looked at Fleur, and that is when we realized that the decoy was not the boy, as we previously believed, but the car. Large parcels and belong-ings would soon change owners" (143). In the end, Fleur wins back everything, including the car. "As for the Agent, the car, you do not feed bait to a gasping fish. . . . You simply extract the hook" (145).

This humorous scene is also a metacritical "picture" from which the alert reader may learn much. It is rife with cues apprising the reader of Erdrich's reappropriative aim, which, ironically, succeeds best in the case of the adept reader who has played the textual game fully enough to be thoroughly, but not naively, hooked into Erdrich's design. In this game, Erdrich as author corresponds to Fleur, the designer of the game. The reader corresponds to the sidelined collective narrator, who struggles to perceive Fleur's de-sign, and to Tatro, who must ultimately cede some of his territory. Like Tatro, distracted by the whiteness of Fleur's dress, the white-ness of the Pierce-Arrow, and finally, the eerie whiteness of the strange boy, the reader is distracted by the whiteness of the page into thinking that he or she is engaged in the simple ("white," Eurocentric) "game" of *merely* reading a story. Such a reader does not at first, or perhaps ever, consciously realize that some of his or her mental space has been appropriated by a member of a "tribe of pressed trees." Though neither this metaphor of the reader-as-gasping-fish, nor the earlier metaphors of the reader as snared prey, is especially flattering, the fact is that, like Lipsha, Tatro, and Clarence Morrissey, we "are caught"—in a new frame of reference, the "trap" of the counter-colonial design of Erdrich's story.

Counting Coup on Postmodern Narrative

In many Indian tribes, a warrior's bravery was traditionally gauged by his success at "counting coup," getting close enough to the enemy to touch him or to appropriate his belongings.[77] Contemporary Native American writers might be viewed as successfully "counting coup" on postmodern narrative, a western genre partly inimical to their ultimate purposes but also replete with narrative features that Indian writers advantageously appropriate. Moreover, contemporary (non-Indian) audience receptivity to such Indian literature might be, in part, a result of postmodern developments and the transformation of reading practices that postmodernity engenders. Although in general, Eurocentric narrative forms powerfully resist many aspects of nonwestern expression, postmodern narrative is less resistant to such expression.[78] Like so many recent Indian narratives, postmodern texts either take for granted the reader's sophisticated awareness of the role of semiosis in the construction of art and reality, or they set out to instruct and, to some extent, create such an audience through metacritical commentary.[79] Certainly, the reader who is familiar with the foregrounded semiotic play of the postmodern novel is better prepared to encounter works by Native American writers, from Momaday and Silko to Vizenor and King, than is the more conventional reader, who expects "irreversible logico-temporal order" and mimetic verisimilitude, both of which camouflage semiosis.[80] The ideal receiver of many contemporary Native American texts is, of course, the bicultural Indian reader who (like the Indian authors themselves) is well versed in western narrative traditions, including postmodernism, and in semiotically self-reflexive oral storytelling and ceremonial traditions.[81] At least one aim of today's Native American writers appears to be the expansion of this audience of ideal, bicultural readers through the use of metacritical and other outwardly "postmodern" strategies.

We are now well aware of how postmodern strategies, including narrative techniques for evoking character and narrator identity, resemble traditional Indian storytelling practices. Both postmodern readers and the traditional Indian audience, for instance, have internalized rules of text production, and both are aware of their responsibilities as participants in storytelling (though such "re-

sponsibility" is quite differently conceived in either case[82]. However, encoded with more than one interpretive frame of reference
or "reception regime,"[83] contemporary Native American cross-
coded narratives demand even greater mental agility on the part
of the reader. To decode these texts successfully is to understand
that notions of "truth," "reality," and "identity," for example, are
culturally determined products of semiosis, that a reader always
reads from within some predetermined cultural frame of reference, and that at times, one's particular frame of reference may
be inadequate to the interpretive task at hand. Even more than
the postmodern novel, which operates within western hermeneutic
boundaries, Indian writers' cross-coded narratives demand flexible and revisionary interpretive capacities. Successfully "counting
coup" upon postmodern forms means not only appropriating the
semiotic "property" of the Other, but also reinventing it by making
it serve "Indian" ends within the mainstream culture.

Capitalizing on the modalities of power encoded in western
narrative forms, Momaday, Silko, Erdrich, King, and others exercise narrative resistance to the habitual construction of the world
according to dominant, ethnocentric "rules." In so doing, these
writers thoroughly and systematically contest the western stereotypical notion that "power and control [are] outside the range of
the Indian imagination."[84] Their works also testify to the fact that
the dominant discourse is always "at risk of disruption"[85] by contradictory statements formulated within the strictures of that same
discourse. Unfolding within the strictures of Eurocentric written
narrative, these texts nevertheless demand non-Eurocentric interpretations based on nonwestern worldviews. Thus the dominant
discourse is readily "counter-colonized" by "subversive" semiotic
practices that, in turn, become a part of the dominant discourse.
Such counter-colonizing texts expand the Euro-American epistemological frame and facilitate the entry of other such texts—and
their concomitant worldviews and "realities"—into the dominant
domain. Indeed, herein might lie the most revolutionary of all destabilizing effects that a novel may achieve by exploiting the power
relations inherent in narrative. Just as Cortés exploited the possibilities inherent in Aztec semiosis even as he subverted the reality
it upheld, contemporary Indian authors have developed an art of
resistance carried on within, and in opposition to, the dominant
discourse. As readers of contemporary Native American writing

increase in number and develop a range of appropriate interpretive responses to these works, we begin to see how Indian writers' management of discursive power results, ironically, in greater solidarity between a now less marginalized group of artists and a less "mainstream" group of readers. "Margin" and "mainstream" are thus likewise exposed as fluid semiotic constructions, as we shall further observe in Chapter Five.

Chapter Two
Imagining the Stories: Narrativity and Solidarity

Almost learned how to read from books that had been burned in a fire at the reservation library. The books were burned on the sides. He read the centers of the pages and imagined the stories.[1]

As we have seen in Chapter One, narrative management exploiting power may frustrate narrativity, the process by which a reader constructs a story based upon expectations and textual cues. Such experience, in turn, might generate in the reader an expanded repertoire of semiotic practices pertaining to texts and world. We have also seen how highly resistant narrative such as Momaday's *House Made of Dawn* might drive the reader's effort to decode the work beyond the margins of the text to extratextual references. Momaday's is a useful technique for transforming the actual reader as thoroughly as possible into a projected, biculturally informed ideal audience; certainly, Momaday has announced his intention of "creating his listeners" on more than one occasion.[2] However, the actual audience for *House* and for other ethnic literature probably consists of only a few who are likely to play a textually mandated reader-as-researcher role. Indeed, today's widened audience for Native American literature has partially resulted from deliberate efforts by authors to foster solidarity with a non-Indian audience without *necessarily* demanding extensive, extratextual detours.

Metapattern Expansion and Solidarity

Achieving solidarity with an audience involves more than the initial deconstructive act of frustrating narrativity. Indeed, if "absence or disruption of cohesive devices [characteristic of resistant narrative] are transparent signifiers of repudiation of social relations,"[3] then a narration of resistance alone lacks the implied world-healing telos of American Indian "story." The reformative aim of resistant narrative depends for its ultimate fulfillment upon the reader's reinvestment in a community of semiotic agents, defined not as passive consumers of dissenting discourse but as responsible participants in storytelling as world-making.[4]

As my discussion of narrational power reveals, one (paradoxical) way of achieving solidarity with an audience is through power tactics, for "solidarity is an effect of power," just as "power is an effect of solidarity."[5] That is to say, as authors variously deconstruct conventional narrative modes and their readers' interpretive practices, they simultaneously instate and foster alternatives to these modes and practices. When shared, these alternatives constitute solidarity bonds. (Solidarity becomes power when a group's production and reception agendas are widely enough ensconced within the dominant discourse to exert significant destabilizing force and to vie for dominance.) Revised social relations of the type that many Native American writers treat thematically in their texts are achieved primarily through regenerative narrative strategies that produce different kinds of solidarity with the audience.[6]

Silko's *Ceremony* provides an interesting case in point regarding solidarity as an effect of managed narrative power. As we have seen in Chapter One, the structural dynamic of Silko's novel derives from encoded semiotic instability, a dynamic that is overdetermined at mimetic (or content) and semiosic (or metasignifying) levels of the text. One syntagmatic chain of references that profoundly reinforces Silko's structural episteme and also fosters solidarity with a broad general audience involves Indian and non-Indian codifications of physical space. In response to these codes, the reader ideally undergoes both frustration of narrativity and induction into a "ceremony" of reclamation. Ultimately, readers are stimulated to change our way of living on the land by first recognizing and transforming our semiotic relationship to it.[7]

In *Ceremony*, an "Indian" relationship to the earth is encoded through a chain of accumulated associations with the color blue that define Native American conceptions of space. Extremely important in the ritual process that Silko inscribes in her text are sandpaintings (or drypaintings) and chantways—ceremonial healing rites that invoke powers associated with colors.[8] Blue appears most often in rituals concerned with healing disharmonious relationships with the earth—especially the land in its maternal aspects. In *Ceremony*, Tayo's relationship to nurturing forces in the land needs healing. Among his many problems, Tayo has offended Reed Woman by cursing the rain. To be cured, he must discover his proper role (of ritual storyteller) in the Laguna community and help make the land "green again."[9] Betonie's healing ritual places Tayo in the middle of a ceremonial painting invoking the powers of the Bear People. Embodying the forces which Tayo most needs to internalize, Pollen Boy occupies "the center" of the painting with his eyes, mouth, neck and joints drawn in blue pollen (141). To restore Tayo's connections with the appropriate Holy People, Betonie also paints a rainbow with a blue stripe, a blue mountain range, and blue bear tracks, in which Tayo carefully steps as he walks "back to belonging / . . . home to happiness / . . . back to long life" (144).

This chain of references to the color blue occurs within (at least) a double frame of potential meanings, for the color blue conveys meanings within Euro-American as well as Pueblo-Navajo extratextual fields of reference. Though non-Indian readers may know little of the Pueblo-Navajo context of Silko's particular references to the color blue, many will likely be generally acquainted with color symbolism in western culture. Moreover, these references to blue may evoke common romantic ideas about therapeutic nature and the American landscape even in the reader who is ignorant of the Navajo cosmology informing Betonie's drypainting. Thus, in addition to the Navajo context, Silko evokes a second (Eurocentric) referential ground through her code of the color blue.

In *Ceremony*, the color blue directly describes sky, mountains, and the apparel of two women characters. One woman's name is "Montaña" (Spanish for "mountain"); her name underscores the equation of "blueness" with earth (specifically with the sacred mountains where the Holy People dwell). Silko's female, nurturing characters in *Ceremony* signify within the typical, Euro-American reader's conception of the earth as female.[10] The color blue—especially as associated with female presence and power—becomes a key term in Silko's revisionary semiosis: if woman and earth are equated (both cultural contexts), and if woman and blueness are equated (Navajo context), then the equation of blueness and earth becomes axiomatic in an expanded "metapattern," or "revised" reader frame of reference. Not all readers will achieve the same awareness of how or in what terms their repertoire of meanings has been expanded; nevertheless, these "new" possible meanings remain available to all of them. As we will see in this and subsequent chapters, the gradual influx of possible meanings and reader-responses from "marginal" to "mainstream" texts may lead to an amplified dominant discourse.

Guided by Silko's textual cues, a careful reader is drawn back to the Navajo material; this time, however, such a reader is better prepared to decode Silko's references to blue in their "ceremonial" context, where the "ceremony" concerns healing by reconnecting humanity with the earth's vertical, metaphysical, and "female" or nurturing dimensions. Thus Silko affords the reader an experience parallel to, if not the same as her protagonist's. Both the reader and Tayo must expand their vision, the reader by making the necessary inferences cued by Silko's text,[11] and Tayo by ceremonially walking through the drypainting. Both must find a new way of interpreting experience within a metaphysical frame of reference that is, in particular, respectful of nature and of the human capacity for environmental destruction.

Rife with meanings drawn from multiple cultural contexts, Silko's blue code becomes a semiotic bridge between dually inscribed cultural content. Therefore, no matter which informational context a reader initially draws on, Silko's blue code will not only signify, but also deliver the alert reader, now more adept at code-switching, into a wider interpretive field. Within this field, however, an Indian vision is emphasized in an authorial gesture designed to produce ideological and emotional change in the reader. For example, blue equals woman equals earth, where both woman and earth are defined for the reader primarily in Silko's "Indian" terms. Though *Ceremony* is not polemical in its message—indeed, it straightforwardly states that both Indian and non-Indian must change—this strategy of overdetermination is designed to preclude a one-sided, Eurocentric reader-response. The novel attenuates the western romantic vision of the earth that typically equates woman and nature, but that also typically commodifies both. Silko deploys Eurocentric cultural information within an interpretive field widened through the introduction of Pueblo-Navajo cultural material; with readers who perform her revisionary interpretive tasks, the author achieves a type of solidarity emphasizing complementary environmental and feminist values.[12]

Louise Erdrich aims for similar ends, though the solidarity bonds that her works generate are more abstractly philosophical by comparison with Silko's activist agenda. In *Love Medicine*, for instance, a string of Cree prayer beads appears at first to be a symbolic bridge between Christian and Native American spirituality. Raised Catholic and even once a postulant nun, Marie Kashpaw sometimes calls these beads a "rosary," a word most commonly used to describe Roman Catholic prayer beads. As Cree beads, they speak to Marie's mystical nature (she is a sorcerer and healer); as a rosary, they appeal to her somewhat more orthodox Catholic sensibility. However, because she is spiritually liminal—both Catholic and Cree, but fully neither—touching the beads creates in her a special type of awareness: "I don't pray, but sometimes I do touch the beads. . . . I never look at them, just let my fingers roam to them when no one is in the house. It's a rare time when I do this. I touch them, and every time I do I think of small stones. At the bottom of the lake, rolled aimless by the waves. I think of them polished. To many people it would be a kindness. But I see no kindness in how the waves are grinding them smaller and smaller until they finally disappear."[13]

To think of the Cree beads/rosary as mere stones is to verge on epistemological insight. The beads *are* stones, called "prayer beads" by Crees and "rosary" by Catholics, according to two different religious frames of reference. These frames of reference are yoked but not conventionally reconciled in the literary symbol of the beads. Able to see from both perspectives, Marie has developed what Todorov calls a "double exteriority" in her outlook on the world; that is to say, the price of a cross-cultural vision is sometimes to become a wistful outsider to both worlds, as we saw with Clarence in *Tracks*.

Furthermore, Erdrich's metonymic substitution of stones for beads potentially directs the reader's attention back to another, associated chain of references to stones that likewise emphasizes Todorovian "exteriority." Water-worn stones, along with water itself, as we saw in Chapter One, are part of a pattern of references in the novel that suggests diminishment of human beings by life.

When Nector feels the course of his life change, he feels "Time . . . rushing around [him] like water around a big wet rock. . . . Very quickly [he] would be smoothed away";[14] and Henry Lamartine, Jr.'s face is described as "white and hard. Then it broke, like stones break all of a sudden when water boils up inside them" (52). In the passage concerning the prayer beads, people, beads, and stones are equated through metonymy. This equation of humans and prayer beads with stones effaces the sacral dimension of existence and re-duces everything to merely phenomenal status.

In such an associational field, the rosary/prayer beads are not a bridge between religions or an expression of synthesized religious values; instead, they remind us that noumenal aspects of material existence provoke a spiritual yearning that religion does not neces-sarily satisfy. A similar eradication of the sacral dimensions of exis-tence occurs when emotional intimacy is described as the touch of "angel wings"; "angel wings" is also, however, the name of an alcoholic beverage—the ruin of many a Native American life. In instances such as these, Erdrich sometimes achieves solidarity with her readers by delivering a kind of existential shock that refocuses our attention onto the things of this world. This shock admonishes any reader prone to totalizing visions of the Indian Other as pos-sessing absolute spiritual knowledge; after all, her comic shaman, Lipsha, is frequently inept, and her wise trickster, Nanapush, ac-knowledges mystery as the ultimate characteristic of the universe.

Sacramentality is likewise subverted in *The Beet Queen* when Mary sees Karl's face in the snow, the nuns see Christ, and Celestine James sees nothing but an indentation in the snow. The "miracu-lous" image is reduced to the merely phenomenal; the sacral di-mension is part of the nuns' frame of reference, and Mary's more imaginative reaction possibly results from her own way of seeing. When the snow melts in the spring, Mary describes the disappear-ance of the image in mystical terms, but Erdrich has nevertheless made her point about the perplexing nature of interpretation. Overall, Erdrich's novels (recalling Silko's manner of narration in *Ceremony*) confront problems of the origin of knowledge, and so re-sist any interpretive urge founded on epistemological or theologi-cal certainty. In these passages Erdrich seems to imply that, while cross-cultural vision may in fact unite those who share it, solidarity may encourage political action less than a contemplative awareness of the human condition. Like Lipsha Morrissey observing his submerged ancestral lands in *Love Medicine*, we may feel displaced and only vaguely comforted by our "perspective on it all" (211).

Employing these narrative power tactics, Silko, Erdrich, and others play the role of the ritual artist described by Victor Turner and other cultural anthropologists. The ritual art of liminality sets out to expand cultural "metapatterns"—interpretive frames of reference through which new experience is both achieved and explained and through which intellectual, emotional, and social transformation of individuals and cultures takes place.[15] Such experiences perhaps prepare the reader to say with Momaday's Father Olguin, "I understand!"[16]—the author's metatextual expression of solidarity achieved between producers and receivers of cross-coded Indian texts. Metapattern expansion that evokes solidarity is also achieved in contemporary Native American narrative by a number of other means—through overt, metatextual instruction of the audience, through textually induced experiences of semiotic disorder that subtly expand the codes of the "mainstream" readership, and through reimbrication of verbal and visual icons drawn from the dominant culture.

Metatextual Instruction

Semiotician Michael Riffaterre has described the encoded reader's response to certain texts as precisely analogous to a musician's response to a musical score: reading amounts to a performance.[17] We have already remarked at length how often the Indian author's assumed persona derives from oral, performative traditions. Semiotic analysis may enable us to understand further how Native American authors likewise imagine their audience's role as primarily a performative act. Solidarity between authors and readers of contemporary Native American narrative results from, as it were, carefully orchestrated texts encoded with vast and complex messages, including metatextual instructions to the reader about the author's apparent assumptions, expectations, and visionary-revisionist intent.[18]

Strategies for delivery of instruction vary. Some writers directly address the subject of writing and its powers, which range from mystical to political. Some (like Erdrich, and like Silko in *Ceremony*) treat the audience gently, while others (like Vizenor in *Bearheart: The Heirship Chronicles* [1990], and like Silko in *Almanac of the Dead*) intend to make their readers uncomfortable. Some writers develop narrators and characters who straightforwardly assume responsibility for guiding the audience and whose remarks provide a context for interpreting other metatextual passages containing subtler cues to the reader. Instructive voices range from earnest, such as those in Silko's *Ceremony* and Walters's *Ghost Singer*, to comedic, such as Erdrich's Lipsha or King's Coyote. The latter types sometimes represent the naive or outsider-reader's point of view through their "dumb" questions and musings even as they focus audience attention on whatever an author means for us to notice. In *Green Grass, Running Water*, for example, when Coyote cues the reader that "all this water imagery must mean something,"[19] his comment is multiply nuanced. The quintessential trickster, he plays a triple role of the dull reader who struggles to interpret image patterns, the clever (western) image-hunter who nevertheless misreads according to a non-Native frame of reference, and the candid instructor of the reader, for as it turns out, all the water imagery *does* indeed "mean something." The reader should, ideally, be aware of all three possibilities at once. Coyote's remark may remind us of what we have seen in connection with culturally cross-coded texts; frequently, as Riffaterre reminds us, two or more simultaneous interpretations of any passage are called for: "the interpretation that the metalinguistic statement of intention seems to require" (King's satirical point that Euro-American readers sometimes mistakenly hunt for meaningful image patterns in "Indian" writing) and "the interpretation indicated by the shape of the utterance which is the object of this metalanguage" (the water imagery *does*, literally, "mean something").[20]

Silko's *Ceremony* provides a paradigmatic example among contemporary Native American literature of the use of overt metatextual instruction. This instruction is part of an overall "elaborated code"[21] in a novel that begins by assuming little or no solidarity with a non-Indian audience but that in the end produces a high degree of solidarity by virtue of having instructed the reader. (By contrast, offering much less metatextual instruction, Momaday's *House Made of Dawn* features a "restricted code" that assumes high solidarity with a literate Indian audience and much less with a non-Indian audience; in the end, however, his restricted code produces less solidarity with his "marginalized," non-Indian readers than does Silko's *Ceremony*.[22]) Consequently, *Ceremony* seems designed especially for a non-Indian audience, though like *House* it develops the highest degree of solidarity with a literate, Native American audience. Lying somewhere in between *Ceremony* and *House* with regard to "elaboration" versus "restriction" of codes is a novel such as King's *Green Grass*, which resembles Vizenor's fiction in exploiting more decidedly postmodern, language-game strategies as its means of "elaboration." In King's and Vizenor's works, metatextual assistance is most readily discernible to the reader who is already adept at postmodern semiotic play, as we shall presently observe.

In *Ceremony*, narrating voices assist the reader as straightforwardly as Ku'oosh and Betonie assist Tayo. Silko includes instructions to the reader about how to participate in her semiotic "ceremony" of healing. Like the ceremonial bear tracks which guide Tayo's steps "home [and] back to belonging" (144), parts of Silko's ceremonial narration and dialogue guide the reader through the potential confusion of the text to an understanding of the power of the creative imagination—the place where "the stories fit together . . . to become the story that [is] being told" (246). Silko specifically addresses the role of thought and semiosis in the construction and destruction of reality. Ku'oosh, for example, tells us that "the world is fragile" (35). The narrator explains his meaning: "The word he chose to express 'fragile' was filled with the intricacies of a continuing process, and with a strength inherent in spider webs. . . . It took a long time to explain the fragility and intricacy because no word exists alone, and the reason for choosing each word had to be explained with a story about why it must be said this certain way. That was the responsibility that went with being human, old Ku'oosh said, the story behind each word must be told so there could be no mistake in the meaning of what had been said" (35–36).[23] Betonie likewise explains Silko's apparent conception of the relationship of words to the world. He teaches Tayo that contemporary evil originated in a malign "story" told by "witches" showing off their magical powers through a "contest."[24] The narrator reinforces the message about story: indeed, the narrator tells us, "the world" is "made of stories" (95).

Silko's dialogue also contains straightforward and literal cues to the reader about the nature of the author's narrative strategies. Various characters, particularly Ts'eh (and her counterparts, the Mexican captive and Night Swan), Ku'oosh, and Betonie provide instructive comments addressed to other characters (usually

Tayo) but rife with information for the reader who, in response to the numerous strategies of destabilization that I have described in Chapter One, struggles to maintain interpretive bearings throughout the text. Thus the dialogue becomes a narrative means of establishing solidarity with the industrious reader who has adequately responded to the destabilizing, "power" tactics of the text. Silko's dialogue fills a liminal space between the reader's presumably untutored consciousness and Silko's represented "Indian" world. The dialogue bridges worlds the way Betonie's verbal and visual cues help mend the rift between Tayo's disorderly mind and spirit, and the Southwestern land. Obvious "performative action" is required from both Tayo and the reader. Solidarity results when author, characters (including the narrator), and audience no longer inhabit mutually exclusive realms of understanding.

Ceremony rewrites the rules for reader performance under maximum conditions of semiotic instability in order to reveal the ways in which "story" makes reality or, in the words of Thomas Sebeok, the ways in which "life modifies the universe to meet its needs, and accomplishes this by means of sign action." [25] By heightening our awareness of the ways in which we make and receive meaning, *Ceremony* instructs us concerning the logonomic (rule-bound, discursive) interface between the "world" of the text and the "text" of the world. The reader who becomes aware of this interface and empowered by such awareness understands that a "story" may lead to a world with atomic weapons, but also that such a world may be "re-read" as a "story" and revised.

The idea of the world as a story under revision by competing stories likewise appeals to Linda Hogan, who instructs the reader directly concerning the "medicine" powers of writing and textuality in *Mean Spirit* and who presents her own text as the semiotic equivalent of a medicine bundle.[26] Though her narrative resides materially in "this world," as we read we realize that it resembles Joe Billy's medicine bag passed down to him from Sam Billy, for it contains other worlds, "wanting out." [27] In Hogan's layered novel, an outer narrative recounting episodes in Osage history and the daily lives of a variety of characters envelops an in-progress, prophetic, inner narrative, *The Book of Horse*, being written or possibly transcribed from spiritual sources by Michael Horse. The "Indian" story implied in the inner narrative juxtaposes the outer narrative, a more Eurocentrically constructed story of the Osage past. This outer narrative (punctuated throughout by the chiming of a clock measuring western mechanical time) reads much like a traditional historical novel. It invokes Eurocentric habits of interpretation, and we are encouraged to view history as a linear, indeed a millennial, story with gaps that need filling until at some point we obtain the complete truth. Even Michael Horse himself for a time shares this millennial vision as he wonders whether *The Book of Horse* might be considered one of the missing books of the Bible.

However, the inner narrative, Michael's in-progress book, defies Eurocentric generic classification. It is the fluid, indeterminate story of a yet undisclosed future. Within Hogan's narrative, references to Michael's book—rather than passages from it—signify its existence; so long as it exists as pure, semiotic potentiality, it cannot be misappropriated. When Michael considers offering his prophetic book to the world as one of the lost books of the Bible, Hogan reminds us that the stories (and histories) of nondominant groups are always threatened by co-optation, or "incorporation" into the dominant discourse. There they are "naturalized," or misread within the semiosic boundaries of the dominant society. When, at the last minute, Michael and his book escape the semiosic domain of history implied by the outer narrative, Hogan reveals her apparent understanding of "writing" Indians' "medicine." *The Book of Horse*, its author-transcriber, and its presumed audience disappear from the mimetic plane at the end of the novel. The predicted fires come, the parrot flies away south, and the "Indian" characters, without literally dying, join the spirits called the Hill People who have gone away, obscuring the "good Red Road" behind them. "They looked back once and saw it all rising up in the reddened sky, the house, the barn, the broken string of lights, the life they had lived, nothing more than a distant burning. No one spoke" (375). Her characters take the good Red Road into an ahistorical dimension, hide the road behind them, and leave us with a message resembling Silko's in *Almanac* and Vizenor's in *Bearheart*: history is not a fixed set of facts or a story to be revised until complete and correct. On the contrary, these writers suggest that history—like the future—is indeterminate and subject to the vicissitudes of the present, or "sacred time." These vicissitudes include the interpretive acts of participants in storytelling. By collapsing the familiar material world described in the outer narrative into the spiritual plane evoked by *The Book of Horse*, Hogan at the novel's end instructively abandons readers in a silent emotional and intellectual space encouraging us to reconsider the nature of our participation. In *Mean Spirit*, Hogan portrays "Indian" realities on the verge of eclipsing dominant, or Eurocentric realities. Outer and inner narratives in this novel recall the oppositional discourses of Silko in *Ceremony* and Momaday in *House*, for they unfold according to different and conflicting systems of rules for producing (and receiving) meaning. Consequently, Hogan subverts the Eurocentric boundaries that for some readers define "reality" as well as many of the conventions for its representation in language. Hogan shows us what might happen should Eurocentric "reality" (described in one narrative layer) give way to the "Native American" reality (described in the other narrative layer). "Re-signing" the boundaries of reality and representation in "Indian" terms, Hogan exploits the considerable, world-altering political power implicit within aesthetic form. Oppositional discourses in *Mean Spirit* semiotically embody the collision of Eurocentric and Indian worlds, and potentially renegotiate the rules by which we construct the future. For Hogan, solidarity is achieved with readers who stand poised in the narrative silence at the end of the novel to begin this profound renegotiation requiring the responsible management of verbal, political, and ceremonial power. Stace's interior monologue toward the end of *Mean Spirit* reminds us that "stories" teach us "that there [are] times when a person could do nothing but wait and be silent, that an answer would sometimes come out of nothing" (348). "Answers" to the reader's questions about the apocalyptic ending of *Mean Spirit*, however, come not "out of nothing," but out of the semiosic plane of the text, the level of metasigns, where we learn to recognize Hogan's "Indian" cues instructing us in how to interpret the text, in how we might escape the tight hermeneutic circle of Eurocentric response to the world.

Direct metatextual instruction of another type occurs in Walters's *Ghost Singer* and, comparably but less successfully, in Robert J. Conley's *Mountain Windsong*. The two authors' very different strategies for integrating historical information lead to "strong" and "weak" solidarity bonds, and to greater and lesser metapattern expansion, respectively. ("Strong" solidarity bonds describe intimacy, whereas "weak" bonds constitute more polite, respectful distance.[28]) Walters brings her non-Indian reader farther into her represented Indian realm than Conley manages to do, and she builds solidarity with her audience that potentially bridges cultures. By contrast, Conley's attempt to force extratextual historical matter into aesthetic bounds, though instructive, produces weaker solidarity and, probably inadvertently, a more complacent acceptance of irreconcilable "Indian" and "white" worlds.

To appreciate the terrifying spiritual phenomena surrounding Indian artifacts at the Smithsonian Institution in Washington, D.C., as portrayed in *Ghost Singer*, readers need to know (though most will not) a fair amount of the history of the Southwest, particularly of the Navajo. Moreover, the reader must know that the "official" or "history text" versions of this past, insofar as they are recorded, are different from the Native oral record. Like any writer of historical fiction, therefore, Walters faced the difficult challenge of integrating such material aesthetically. An additional challenge arose when she decided to attempt to revise the official history even as she recorded it. To succeed in her apparent revisionary mission, Walters had to provide not only alternative historical material, but an alternative frame of reference for its construal by non-Indian readers, as well.

Comparably to Hogan's *Mean Spirit*, a Chinese-box narrative pattern in *Ghost Singer* calls attention to, and ultimately disrupts, semiotic and epistemological boundaries defining "Indian" and non-Indian realities. In Walters's *Ghost Singer*, a yet-to-be-written text by David Drake constitutes an inner narrative positing "truths" in the mimetic (or content) plane of the novel that conflict with (and are ultimately silenced by) those of the Indian world sustained by the outer narrative. In the semiosic (metasign) plane, this proposed historical narrative—a presumptuous white man's story of the Navajo to be told from the "Navajo point of view"[29]—likewise contrasts with the outer narrative, for it encodes rules for worldmaking that conflict with those operative in the outer narrative describing an "Indian" world. Walters need not actually produce Drake's history within her text in order to deploy its oppositional power, for the reader already knows how his story will go, having in various ways already read white men's histories of the Indians, possibly even those written by David's nineteenth-century namesake scholars, Benjamin Drake and Samuel G. Drake. The generic, history-textbook story of Native Americans told by cultural outsiders is thus invoked through a fictional name redolent of nonfictional agents. The potentially silencing power of the dominant culture is thereby invoked as a story against which the outer narrative may be read and interpreted.

Meanwhile, the outer narrative plays out a compelling mystery centered around Indian artifacts and spiritual phenomena at the Natural History Building of the Smithsonian Institution. However, the Eurocentric reader who might expect this outer narrative to "make sense" or to cohere according to the rules of conventional ghost story, mystery,[30] or historical fiction is soon frustrated by the ways in which pieces of the story resist merger into any anticipated, seamless whole. Certain parts of the story, in fact, cannot adequately be explained within any traditional western frame of reference, though they do lend themselves to standard misinterpretations. Indeed, as Walters subtly informs her readers, Indian and non-Indian ways of seeing and "making sense" of the world, past or present, are not the same.

To realize her ambitious, historically instructive project, Walters provides metatextual instruction through dialogue among characters who are variously informed about the Navajo past. By developing characters with fragmentary knowledge of their tribal and family histories, Walters emphasizes the liabilities of oral record keeping even as she criticizes western conceptions of authority and cohesiveness that are structured into written historical narrative. For example, Jonnie Navajo knows bits of the past and wants to know more; a failed liaison between him and a white historian, David Drake, points up the deficiencies of each culture's efforts to construct the past. In his reliance upon oral, regional histories, Jonnie's knowledge is only as extensive as his social network. Drake, on the other hand, to whom vast amounts of written historical information are available, and with whom Jonnie has tentatively agreed to share his tribal knowledge, is limited by his own western conception of historical authority. For him, Jonnie's tribal record is not "legitimate," nor are the obscure individuals from the past (such as Red Lady and her baby, in whom Jonnie is primarily interested) the "proper" focus of historical inquiry.

For Jonnie, history is primarily the intersecting stories of many private individuals, while for David, history is the record of a few "significant" public figures and grand events already identified in a Euro-American master narrative. Arrogantly, David plans to retell Euro-American history from the Navajo point of view. However, as Jonnie remarks to David, " 'you and me is different. Not in our

skins, but in our minds.' "[31] He sounds the depths of David's ignorance of how different cultures inhabit different worlds and of how
the histories of these worlds are constructed according to different
logonomic rules. Indeed, Jonnie's and Wilbur's "Indian" vision can
account for phenomena such as the ghostly warrior in the Smithsonian that David Drake can only dimly perceive. Walters represents "Indian" reality as vaster and more spiritually sophisticated
than the conventional white man's materialist vision allows him to
see. Consequently, though he is well situated to do so, David remains unable to piece together the fuller story of the Navajo people
that he desires to tell.

Only Walters's reader can eventually put together the pieces of
the story of Red Lady's abduction into slavery in the 1830s and see
this story in the context of the larger story of Indian oppression
in the southwest. The reader knows the story that Jonnie Navajo
longs to hear but never does—what happened to Red Lady and
her child, Jonnie's ancestors. Conversations among Willie Begay,
George Daylight, Russell Tallman, and Wilbur Snake provide even
more important information for the reader, whose role in the novel
sometimes resembles that of the reader of mystery and detective fiction. It is our responsibility to notice the cues and clues about how
all the pieces fit together. However, the strongest solidarity bonds
uniting Walters with her audience consist of our deeper understanding that sometimes the pieces do not fit together until we
comprehend how Indians and non-Indians are "different . . . in our
minds." Walters's projected readers become part of a cross-cultural
community sharing solidarity with Walters, with each other, and
perhaps with Navajo and other American Indian authors we might
encounter in the future. Ultimately, Walters's advice to the Eurocentric reader recalls Wilbur Snake's advice to the noisy white
woman in the museum: "Be quiet," he warns her, for her chatter
not only endangers others; it is the outward sign of a closed mind.
Likewise, Russell Tallman eventually shouts at Donald Evans, "You
have a fantastic opportunity here to learn something, something
about yourself, and the world around you. At this moment it is possible to . . . learn some secrets of the universe. . . . Open up your
mind and prepare to learn something" (211). Walters constructs an
outer narrative encoding an "Indian" interpretive frame of reference that successfully eclipses the Eurocentric frame of reference
invoked by the implicit inner narrative (Drake's stillborn account

of the same events). Thus the outer, or "Indian," story silences the white man's story; *Ghost Singer* requires non-Indian readers to "be quiet" and "open up their minds" to alternative accounts of phenomenal reality.

Indeed, the ideal reader of *Ghost Singer* is better prepared to explain why some Native American novelists are more successful in their didactic missions than others. Robert Conley in *Mountain Windsong*, for example, apparently sets out to accomplish many of the same ends as Walters in *Ghost Singer*. He juxtaposes chapters containing "official" U.S. history with narrative sections telling the story of two young Cherokee lovers separated by the Trail of Tears. Despite the fact that the historical matter honestly exposes the evils of Jacksonian Indian policy, the separation of historical, public discourse from the storyline dilutes Conley's message (reminding us of Walters's) that history is also the story of individuals' personal agonies viewed from within frames of reference different from those of the mainstream society.

Moreover, unlike Walters's novel, Conley's leaves inviolate the logonomic system within which U.S. political history is produced. Primarily through the instructive dialogue of semiotically sophisticated "medicine" characters such as Wilbur Snake, Walters sends a shock wave through the logonomic system constructing the official history of the Navajo; she thereby deconstructs the system, by exposing not merely its falsehoods and inaccuracies, but also the semiotic means of its inadequate construction by cultural outsiders. The end of the *Ghost Singer* is particularly insistent on this issue when we learn what Wilbur Snake learned from LeClair, and what Wilbur then passes on to Willie Begay about the intersection of dreaming and language: dreaming is a source of knowledge of the material world, which is manipulable through language. Consequently, Walters takes her readers to the source of world-making in sign action, thereby disrupting her readers' confidence in the truth-claims of any society's discourse but also fostering in the reader a sense of power through responsible storytelling. In contrast, Conley leaves the reader merely with a sense of the irreconcilability of worlds, the injustices of the past, and with no appreciation of the linkages between logonomic rules and the ostensibly fixed reality we inhabit. Unlike Walters, Conley cannot release Indian ghosts from the constructed past to haunt the reader's imagination by insisting upon the presence of the past.

An Excess of Disorder

In the cases of Silko's blue code, Erdrich's bead code, and Hogan's and Walters's management of the conventions of the historical novel, we have seen examples of how Native American authors may broaden our repertoire of meanings and interpretive habits through strategic appeals to what is already familiar to readers. According to Eco, semiotic "codes allow us to enunciate events that the code [does] not anticipate as well as *metasemiotic* judgments that call into question the legitimacy of the code itself." Eco claims that such a characteristic of semiosis explains how the "literary" eventually "becomes culture" or "knowledge." [32] That is to say, when a writer first introduces a figure of speech or a new field of meanings for a conventional structure, it strikes the reader as unique and strange (recalling early formalist arguments concerning "defamiliarization" as a literary device [33]). However, what is "literary" becomes "culture" when it becomes part of our internalized repertoire of codes. Postmodern art forms, for instance, have "become culture," for most of us now expect to encounter their characteristic disjunctive and self-referential features, including their metasemiotic tendency to "question the legitimacy" of interpretive practices in general.

Before a device falls into a reader's set of standard expectations, however, it must be met and negotiated repeatedly in order for the reader to attain a full sense of its semiosic potential. Eco argues that "metaphors [for example] . . . tend to resist acquisition. If they are inventive (and thus original), they cannot be easily accepted; the system tends not to absorb them. Thus they produce, prior to knowledge, something which, psychologically speaking, we could call 'excitation' and which, from a semiotic point of view, is none other than 'information' in the most proper sense of the term; an excess of disorder in respect to existing codes." [34]

Much of contemporary Native American narrative does, indeed, produce for its audience(s) such "an excess of disorder in respect to existing codes." [35] As I have already suggested throughout this study so far, negotiating various types of semiotic disorder is a primary task of the reader of contemporary Indian writing. With reference to works by Gerald Vizenor in particular, I will argue further that solidarity with readers occurs when they discover how metacodes dispel apparent semiotic chaos; such metacodes consist of metaphors and other devices that order the disorder or, in Silko's terms, show us how "the stories fit together."[36] In *Ceremony*, for instance, Silko's references to sandpaintings provide a meta-code for deciphering the analogous relationship of atomic energy and storytelling that her novel suggests. Such biculturally inscribed metacodes, in turn, are frequently conventional enough to inter-face with what the reader already knows as mainstream "culture" or "knowledge," yet they amplify this field with meanings drawn from the marginal society. When we perceive, for example, in *Ceremony* how the atomic test crater at White Sands, New Mexico is a kind of sandpainting, we have learned something not only about Navajo ceremonial ritual but also about the nature of human cre-ativity and destruction as expressed in any culture.

Unlike Silko and others whose works seem to encourage a socially transformative slide from "literature" to "culture," however, Gerald Vizenor in his works appears deliberately to resist the process. In-deed, he has declared many times, in different contexts, that "cul-ture doesn't exist" and that "colonizers" such as anthropologists have "invented it."[37] Vizenor's invectives against "culture" and "ter-minal creeds" are statements about the problems involved in "fa-miliarization" of the disorderly "information" that creative artists deploy. Consequently, as an author, he treads coyote-like on the narrow border between semiotic overload and audience accom-modation, apparently so that he may delay as long as possible any paralyzing shift of his creative energies into the reader's repository of formulated "knowledge." This feature of his works might at first seem to gainsay solidarity but, ironically, such resistance becomes an aspect of an admittedly problematic solidarity that he eventu-ally achieves with some readers.

A novel characterized more by high-level, semiotic energy than by formulable, mimetic content is Vizenor's *Darkness in St. Louis Bearheart* (1978), reprinted in 1990 as *Bearheart: The Heirship Chronicles*. When it first appeared in 1978, the analogues for read-ing it that existed within the dominant discourse included the postmodern novel and science-fiction. *Bearheart* conforms to both sets of conventions, but this novel's grievous publication history in manuscript and print prior to its re-release in 1990 reveals just how few readers in the late 1970s were equal to the considerable challenges it posed.[38] *Bearheart* confronted most readers (except perhaps for a very small coterie of postmodernist, literary Indians like Vizenor himself) with nearly insurmountable interpretive obstacles and an almost overwhelming experience of cultural marginalization.

Published for a second time, Vizenor's text reemerged in the 1990s within a greatly transformed dominant discourse. Since the late 1970s, works by many contemporary American Indian writers, including some of Vizenor's own, have created for *Bearheart* a new, more receptive audience. Nevertheless, it remains a difficult book. A carnivalesque satire on almost every aspect of late twentieth-century existence, the novel confronts the reader with excessive violence and deviant sexuality (even by 1990s standards), racial fury, a gnomic plot line, and postmodern, complex verbal gamesmanship. Consequently, a disproportionate measure of its content amounts to what Eco calls "information"— "an excess of disorder with respect to [the] existing codes" that readers expect to engage in their interpretive efforts. Not only are its postmodern, disjunctive manner of narration and Vizenor's verbal gamesmanship quite demanding for the reader, but a formidable amount of "Indian" cultural content must also be negotiated. In fact, Vizenor's book is so "original," in Eco's sense of the term, that it constitutes a multiple challenge to almost any reader, even a literarily inclined or "academic" Native reader.

To appreciate how Vizenor's "disorderly," potentially alienating discourse engenders audience solidarity, we may reflect on scenes of the contest between the Evil Gambler (Sir Cecil Staples) and Trickster (Fourth Proude Cedarfair) that comprise the narrative center of the text. The Evil Gambler is a pan-tribal character who appears frequently in the stories of Anishinabe people.[39] However, Vizenor's Evil Gambler is different from all the others. He is not simply drawn from Chippewa stories nor, despite Vizenor's self-consciously managed intertextual plunderings, is he borrowed intact from the fiction of other contemporary Native American writers. Vizenor's Gambler in *Bearheart* is a vicious gasoline tycoon in an era of near-total environmental breakdown. Though he retains many traditional tribal features, Vizenor's Gambler is first and foremost the degenerate inhabitant of a socially disordered, postmodern America. His "mother," we learn, trafficked in pesticides and kidnapped children, and the Gambler attributes contemporary indifference toward his own variety of sadism and mayhem to government and corporate policies that numb human sensitivity to environmental destruction and murder.

The contest between the Gambler (Sir Cecil) and Trickster (Fourth Proude) occurs precisely halfway through the novel, and it marks the narrative center in several ways beyond the literal. By placing the contest to "balance good and evil"[40] at narrative center, Vizenor prepares his audience for developments in the second half of the novel that balance those in the first half. These developments include the return of "myth" as "the center of meaning" (162) that displaces "terminal creeds," the emergence of a redemptive, Earthdiver dimension in Fourth Proude Cedarfair (143), and Proude's subsequent leadership of the Pilgrims to the Chaco Mountains, where they join the visionary Bear People in the next world, home of the prophetic, Bear-authored, Bear-narrated *Heirship Chronicles*.

The apparent disorder of Vizenor's narrative is dispelled when we perceive at narrative center the metacode inscribed in the "balancing" contest. The Gambler-Trickster pair comprises a semiotic force—the play of fixed and rigid systems of meaning (Euro-American historical master narrative, conventional modes of interpretation, terminal creeds, the Gambler's culture of death [132]) versus the indeterminate, the wildly disruptive and constantly transformative power of signification. This latter power is also represented by the pure semiotic potentiality implied in the absent *Chronicles* manuscript (reminding us of similarly absent, but highly generative texts embedded within other novels— *The Book of Horse* in Hogan's *Mean Spirit*, Drake's stillborn history of the Navajo in *Ghost Singer*, and the ancient codex in Silko's *Almanac of the Dead*). At the heart of Vizenor's text, in other words, lies a metatextual message about how the dominant discourse (in *Bearheart*, the Evil Gambler's discourse) is rife with potentiality for its own destabilization by the semiotic action of the Other (Fourth Proude Cedarfair's oppositional discourse). In a novel that dubs itself a visionary "window" (242) into the next world, this metacode affords us a view, beyond narrative disorder, of the "Bearheart" (bare heart) of the text— not a view of some binarily opposed order, but of an apparently semiotic, ordering-disordering principle of the universe itself.

In terms of this metacode, we may begin to understand the primary purpose served by many of the otherwise chaotic gestures of the novel, particularly the wordplay. Vizenor's pyrotechnical display of puns and other verbal witticisms becomes almost distracting as the reader labors to negotiate the centrifugal force of Vizenor's narrative, always on the verge of spinning out of our interpretive control. However, when we consider Vizenor's dizzying transformations of words (bear/bare, heirship/hairship/airship, etc.) in light of his metacode, we detect the same deconstructive energy represented in the struggle of Trickster and Evil Gambler—the energy intrinsic to sign systems that allows one word so easily to transform into another through the smallest orthographic or aural change. What is fixed gives way. As the Gambler proclaims during the contest, "What holds us to believe in the rules of our own games? . . . [A]t the end . . . we will find a new game, because we are after all bound to chance" (131).

The game, then, lies in our self-conscious invention of the rules for playing, not in playing by the rules. Solidarity among Vizenor's readers depends upon our relative comfort within an unfixed reality, free of terminal creeds and characterized by ceaseless making and unmaking of worlds, especially when they become oppressive. As one particularly astute critic of Vizenor's *Bearheart*, Jon Hauss, has remarked, this novel affords "a privileged site within which to study both the . . . dominant American culture, and the elaboration of a whole series of counter-hegemonic cultures which begin imaginatively to limn . . . a radically democratic connective culture." Hauss's analysis implies that this "connected" reader will resist "fantasies of social wholeness" and all manner of "essentialisms."[41]

Judging from the humanistic messages conveyed by Vizenor at the mimetic level of his texts—especially in the fourth world described in the ending of *Bearheart*—Vizenor indeed appears to envision such a "democratic connective" culture. However, his implied ethos (connectivity) seems compromised by his carnivalesque celebration of semiotic instability for its own sake and his implied absolute resistance to all creeds. To remain forever locked into Derridian aporia might be to resist "essentialisms," but to precisely what sort of human "connection" this radically skeptical position may lead remains unclear.[42] Vizenor's parodies of his Native American "essentialist" contemporaries such as N. Scott Momaday and Heyemeyohsts Storm ("romancioso momaday" and "arrowshow storm" in *Bearheart*) suggest that, although he endorses their belief in the regenerative power of visions in general, *particular* visions are "terminal" and objectionable. The way out of this dilemma is obscured by Fourth Proude Cedarfair's disappearance at the end of *Bearheart*. At first burlesqued for pandering to the empty rituals of "New Age . . . pantribal urban emptiness" (16), at the end of the novel Proude follows the Vision Bears into the next world that is free of "word wars," but he leaves behind "old men" storytellers to guide this world with (presumably) specific dreams and visions. Moreover, Vizenor's references to myth as the "center" of meaning, and the centered architecture of the novel itself expose a probably unavoidable internal contradiction within Vizenor's proclaimed philosophy.

Among Vizenor's more recent works, the stories in *Landfill Meditation* (1991) perhaps afford some insight into how he resolves this philosophical dilemma for himself, and into how we might finetune our understanding of the kind of solidarity relations his fiction intimates overall. Consider the quotation from *Landfill Meditation* that appears as the epigraph to this chapter: "Almost learned how to read from books that had been burned in a fire at the reservation library. The books were burned on the sides. He read the centers of the pages and imagined the stories." Here Vizenor implies that the reader's task and responsibility lie in the act of completion— the act of granting the author's creation some space within one's own imagination to become what it will. Other works by Vizenor elaborate upon this basically phenomenological view of art. They insist that "completion" of a text must not lead to stale interpretations (in Eco's terms, they must not "become culture"); instead, a work must be allowed to unfold repeatedly with different results within the same reader each time it is read.

Even more adamantly than the "burned books," Vizenor's "blank books" reiterate this phenomenological readerly role. Like the books that are "burned on the sides," the blank books demand to be filled in by the reader's imagination. However, the blank books that Almost and his partner sell on the college campus are not quite blank. Each contains "an original tribal pictomyth painted by [Almost] in green ink, a different pictomyth on a different page in every blank book. Yes, pictomyths, stories that are imagined about a picture, about memories. So, even our blank books had a story. . . . Our blank books said everything, whatever you could imagine in a picture" (9–10).

Vizenor's equation of "pictomyth" and story reiterates his phenomenological view of reading and implies that after all, behind his scorn for Momaday's essentialist thought, he may share more assumptions with "romancioso" than he appreciates. As we shall see in much more detail in Chapter Three, Momaday believes that "writing is . . . a kind of drawing,"[43] not only because writing involves putting marks on paper, but also because writing—narrative—is in some ways iconic in the way that it communicates to the reader. Like an icon, it generates ideas and initiates interpretive processes in the reader that exceed the artist's intention or control. Momaday favors "blurred edges" and "buried outlines" because, as he says, "I don't want to enclose the thing I'm drawing in a precise outline. Giving a thing such definition sometimes reduces it" (173). And as a creative writer, he favors "emblematic" methods over "linear exploration" (55), implying that the former allow for the creative participation of the mind of the reader. With his pictograms and his blank books, Vizenor seems to be elaborating a quite similar view of the "emblematic" or "iconic" nature of narrative. Solidarity for Vizenor as for Momaday consists of a shared pact between author and reader to participate responsibly and creatively in storytelling, and to resist the hard "edges" and "outlines" of fixed definition. For Vizenor, however, definitions to be most vigorously resisted are all definitions of the "Indian," especially perhaps, those formed by achieving solidarity with Native American writers (in *Bearheart* satirically dubbed "romancioso momaday," "somewhere silko," "earthboy welch," "stoutword deloria," "arrowshow Storm")—even including himself ("visitor vizenor").

Reimbrication

In an interview with Laura Coltelli, Vizenor notes Susan Sontag's observation that whoever controls representation also to some extent controls culture. According to Sontag, there is world-making power in a photograph or an image and, in Vizenor's words, "because it has power, you can . . . change the images and people might believe that you've actually changed social conditions. And of course, you haven't done anything. You've just changed the photos."[44] The question of whether the manipulators of images have or have not "done anything" appears to be especially intriguing to contemporary Indian writers. Several of Vizenor's Almost Brown stories in *Landfill Meditation* and elsewhere entertain this question at several textual levels. Almost's laser holograms, in particular, bear a powerful and immediate impact on social reality. Preoccupation with the control of representation likewise characterizes Thomas King throughout many of his stories and especially in his comic masterpiece, *Green Grass, Running Water.* Among numerous memorable scenes in this novel, passages describing the altered videotaped versions of classical, cowboy-and-Indian movies and the videos' effects on the audience underscore King's point about the semiotic origins of social transformation. Indeed, King's works provide an excellent opportunity for exploring yet another transformative strategy that Indian authors have developed, the reimbrication of cultural icons of the dominant society. Reimbrication not only revises "reality" and social relations by expanding the audience's repertoire of possible responses to familiar images; it also promotes solidarity within a bicultural audience by reducing the sometimes exaggerated notions of the "Otherness" that different cultural groups frequently project upon one another.

We have noted Eco's remarks about "new" or "original" material. While a figure of speech or a narrative structure remains idiolectic (operative or meaningful only within the specific discourse where it first occurred), it remains "literary." When the "literary" becomes familiar (or sociolectic — a part of the extraliterary information that readers commonly possess), it becomes "knowledge," according to Eco. "When, finally, metaphors are transformed into knowledge, they will . . . have completed their cycle: they become catachreses. The field has been restructured, [and] semiosis rearranged."[45] Most semioticians would agree that familiar cultural icons are catachreses. They are so heavily encoded with sociolectic baggage that an author who interjects cultural iconography into a work of art must work against its tendency toward cliché. However, the American Indian author-as-bricoleur subversively "rearranges semiosis" with respect to cultural icons, converting already heavily encoded images into reservoirs of nondominant meanings and associations.

A consummate, subversive bricoleur among recent Native American fiction writers, Thomas King in *Green Grass, Running Water* and in the short stories included in *One Good Story, That One* (1993), attacks the Indian of American myth as well as the primarily iconic means by which such myths arise and are perpetuated. Like Vizenor, Momaday, and others, King apparently contrives to demolish in particular the mainstream society's clichéd conceptions of Indians that blind so many, Native and non-Native alike, to social realities, past and present. Like Vizenor's deconstructive satires, King's works open the semiotic space of cultural icons to the fuller participation of the responsibly creative imagination of the reader.

In *Green Grass*, King wreaks semiotic havoc upon a variety of mainstream literary and biblical icons. In the novel, four "old Indians" periodically escape the psychiatric ward of a hospital and, along with Coyote, tell the "stories" that have created the world. Assuming the names of Hawkeye, Robinson Crusoe, the Lone Ranger, and Ishmael, the old Indians make repeatedly aborted efforts to tell their stories correctly so that reality, semiotically damaged as a result of previously botched "versions," may be "fixed up." The storytellers and Coyote argue, interrupt one another, and otherwise compete for dominance. They hopelessly mix Indian and Judeo-Christian creation stories in their efforts to account for the sorry consequences of the behavior of the first man—Ahdamn—whose orthographically altered name in this novel suggests his ineptitude in getting the world off to a good start. The miscreant storytellers in King's novel, however, agree upon one thing: "All this water imagery must mean something."[46] King organizes his text around the biblical and pan-tribal icon of the flood to suggest that cultures tell different stories about many of the same universal mysteries. Both the biblical account of The Flood and Indian accounts of primordial watery disasters suggest to King that the Creator is a raconteur who simply cannot get the story right and has to keep "fixing" things through destructive erasure-by-water. Coalescing the iconic meanings of Indian and Judeo-Christian floods, King implies that all human beings have the same ultimate questions about life: one section of the novel consists of several characters, representative of diverse groups, asking (along with God, a few pages earlier), "Where did all the water come from?" (31, 81). In the novel, water (incidentally, a motif suggesting an intertextual link to Erdrich's novels) signifies the supremely powerful, creative-destructive energies of a universe in constant motion. Coyote, a pan-tribal figure who insists that we must explain "all the water," has pan-cultural equivalents in Trickster figures the world over. King's comic focus on the flood as a cross-cultural icon melds together the meanings that all cultures have attributed to the universe in their different stories explaining fundamental human situations. King reduces the "otherness" of diverse groups by suggesting that we are all, as it were, in the same "ark." Moreover, readers of his novel appreciate the fact that spring-like new beginnings ("green grass") and eternally transformative force ("running water") lie behind the storytelling efforts of Indians and non-Indians alike. (Naturally, we might also perceive great irony here, for King's title alludes to broken treaties with the Indians regarding lands they would allegedly retain, in Andrew Jackson's illustrious words, "as long as grass grows and water runs.")

Erdrich similarly enjoys reimbricating Judeo-Christian icons with "Indian" meanings to afford the reader a broader, cross-cultural view of human community. In *Tracks*, she evokes and yokes together in an elaborate, syntagmatic network at least three distinct Christian icons—the weeping Madonna, the fisherman-Christ, and Christ in the Garden of Gethsemane. In each case, the reader's full decipherment of the passages in which an icon appears depends on his or her observation of how the image works like a visual pun: we *almost* simultaneously construe the image within two, irreducible frames of reference at once. The result is the same type of pleasant shock we experience when we see, first the "rabbit," then the "duck," for example, in the now famous trick drawing made famous by Wittgenstein.[47] Though Erdrich's iconic "puns" do not erase cultural difference, like Wittgenstein's "duck and rabbit," they do bring about in the audience a heightened sensitivity. Having seen both "duck and rabbit," we cannot see one without remembering the other. Our overall awareness of the "whole picture" exists, whatever our particular focus.

Erdrich's weeping-Madonna trope signifies in connection with a highly elaborated water motif[48] (that proffers a double interpretive frame) running throughout *Love Medicine*, *Tracks*, *The Beet Queen*, and *The Bingo Palace*. Informing this motif is, on the one hand, the Anishinabe belief that the spirit of a drowned person cannot depart down the "three-day road" to the realm of the dead, and on the other, the numerous Christian practices involving water, from baptism to sacramental purification (Catholics' use of "holy water," for example, to anoint themselves when entering and exiting a church). In Fleur Pillager, a character who is heavily encoded through water imagery, we see Erdrich oppose these Chippewa and Christian frames of reference. As the fearsome consort of Misshepeshu—the lake monster of Matchimanito—she can drown people, sometimes as sacrificial substitutes for herself; she is also a Christ-like revenant who has herself drowned three times and returned to life. A variety of references to Fleur Pillager and Christian iconography tempt us (as they do Pauline) to understand her within an ultimately inappropriate frame of reference; however, when in our imaginations we eventually divest Fleur of any Christian associations to see her as she is, we "remember" the alternative interpretive possibilities.

Another instructive juxtaposition of these Christian and Chippewa frames of reference involving Fleur occurs when Clarence in *Tracks* uses the statue of the Virgin Mary to break Pauline's spell on Sophie. Pauline reports that the statue cries tears (water) when it is held to gaze down on Sophie, and that with the flow of these tears the girl "thaws" out of her trance. In the opening of this scene, however, not the Virgin's but Fleur's gaze falls on Sophie, who kneels before her to beg forgiveness for seducing Eli. By "substituting" the Virgin for Fleur, Erdrich suggests an odd equation between them, which she elaborates even further. An icon of motherly mercy and forgiveness, the Virgin at first seems the complete opposite of the frightening, sexually provocative Fleur Pillager. However, Pauline reminds us that heavenly sympathy is rooted in empathy—that the Virgin Mother, like Fleur herself, understands the desires of the flesh that led Sophie astray. Pauline sees humanity and compassion as traits that Fleur and Mary share. The statue, miraculously expressing these qualities for Fleur, releases the girl from her repentant rigor. Other traits linking Fleur and the statue are their brown eyes, their overall powerful appearance [49] and their mutual representation with serpents and water (the lake and the flowing tears, respectively).

Perhaps reminding us of its use in King's novel, water imagery further elaborates Fleur's characteristics and links her not only with the all-forgiving Virgin Mother, but also with Christ himself. Throughout Erdrich's novels, Christ is a "fisherman" of souls. Fleur is likewise both fish and fisherman. She "reels" people into her traps and schemes [50] in an odd reversal of Christ's redemptive efforts. Like the weeping-statue substitute for Fleur, Christ "wept a river" in Gethsemane (149). An array of "temptations" arise for Erdrich's reader, who may struggle to discover some universalistic vision in Erdrich's texts. In the long run, however, Erdrich's texts seem to confront us with the verbal equivalent of visual puns that exercise our perceptual faculties while underscoring their unreliability.

Leslie Marmon Silko's works also devote serious attention to reimbrication of cultural icons and, like King's and Erdrich's, her novels instruct readers about the interpretive codes as well as the content of messages inscribed in verbal and visual images. Silko's reimbrications tend to be secular more than religious, however. For instance, an American story (complete with Silko's revisions) is told through the iconography of the Coca-Cola calendar that Silko describes in detail in *Ceremony*. The advertiser's image of the girl in the blue twirler's suit reminds Tayo of a stuffed bobcat and almost speaks for itself as an icon of Euro-American commodification of woman and the American West. Responding to Silko's code of blue that we have discussed earlier, however, a reader might find the following revised "story" in the calendar: the dominant culture commodifies woman (the twirler) and nature (waxed and bleached horse) by using them for the purposes of an advertisement which sells not only Coca-Cola, but also a hyperreality—an image of the West full of blond girls and perfect horses. Made-up and packaged as "American girl," the twirler is like the bleached and waxed horse who is unnaturally represented; the twirler is also, in fact, a "dead bobcat," for both girl and cat are "trophies" hung on a wall. However, in light of Silko's code of blue, the girl's blue suit connotes her vestigial female power, though it is nearly eclipsed by the dominant culture's countersigns. Even so, such a vestigial trace in the reference to blue is perhaps just enough to alert the reader to a more complete story encoded in the calendar.

To benefit from the "offering" of healing in *Ceremony*, the reader like Tayo must learn to read these and other diminished signs to perceive the sacramentality submerged within them. Silko implies that the desacralized symbols of Native American culture, such as the eagle emblazoned across the property of the U.S. Army, that are displayed in stores and at annual tourist events at Gallup must be reclaimed. The army eagle signifies Euro-American, nonsacramental appropriation of Native American sacred symbols; it also signifies U.S. appropriation of Native American bodies to fight in the war. Under the sign of the eagle, army recruiters come to the reservation to declare that " 'Anyone can fight for America . . . even you [Indian] boys' " (64). The eagle signifies doubly for Tayo as a half-blood soldier returned to America with "battle fatigue." Service in the army under the sign of the eagle leads to his need for a healing ceremony; this ceremony, in turn, awakens him to his shamanic role of making changes in the old ceremonies that began and continue with "the aging of the yellow gourd rattle [and] the shrinking of the skin around the eagle's claw" (126). The new ceremonies, says Betonie, the mixed-blood Navajo singer, will have to be powerful enough to heal the planet. They will have to reach across continents and cultures, lest those who remain sick should "take this world from ocean to ocean / . . . [and] explode everything" (137).

Like King, who manages cultural icons to reduce "otherness" while insisting upon audience acknowledgment of the actual, historical past, and like Erdrich, who emphasizes irreducible otherness yet suggests that all views are a part of a larger, mysterious "picture," Silko potentially outlines an alternative, transcultural set of values. The aesthetic, humane, and spiritual values inscribed through Silko's blue code prevail over the material values inscribed in the codes of Euro-American colonized space. For King, Erdrich, and Silko alike, however, the stories are "alive" and thus defined by semiotic open-endedness. Solidarity therefore amounts to participation in a semiotic process rather than reception of any fixed message. Readers are performers of certain actions that bind them together. These actions include first and foremost reading within a tutored, evaluative frame of reference. A survey of contemporary Native American authors will reveal others whose works similarly amplify the meanings of cultural icons. Hogan in *Mean Spirit*, for instance, reimbricates fire as a cultural signifier by invoking oppositional biblical and Osage meanings. Momaday reinscribes an icon of the American West, "Billy the Kid," with essential predatory qualities, as I demonstrate further in Chapter Three in connection with social semiotic constructions of self.

Chapter Three
Re-Signing the Self: Models of Identity and Community

> The last superstition built into memory is that you exist as you think you do.[1]

Contemporary fiction by Native Americans frequently traces crises of self-transformation.[2] Unique complications in the transformational process arise for Indian characters, sometimes on account of their half-blood or mixed-blood status, sometimes owing to their efforts to sustain tribal values in a white world, and other times due to their attempts to live by the rules of the dominant society. In the end, such characters usually shape themselves less according to traditional models drawn exclusively from a particular culture than to models that they half-invent and half-discover through bicultural experience. Thus, in their patterns of character development, American Indian narratives emphasize flexibility and fluidity as important values; indeed, contemporary Native American writers often equate such malleability of self with the dynamic motion of nature.[3] They see nature in contrast to the rigidity that some of them attribute to Eurocentric culture and art. For instance, one of Thomas King's characters in *Green Grass, Running Water* warns another, " 'Things that stand still, die.' "[4]

Likewise, in Leslie Marmon Silko's *Ceremony*, Betonie, a Navajo singer, warns Tayo that "things which don't shift and grow are dead things.' "[5] Suggesting the important relationship between art and both individual and cultural identity, Silko's narrator sees western art as "dead objects . . . . [h]ollow and lifeless as a witchery

clay figure" (204). Accordingly, Betonie instructs Tayo about flexibility, saying that "long ago," even before white people came, "the
changing began . . . in the different voices from generation to generation. . . . I have made changes [in the traditional ceremonies]
. . . . The people mistrust this greatly, but only this growth keeps
the ceremonies strong" (126).

Tayo understands Betonie's lesson well by the end of the novel,
when he contrasts the "relentless motion of the stars" in the sky with
the "motionless dead stars" that the "destroyers" paint "in black
ash on cave walls" (247). His objection to stasis and fixed form
has obvious aesthetic implications and hints at why many Native
American storytellers have resisted writing in favor of oral and
performative art. As we have seen in our discussion of narrative
power and solidarity, however, such apparent rigidity and stasis are
more perceived than actual (since the dominant discourse contains
within itself the potential for its own disruption). Moreover, despite
some fairly dogmatic statements about Eurocentric art proclaimed
through their characters, the Native American writers whom we
have considered seem quite aware of the revisionary potential contained within the Other's discourse.

For instance, through Betonie and other characters including
the narrator in *Ceremony*, Silko criticizes white society and art for
their resistance to nature's fluid example; still, she issues no simplistic call for a return to traditional tribal ways. By focusing on
the need for change, not to mention its inevitability, and by writing her stories instead of speaking them, Silko emphasizes her own
"kinship" to Betonie, the not quite traditional, mixed-blood medicine man who knows he must adapt his healing art to present-day
exigencies. Indeed, despite objections to a perceived Eurocentric,
formal "rigidity," Indian writers like Silko and Momaday seem especially adept in their management of the formal elements of narrative, including its iconological power, as we will presently see.
Silko casts herself in the role of the artist as healer, transforming
the genre's formal features to her own "ceremonial" purposes as
well as exploiting the novel's inherent, dialogical evasion of formal
rigidity. Moreover, in her concern with social and personal transformation, Silko exposes what Paula Gunn Allen calls the " 'last
superstition built into memory'—the idea "that you exist as you
think you do.' " Silko invites both Indian and non-Indian readers of

Ceremony to "accept this offering" of a new "story" with alternative, cross-culturally evolved models of self and community (262).

This chapter examines issues of identity and otherness as they develop in a variety of contemporary Native American narratives. In particular, I am interested in how certain texts imply that vital aspects of "self" arise through a semiotic process encoded within and susceptible to manipulation by narrative forms, including but not limited to art. Partly through a dialogical relationship to their western generic counterparts, these contemporary Indian narratives rewrite some of the rules for production of identity in texts and in the world.

Re-Drawing the Boundaries of Self and Other

In any culture, the definition of a "self," or of "individual" or "personal identity," depends partly on how the culture defines "truth" and "reality." To a great extent, individual conformity to normative definitions amounts to "community," while degrees and kinds of nonconformity result in Otherness. Personal identity partly reflects the measure of one's conformity to, or divergence from, social and cultural norms. Understanding Euro-American and Native American normative definitions of the individual and some of the mechanisms of their cultural construction is fundamental to a study of Indian cross-cultural storytelling. This kind of fiction demands a reader-participant who recognizes and respects the point of view of the cultural Other, who attempts, insofar as possible, to entertain this point of view as a reader, and who is ready to question ingrained assumptions about personal identity, including the ways in which identity is evoked in narrative from culture to culture. The non-Indian reader-participant must resist "naturalizing" the Indian material of cross-cultural literature (that is, making "repeated analogies to familiar western forms" to decode the discourse of the Other).[6] Such mistaken equations emphasize how much rules of reading are culturally prescribed, and how much the misapplication of rules to text can produce a meaningless story, or distort complex characters and worldviews.

Owing to these and other impediments to cross-cultural communication, semiotic analysis is especially appropriate to contemporary American Indian representations of self. Recent developments in semiotic theory afford insight into the complicated process of becoming and sustaining a "self" in relation to the Other, the community, and the phenomenal world. Semiotic studies also illuminate the even more intricate processes of encoding and decoding such information in written works. Semiotically self-aware, cross-coded narrative emphasizes the "structuration"[7] of "western" as well as "nonwestern" epistemological screens and potentially liberates readers from many restrictive patterns of thought. Perhaps more dramatically than any other kind of narrative, it opens the imagination to social, political, and aesthetic alternatives to the global status quo. Indeed, when asked about the contribution of North American Indian writers to contemporary society, Beth Cuthand, a Canadian Cree poet, declares: "there's something happening in Native American writing . . . . There are a number of us who are . . . telling a contemporary story [that] . . . down the road, someday . . . [might help people] come to terms with cultural differences, with racism, and . . . free up humanity to do better things than to kill each other."[8]

Semiotic analysis can reveal how Native American authors of cross-coded narratives often attempt to "free up humanity" by dismantling the belief that any essentially "western" or "Indian" self exists independently of semiotic practice. As Gerald Vizenor implies when he claims that "culture doesn't exist; [anthropologists] invented it,"[9] definitions of identity, alterity, and community rest upon a ground of assumptions. Deconstruction and other poststructuralist developments have intensified our awareness of such epistemological problems. These developments underscore the perils of establishing binary oppositions such as "western" and "nonwestern" that, to a degree, create conditions we then analyze as though they were grounded in the absolute. Despite the lessons of recent intellectual history, however, much contemporary academic discourse continues to harbor insufficiently examined assumptions and generalizations about "western" versus "nonwestern" people, even though the "west" includes an extremely diverse collection of countries, nationalities, and ethnic groups, and "Native Americans" consist of hundreds of different tribes in the United States alone. Even those academic works that directly challenge stereotypical cultural categories sometimes refer to the "west" and to "American Indians" (and other groups) as though the terms denoted homogeneous sets of people and ideas.[10]

Certainly, we must resort to these generalizations at times, lest we become like the character in Jorge Luis Borges's "Funes the Memorious" (1962), idiot savants lost in the rich detail of experience and unable to formulate concepts. Although the "practice of semiotics is . . . itself inevitably a semiotic act, unable to declare absolute truths about absolute reality, while constantly doing so,"[11] the practice of semiotics also explains why we may, without invoking absolute referents, *cautiously* but legitimately employ code words such as "western," "Euro-American," and "Indian." Referents for such terms reside in the sociolect, an encyclopedic reservoir of not necessarily "true" or correct information that nevertheless enables us to interpret specific statements; the sociolect, in turn, is continually modified by acts of interpretation and signification that add to, qualify, or correct the general body of information. Signification does not necessarily serve absolute "truth," but it *makes sense.* Moreover, as Derrida's apologist, Christopher Norris, argues eloquently in his defense of deconstruction,[12] understanding the troublesome relationship between words and the world does not simplistically negate all positive claims staked in language. Predicated upon the existence of a sociolectic reservoir of meaning, the rules of discourse allow us to discuss sameness and difference and to arrive at some reliable (and flexible) conclusions without invoking a "transcendental signified" or forgetting that our generalizations frequently break down when applied to specific "western" or "Indian" groups or persons. On the contrary, this inevitable breakdown forces us to modify our general concepts, a fact which culturally cross-coded, semiotically self-reflexive texts exploit. For example, contemporary Native American writers modify and expand the sociolect of the average reader by replacing "cowboy and Indian" stereotypes with accurate information about individuals and cultures.[13]

I rehearse these obvious points because I wish to avoid the trap of *unexamined* generalizing about identity and difference. Furthermore, my study rests on the assumption (shared with the writers I discuss) that human beings are not defined within rigid ethnic or cultural categories, and that cultures are at every moment undergoing transformation through some variety of sign action. In Vizenor's words (recalling Betonie's to Tayo, cited earlier): "Cultures are not static, human behavior is not static. We are not what anthropologists say we are and we must not live up to a definition. . . .

We're very complex human beings, all of us, everywhere."[14] Indeed, a major difference between western and Indian people lies not in their relative complexity and simplicity (as Euro-Americans for so long prejudicially maintained), but in their sometimes vastly different ways of expressing their complexity.

The complexity of western people, for example, is overtly demonstrated in the effort to explain experience in analytic discourse. Though all cultures apparently contain members capable of reflecting upon their own epistemological frames of reference, western society is especially characterized by the development of formal metacognitive discourse. Descartes's elegant and apparently simple equation of human identity with consciousness, for example, has generated volumes of discourse probing ontological, epistemological, and even theological questions. Ironically, this western tendency to think, write and speak extensively about thinking, writing, and speaking frequently curves back upon itself—the trajectory of western radical skepticism—to undermine the "truths" upon which western society is founded. Even more ironically, the same antifoundationalist energy that drives modern and postmodern art also galvanizes contemporary Native American authors' efforts to re-invent their own and western cultures by re-encoding narrative with alternative paradigms of identity.

For example, western self-conscious discourse inspires Tosamah's humorous sermon in Momaday's *House Made of Dawn*. Tosamah chides St. John for talking too much to explain the statement, "In the beginning was the Word."[15] Tosamah implies that too much verbal elaboration amounts to "fat."[16] St. John "was a preacher, and he made a complex sentence of the Truth, two sentences, three, a paragraph. He made a sermon and theology."[17] Theology, like philosophy and other modes of discourse, in turn becomes the occasion for further talk, disagreement, doubt, and disbelief. Tosamah implies that an Indian version of St. John would have been silently receptive to the "vision . . . in back of his eyes" (92) and thus to spiritual revelation and wisdom. Like Tosamah, Wilbur Snake, a laconic Ioway medicine man in Walters's *Ghost Singer*, sums up many a contemporary Indian character's advice to white people: "Quiet . . . be quiet."[18] Erdrich's Nanapush can use words to "cure or kill,"[19] and Silko's "destroyers" conjure up nuclear holocaust in a storytelling contest. According to these writers, self-loss or even self-annihilation may result from too much talk.

Nevertheless, conceptions of "truth," "reality," and "self" that derive from self-reflexive western "talk" are solidly encoded (and multiply overdetermined) in western narrative forms.[20] An atomistic conception of human identity is inherent in western narrative form and, consequently, American Indian writers struggle against the innate resistance of this narrative form to the representation of nonwestern identity. Though postmodern developments in the west attacking atomistic conceptions of human identity have probably facilitated Indian writers' revisionary task, these writers as a group do not endorse postmodern, antifoundationalist conclusions (especially not those concerning identity and the relationship of the word to the world).[21] Still, as we have noted, postmodern art as well as poststructuralist discourse have unsettled the grounds on which western conceptions of self once complacently rested. Thomas Sebeok's notion of the "semiotic self" and Hodge and Kress's social semiotic concepts of "modalities" and of "definitions of the real" are particularly enlightening for anyone wishing to understand the terms of the semiotic counter-conquest of American aesthetic and philosophical space that Indian writers have recently undertaken.

Thomas Sebeok's theory of the "semiotic self" demystifies culturally and historically constructed differences in human identity. Indeed, Sebeok believes that semiosis will one day be understood as a physiological phenomenon and that all such (historical and cultural) differences will be exposed as epiphenomena of universally human neurological traits, many of which are shared even with nonhuman life. He sees the human being as a biological organism endowed with consciousness; through "sign action" (inclusive of more than language), the human being creates the self (not coterminous with consciousness) as a "subject" and the world as a social reality.[22] Sebeok subscribes to what he calls a "variant of the dualist-interactionist theory" of identity. He defines " 'mind' as a system of signs which is, roughly, tantamount to Jakob von Uexküll's *Umwelt,* and 'brain' as a system of signs displayed, for example, as a physical network, or structure, of neurons" (126). Sebeok believes that "self" consists of a "coherent and personal narrative schema" (9) constructed by consciousness partly through interaction with the environment and partly from memory. Thus, Sebeok is also particularly interested in the mechanisms of memory: "The question to be investigated is how mental manifestation of the information in the

mind is transcoded into our central nervous system, and vice versa."
Answers to this question, he argues, must come from "neuroendo-
crinology. . . . It is precisely in the dynamism of the brain and the
self-organizing properties of neural networks, driven, as they are,
by experience throughout life, where the next and perhaps final
frontier of semiotic inquest will find its be-all-and-end-all resolu-
tion" (114).

One mode of interaction with the world involves "specular
semiosis," which Sebeok defines as the process of encoding meaning in the mind by looking at objects in the world. Exterior objects
become "iconic spatial expressions" of meaning and are often
internalized as representations of self.[23] For example, Sebeok explains that part of his personal identity as a male growing up
in a patriarchal European culture was acquired by looking at his
father's iconized representations of authority as head of the table
at dinner.[24] Such "iconic spatial expressions" help a person to construct and maintain the "*Umwelt*" or "self-world," which includes a
sense of an interior reality as well as an idea of the reality of "the-
world-about-me."[25]

The "narrative schema" comprising the self also derives from
memory, which records the various interactions with the environment and organizes experience and "icons" syntactically according
to the rules of language: "Language is . . . a modeling device, a mental representation of the world which . . . is different from all the
animal models in that it has a feature that linguists call syntax. . . .
[W]ith syntax human beings are able to disassemble the model as
if it were made of Lego building blocks. You can reassemble them
in an infinite number of ways. With syntax you can take sentences
apart and hook them together in different ways. And just because
humans have this ability they can produce not only worlds in the
way in which [nonhuman] animals produce them, but they can
produce possible worlds."[26] In other words, the phenomenon we
call the "self" arises through non-linguistic interaction with the
environment (like that of the "lower" animals), through linguistic
(syntactical, peculiarly human) activity, and through manipulation
and organization of experience in memory. Cultural differences
notwithstanding, all human beings are alike in this fundamental
way. Sebeok's theory implies that differences between selves and
cultures result largely from *different semiotic practices* rooted in a *universal semiotic ability*.

Kaja Silverman's semiotic theory of the "subject," especially her notion of the role of "cultural overdetermination" in the formation of the self, complements Sebeok's "dualist-interactionist theory" of identity as a product of semiosic exchange with the environment (though Sebeok would reject the Neo-Freudian elements of Silverman's thought). Her definition of the "subject," as opposed to the "individual," reinforces Sebeok's observations about the ways in which self arises as a "narrative schema" rather than exists as a fixed quantity. "The term 'subject,' " says Silverman, "designates a quite different semantic and ideological space from that indicated by the more familiar term 'individual.' The second of these terms dates from the Renaissance, and it still bears the traces of the dominant philosophical systems of that time—systems which afforded to consciousness the very highest premium. The concept of subjectivity . . . marks a radical departure from this philosophical tradition by giving a more central place to the unconscious and to cultural overdetermination than it does to consciousness."[27] Like Sebeok, Silverman wishes to liberate identity from its traditional Cartesian equation with consciousness; also like Sebeok, she implies that "self" or "identity" is a construction, while "consciousness" is a biological given.

Both Sebeok's theory of the "semiotic self" and Silverman's theory of the "subject" afford much insight into the "western" as well as the "Indian" constructions of self that are cross-coded in some contemporary Native American narratives. For instance, Sebeok might remark that when Stephen in *The Woman Who Owned the Shadows* (1983) refers to the "last superstition built into memory" as the belief "that you exist as you think you do," Paula Gunn Allen authorially points to a person's mistaken equation of his or her own overall existence with a cultural description of it. Such a person conceives a *narrow* narrative schema, a "semiotic self" unaware of her semiotic origins and thus unable to avail herself of semiotic power. Stephen's remark about existence, and indeed a point of Allen's novel, is that the self is not "fixed": it is not a discrete psychological essence, nor a culturally-bounded, inflexible quantity. Instead, the self is a "subject," a narrative "process" constantly undergoing revision.[28] The world, likewise, undergoes revision through the collective sign action of its inhabitants who "can produce possible worlds."[29]

A number of works by Allen, Momaday, Silko, and Walters suggest that Sebeok's view of personal identity (as arising in connection with social reality and as subject to violation and disruption by one's own and other people's sign action[30]) rather uncannily resembles that of Navajo-Pueblo people. They, like Sebeok, reject notions of self as a discrete "individual" and the world as in any way static. Instead, one's identity develops in relation to cosmological patterns embodied in sacred beings and cultural icons, and is transmitted through elaborately structured semiotic systems. About Navajo culture, Nia Francisco explains that the "events of early childhood and along the path of a Diné [Navajo] person's life are set by the *Diyin Diné'e* [Holy People]. . . . [T]here are major mythical figures that set examples for the personal growth [of a child] . . . . This pattern is best shown by sampling the prominent events in a Diné person's life" (267–68).

Moreover, the Diné child in pre- and post-natal stages of life may be affected by the transgressions of others in the community. A child may become very ill (physically, spiritually, or both) if members of the community, especially his or her parents, do not observe the formal ritual behavior surrounding childbirth and childrearing. And finally, through the appropriate ceremonies, the Navajo child can be given the qualities and powers of sacred animals (270–75). Because no child is a discrete, pre-determined "individual," but each is instead part of a complicated web of interrelationships between the Diné and the *Diyin Diné'e*, every person is obligated to know the "order and structure of things" and "the names of things" so that he or she may act properly in relation to them and, thereby, prevent the world from changing in destructive ways (11). In Momaday's *House Made of Dawn*, for example, Nicolás *teah-whau*, the Bahkyush witch, verbally curses the child Abel, and this sign action has demonstrable effects on his life. Moreover, even though Abel's role as "Monster Slayer" is apparently sanctioned within the overall cosmological scheme, his killing of the albino is wrong because he egoistically confronts evil alone instead of merely playing his role in the overall, communal management of it. In this and other acts, Abel violates a sacred pattern by inappropriately assuming individual responsibility.[31]

The Navajo world view (like many other Native American world views) is semiotically self-aware. It recognizes not only the "structure of things" that must be learned and remembered through language and other sign systems, but also the direct role that sign action plays in the cosmological scheme. The Navajo self as a "narrative schema" (in Sebeok's terms) is formed and re-formed in conscious connection with cultural narratives—verbal embodiments of cultural memory. Navajo chantways, for example, verbally communicate the "order, structure, and names of things" in the universe; ceremonial medicine chantways assume the singer's power to heal by realigning the visible with the invisible worlds, or the world of actual experience with the world of the *Diyin Diné'e* revealed through signs. Pueblo tribes display equivalent semiotic self-reflexivity. In Allen's *The Woman Who Owned the Shadows*, for example, Ephanie revises herself and the Laguna "double woman" (211), or lesbian, paradigm by self-consciously adapting traditional narrative models to the realities of twentieth-century female and Indian experience.[32]

Thus the Navajo and Pueblo world views—and, accordingly, works by writers such as Allen, Momaday, Walters, and Silko that are variously based on them—overtly acknowledge the semiotic processes involved in the formation of self and social reality. These writers construct characters whose emotional, spiritual, and physical regeneration depends, one might say, on revising themselves based on their relationship to the master narratives of Pueblo-Navajo culture. (Writers such as Silko and Allen further imply that the viability of their cultures depends upon the ongoing revision of the master narratives of the sort undertaken by contemporary writers.) Momaday's Abel revises and heals himself according to the chantways sung to him by Ben Benally and others. Eventually, when he is able to sing for himself, he chooses the "Horse Song," part of the Navajo origin story. Emphasizing the act of making— "His mane is made of short rainbows. / My horse's ears are made of round corn. / My horse's eyes are made of big stars . . ."[33]— this sacred song provides a pattern and a model for Abel's recreation of self. Abel constructs a "semiotic self" through reference to "iconic spatial expressions" named in the chantway. "The specific imagery of the prayer dramatically connects horse and rider to sky and earth. . . . This horse is formed of sacred substances, reflecting a kinship of celestial phenomena, water, food, and flesh. The singer's knowledge of these relationships empowers him toward wholeness."[34] The singer's words effect the change.

The Iconology of Self

Perhaps more straightforwardly than any other American Indian
writer, N. Scott Momaday self-consciously develops in his works a
theory of identity that we may advantageously compare to Sebeok's
notion of the "specular semiotic self." Momaday's novels contain
an implicitly stated theory of images and an elaborate, iconological
metadiscourse addressing the profound connections between art
and identity. Indeed, the iconic basis of Momaday's notion of self is
suggested in the titles of the four sections of *The Ancient Child* (1989)
— "Planes," "Lines," "Shapes," and "Shadows." Through his paint-
erly language, Momaday suggests that over time, the self emerges
as a kind of three-dimensional, imaginative construction comparable to a work of art. These titles further suggest the iconicity of
narrative, another epistemic source of personal identity according
to Momaday.

Momaday believes in a distinctively Indian mode of perception of
the world, a decidedly visual mode. In Native historical materials,
Momaday notes an Indian tendency toward "emblematic recollection" rather than "linear exploration"—pictorial calendars, for example, rather than chronicle.[35] In *The Names: A Memoir* (1976), he
traces this "emblematic" perception to its source in the Indian's
aestheticized relationship to land.[36] Though Momaday probably
overstates his case in assuming that such a pronounced, visual-
perceptual mode is distinctively Indian, there is no doubt about
his emphasis on the primacy of visual perception in his art and in
his general sense of what it means to be Indian.[37]

A clear message emerges from Momaday's work overall: for
Native American people (and especially for Momaday himself),
mental, emotional, and spiritual phenomena occur in connection
with powerful visual phenomena, including external objects and
internal pictures in the mind's eye.[38] External images from nature
and culture may become icons for individuals or groups of people.
"Tsoai," the Bear Lodge or "Devil's Tower" in Wyoming, for example, is just such an icon for the Kiowa people, as are horses,
bears, and a host of other animals and mythical, spiritual, and
legendary beings.[39] Resembling Sebeok who espouses a neurological theory of semiosis, Momaday believes that collectively internalized images reside in the "racial memory" and are passed on "ge-
netically"; a Kiowa who has never actually seen Tsoai, for instance,

might nevertheless be affected by this image, or some variant of it, that "surfaces" within his or her mind.[40] In addition to the exterior and "genetic" sources of icons in nature, culture, and tribal memory, other sources of images include dreams, visions, and the individual imagination. Those created by artists and storytellers sometimes enter the collective mind as cultural icons and become a part of the visually-oriented "racial memory," according to Momaday.

Unsurprisingly, given these beliefs, Momaday's storytelling emphasizes visual phenomena. Icons replete with complex, cross-cultural implications are drawn from Plains, Navajo, and Pueblo cultures as well as from Euro-American culture—for example, Devil's Tower, Tsoai-talee, House Made of Dawn, Eagle, Bear, Billy the Kid, and Charlie Chaplin. About the visually-oriented qualities of his works, Momaday explains, "My work probably fits into a continuum of American Indian expression which begins with ledger-book drawings and hide paintings and comes up through a traceable line to the present. I think I can be fitted into that evolution. . . . My father was a traditional Indian artist, and his themes were Indian. He drew and painted peyote figures and buffalo hunters and did various kinds of mystical paintings. I think he comes directly out of the Kiowa artistic traditions which preceded him, and in some ways . . . I follow in his tracks."[41]

Self-consciously following in his father's mystical painter's "tracks," Momaday fully comprehends the role of images in the formation and preservation of Native thought and history. As an Indian, he also understands the traditional responsibility of the image makers to their communities. As so many contemporary Native American writers insist, both power and responsibility lie in the management of aesthetic form, since art not only reflects the natural, aesthetic order of the universe, but also influences that order, for better or worse. As Jeanette Armstrong (Okanagan) explains, "harmony-seeking creative thought-constructs brought forward from . . . ceremonies become symbolic representation in the arts"; such representations affect "societal functioning, which in turn changes the world."[42] The same belief informs the work of Leslie Marmon Silko, whose novel, *Ceremony*, is meticulously structured as an aesthetic act of healing.[43]

Like Armstrong, Silko and other Indian artists, Momaday emphasizes the importance of formal perfection, since "Spirit" or the sacred is expressed through form.[44] Even when practical art objects,

such as profane stories, pottery or trade blankets, have no ceremonial function, they testify to fundamentally sacred principles
of universal design in their construction. The Indian artist rarely,
if ever, creates without acknowledging some spiritual or transcen-
dent source of meaning in a work, meaning that is embodied in
its form.[45] Thus, when Momaday says that "Literature, art, is a
bridge to essence," he means that art does not merely symbolically
evoke an imaginary world that *stands for* or figures the "real." He
means that an ineffable, mystical realm actually exists, and that art
as a formally perfected structure *stands* (and affords exchange) *between* material and spiritual worlds.[46] Momaday also believes that
art "bridges" different cultural worlds and reveals their common
"essence" within the "one great and true story."[47] As we will presently see, Momaday's icons (such as the bear and Billy the Kid in
The Ancient Child) are frequently enmeshed within elaborate syntagmatic networks that reveal to a careful reader their "essential"
or universal significance, though these icons might at first (like
Billy the Kid) seem culturally circumscribed.

Art as both metaphysical and cultural "bridge" must be not only
structurally, but morally sound. Momaday, like most Native American artists, sees creativity as a powerful and inherently moral (or
immoral) act, in that the artist mirrors (or distorts) the intrinsic
morality embodied in the natural order of Creation. *House Made of
Dawn*, for example, records the traditional Navajo fear of witches,
who know how to disrupt the balance of nature by using the
strategies of medicine people, the traditional restorers of harmony
through meticulous adherence to formal design.[48] Witchery introduces "something out of place, some flaw in proportion or design,
some unnatural thing," and thereby causes damage.[49] Morally responsible acts, including art, result from working with, not against,
natural (commensurate with "spiritual") forces in the universe.

For Momaday, the life of the artist is a sacred vision quest resembling Abel's in *House Made of Dawn* and Set's in *The Ancient Child*—a
quest for moral and intellectual clarity that emerges slowly in connection with personal and cultural icons. Studying one of his own
barely begun paintings, Set remarks: "I want to believe that there
are real forms there, unique, intricate forms straightly related to
a deep field of receding grounds, one after another, ranging to a
black infinity, the definite forms of definite things, the very things
I cannot comprehend by other means."[50] Set's spiritual develop-

ment reveals the task of the artist: to confront the mysterious, "black infinity" and to wrest out of it the forms and images that lead through contemplation to knowledge and wisdom. Corroborating Set's spiritually acquired knowledge are Momaday's own paintings,[51] which are much like Set's as described in this partially autobiographical novel. Simple, slightly blurred images emerge out of vague backgrounds, as though the artist has coaxed them from a world of incipient form. Especially startling in their effects are "Anthracite" and "Shaman." In the former, patches of shadows suggest that the spirit of coal bears a human-like face, and in the latter, the shaman appears in a foggy liminal space, as though suspended between material and spiritual worlds. Both paintings remind us of fundamental habits of perception that western tradition rejects, at least in adults—the tendency to see faces in clouds and on the surfaces of rocks and tree trunks. Such habits of perception suggest there is much more in the world than we may actually see. As Momaday says, "I don't want to enclose the thing I'm drawing in a precise outline. Giving a thing such definition sometimes reduces it."[52] Momaday seems to follow the same general rule in his fiction; he resists "precise outline" and reductive "definition" by developing a rich language of images that points to the semiotic processes involved in the formation of identity and community.

Like the narratives of many other contemporary Native American writers, Erdrich in particular, Momaday's novels resist diegesis (the ingrained tendency of the reader to reassemble nonchronological narrative into chronological, cause-and-effect order). This resistance results from the fact that his texts, like his paintings, abide in memory as a collection of fairly simple, related images rather than as a conventional series of events or character interactions.[53] Indeed, whole dimensions of characters and a sense of textual coherence are lost on the reader who misses the paradigmatic and syntagmatic significance of Momaday's images.[54] The opening and closing paragraphs of *House Made of Dawn*, for instance, verbally iconize Abel as Dawn Runner. Implicit in the reader's encounter with this image are several tasks required for adequate understanding of Momaday's nonlinear, nonchronological story: first, we must understand the image thematically within a traditional Navajo-Pueblo context; next, we must understand how this image relates to numerous other traditional and nontraditional images of Abel that occur throughout the text (Abel as Stricken

Twin, Abel as the Bear, etc.). However, Momaday's icons do not merely collectively restate a "theme" in visual imagery; each contains a story or a fragment of a story (from or based on Kiowa, Pueblo, and Navajo culture) that the potential reader interpolates into the ongoing story of Abel. Unlike conventional, syntactic language, Momaday's "language of images" does not depend on linear sequencing to convey meaning. Indeed, the circular relationship of the icons in the novel suggests that no matter where in Abel's story the reader might initially enter (one might begin anywhere), he or she would ultimately end up completing the narrative circle to gain a complete impression.

Ultimately, the opening and closing image of Abel as Dawn Runner is an important part of a series of images forming this narrative circle. As a structural device, the circle not only frames the narrative, emphasizing its formal, geometric design, but also provides a clue to the design of the universe that Abel inhabits and within which his actions must be understood. For the reader, putting the story together is less a matter of deciphering a chronological, causal order of nonchronologically narrated events than it is a matter of "reading" the images and understanding how, in fact, they circularly refer to one another as different pieces or fragments of Abel's life. In Abel's quest for healing, he must assemble and interpret fragments (represented as his own and other peoples' visual memories and imaginings) to arrive at what Momaday calls a whole or complete "idea of himself";[55] the reader's potential response likewise requires the proper interpretation and assemblage of visual elements of the narrative, beginning with the important opening scene which, above all, establishes Abel's fundamental identity against which all subsequent representations of him may be read. In retrospect, the reader might eventually see in this opening scene of Abel as Dawn Runner against the horizon a fascinating metatextual suggestion of how all Momaday's icons are read against a "horizon" (an arc of a circle) of possible meanings, both extrinsic and intrinsic to the text. A compelling question for Abel and for a variety of other characters in the novel—"Do you see?"[56]—is therefore also an important metatextual question covertly addressed to the "reader" of Momaday's elaborate iconography.

While *House Made of Dawn* is fairly subtle in its metatextual statements on looking at images and forming a self, Momaday's second novel, *The Ancient Child,* overtly addresses the subject, primarily by

focusing on a visual artist as a main character. Set's interior mono-
logues and dialogue often concern painting, perspective drawing,
and the implied interconnections between imaginative structures
and personal identity. However, major clues to decoding Momaday's self-conscious language of images in *The Ancient Child* lie in the
easily overlooked references to "pointing" and dimensionality that
occur throughout the text. An important part of the ideal reader's
experience involves noticing these authorial cues, which underscore key images (and constellations of images) requiring careful
interpretation. Such cues also invite us to contemplate the epistemic nature of images. Like Sebeok recalling his father as patriarchal icon, Momaday implies that personal identity is formed partly
in relation to internalized and interpreted images drawn from the
outer world of spatial forms.

Of a total of three strategically placed references to "pointing" in
The Ancient Child, the first is Billy the Kid's humorous advice to Grey.
When using a gun or instructing a horse, he says, "You got to point.
. . . How could he know such things, she wondered. . . . *Ah, what
sagacity perished here!*" (170). Initially, a reader probably laughs at
Grey's hyperbolic response; after all, she is a young girl infatuated
with a fantasy lover, and his "sage" advice seems rather banal. However, subsequent references to "pointing" suggest that perhaps the
visionary Grey understands something in Billy's deceptively simple
words that rewards further thought, at least in the context of this
novel. A second reference to pointing occurs within one of Grey's
visions. She searches among a group of Plains ancestors for her
recently deceased grandmother, Kope'mah, but does not see her.
An ancestor, Mamanti, points to "hundreds of tarantulas" at Grey's
feet, presumably to suggest that Grey has not recognized Kope'mah
in the guise of Grandmother Spider (252). Nor has she recognized
the flood all around her as a sign of "emergence"—the beginning
of a new "calendar" or phase of existence (251).[57] Mamanti, like
Billy, instructs by pointing—directing and focusing Grey's attention on what she looks at but does not yet fully see in her quest for
self-knowledge and self-integration with traditional culture.

Ultimately, Grey herself, as a mature medicine woman, learns
how to "point": "Kneeling, she [drew] lines on the red earth, describing where she and her man must go" (260). Her lines in the
dirt point to Lukachukai in Navajo country, where Grey and Set
begin the next phase of their spiritual journey together, a journey

that unfolds in connection with a variety of sacred images inti-
mating their respective identities. Grey becomes for Set the one
who guides and instructs. She teaches him to heed and interpret
images (bear, centaur, etc.) that he, like her, encounters in dreams,
imagination, and reality.

To understand the pattern unfolding in the images emerging
from Grey and Set's visionary liaison, a reader must heed Momaday's instructions on "pointing." A new "calendar"—a new era represented through visual images that collectively tell a story—begins
with Set and Grey's union at Lukachukai. Momaday's novel proceeds in Native "calendar" fashion as a series of memorable visual
images, among them Mamanti and the ancestors in the flood, Set's
arrival, his ritual initiation with the "centaur" and the bear paw,
and his transformation into the bear. The narrative draws to a close
with an image of Set and Grey's mutual transformation. Set is now
Tsoai-talee, and Grey is "the grandmother": "Grey, sitting away in
the invisible dark, heard the grandmother's voice in her mouth.
When Set raised the [bear] paw, as if to bring it down like a club,
she saw it against the window, huge and phallic on the stars, each
great yellow claw like the horn of the moon" (304). The reader,
like Grey and Set, must look for the "pattern" that these images
together compose: Mamanti points to the spiders and Grey becomes the "grandmother" she had sought outside herself; Perfecto
Atole strikes Set with the bear paw so that Set may, in turn, raise
it to the stars and the moon. These Native calendar-like images
"point" to one another, though they do not relate to one another
according to the reader's conventional expectations of image se-
quences. Momaday teaches the reader to "see," but his method of
instruction seems designed to occlude the western analytical eye
and to encourage more mystically-oriented insights.

Grey's and Set's imaginations render precisely the images they
need to contemplate if they are to honor the universal "pattern"
or story defining their individual existence. To resist the visions
and the pattern brings psycho-spiritual and even physical illness.
Whether humorously, through advice from Billy the Kid, or seri-
ously, through wordless lessons from Mamanti or visions of the
centaur, Momaday suggests in this novel that the human imagination produces instructive mental pictures leading onto spiritual, intellectual, and other paths to knowledge, belief, and moral
acts. Sometimes these mental images are "incised" on "the picture

plane" as art.[58] Indeed, Set uses his own painted images as a guide
on his own path to knowledge.

Beyond their textual confines within *The Ancient Child*, Momaday's references to "pointing" provide excellent metatextual instruction for the reader who delves further into Momaday's language of images. Momaday apparently believes that cultural icons
"point" beyond cultural specifics to "essence." Reminding us of
Sebeok's claim about the physiological basis for semiosis, Momaday suggests that cultures differ in their particular signs and semiotic habits, but that all people are united through sign action in
general. Billy the Kid in *The Ancient Child*, for example, is no mere
Euro-American icon of the old West; for Momaday, Billy iconizes an
essential predatory force within the universe, a force that every culture recognizes but depicts differently. At strategic sites throughout *The Ancient Child*, Momaday paradigmatically equates Billy with
several animals—eagle, bear, and shark (12, 85, 183)—that iconize the predator. Incorporated into this animal iconography, Billy
the Kid loses some of his culturally circumscribed significance as a
romantic Western outlaw, or as merely a sociopathic white man. By
suggesting Billy's predator "essence," Momaday implies that Billy
is simply the manifestation of a universal force expressing itself
through an individual identity. Each animal icon with which Billy
the Kid is paradigmatically equated becomes part of a cluster of
"predator" images. The "predator" icon, in turn, potentially shapes
the reader's response to cultural difference: though Momaday demands reader sensitivity to cultural difference, he also suggests that
many such differences ultimately disappear within what Set calls
the "one great and true story" of life (216)—an admittedly "universalist" view for which Momaday has been criticized.

In the face of such criticism, Momaday defends his belief that
the act of myth-making unites individuals and cultures more profoundly than any particular body of myths distinguishes them.[59]
For example, though Momaday himself identifies strongly with the
Kiowa "bear boy," Tsoai-talee, he also shows in *The Ancient Child*
how all bear stories "point" to some vaguely outlined but essential "truth" beyond cultural difference. Linking Greek mythology
to Kiowa lore through references to Callisto, Ursa Major, and the
story of the Seven Sisters (18, 42), Momaday suggests profound
linkages between human beings across cultures. Set, Billy the Kid,
and Grey (all variously aligned with the bear) are destined, "ar-

ranged in some pattern, like the pattern of the universe," to be part of the one larger story.[60] The "one story" also includes Momaday himself as the "reincarnation" of Bear. Perhaps unsurprisingly, considering this narrative strategy, Momaday's concern with imagistic "pointing" takes a Borgesian turn in *The Ancient Child* when, finally, Momaday uses his own text to "point" to the ways in which one work of art "points" to its multiple and culturally diverse sources in other art; together with an epigram quoting Borges on literature as myth, the opening chapters make the reader especially self-conscious about reading and looking at cultural artifacts, and about the ways in which art serves as a model for other art, personal identity, and even reality itself.

Indeed, Momaday believes that to understand aesthetic form as episteme is to understand how the human mind works: according to his character, Set, "Art—drawing, painting—is an intelligence of some kind, the hand and the eye bringing the imagination down upon the picture plane; and this is a nearly perfect understanding of the act of understanding."[61] Momaday claims that such meta-consciousness is a primary feature of Indian identity; it is a part of the special "aesthetic perception" of the Indian, who is "sure to perceive an order in the objects he beholds, an arrangement that his native intelligence superimposes upon the world . . . . He sees with both his physical eye and the eye of his mind; he sees what is really there to be seen, including the aesthetic effect of his own observation upon the scene, the shadow of his own imagination."[62]

Like his theory of images, Momaday's theory of self derives from his belief in a formless "essence" beyond form and from his idea of himself as an Indian endowed with "aesthetic perception." He sees the self as much like a work of art that is teased out of the realm of pure "essence" with painstaking spiritual and creative efforts such as Set's in *The Ancient Child*. One of Set's art teachers tells him: "you can make something, a line, a form, an image. But you have to proceed from what is already there—defined space, a plane" (55). In both of his novels, Momaday implies that the teacher's advice applies to the formation of a self, as well. Through character development in his fiction, Momaday shows that there is always something "already there" in a person, some essential identity on a spiritual "plane" that requires further shaping into "something . . . a form, an image." In the unformed Abel of *House Made of Dawn* there are the vestigial traces of Monster Slayer, Dawn Runner, Eagle Watcher, and Bear. Likewise, within Set of *The Ancient Child*, Tsoai-talee always exists.

Momaday's graphic "self-portraits" also suggest the emergence of personal identity from a "black infinity" of mysterious, perspectival depths, or "essence." In the painting, "Self Portrait with Leaves,"[63] Momaday depicts himself as the bear. The bear's body and face are etched with lines not quite squarely centered over the shadowy patches defining the spaces of body and face; and slightly to the right and behind the bear's face is the hint of an emerging human head. Perhaps the bear is about to turn into a man, or has just been transformed from man to bear. In any case, the bear-man appears as not quite one being, but one being perhaps superimposed over another, or a series of beings emerging from one plane to another. (In *The Ancient Child*, a psychiatrist and a friend of Set's argue over whether he is a bear trying to be a man, or a man trying to be a bear.) Likewise, in another of Momaday's paintings, "Setangya,"[64] what looks like Momaday's own partially line-drawn face is superimposed over the shadowy image of Sitting Bear.

Both of these paintings (like so many of Momaday's works) seem deliberately to call attention to their status as representations and, simultaneously, to comment upon the role of representation in the specular semiotic process of self-realization. According to Momaday, the self becomes fully dimensional partly through contemplation of the "emblematic" contents of the "racial memory." In *House Made of Dawn*, for example, Abel "remembers" scenes of water (121), some of which have actually occurred in his life, and some of which have happened to him on a spiritual plane as the embodiment of "Born for Water," Younger Brother of the Stricken Twins. No healing is possible for Abel until he understands how such images are related and how they are the key to his own identity, and until he acts responsibly upon this dual knowledge. Likewise, in *The Ancient Child*, inklings of something "beyond [conventional] memory" (45) from his tribal ancestry attract Set, as a child in a Catholic orphanage, to western myths and images of bears. Long before he learns the Kiowa story of the Seven Sisters and the "boy bear" who spiritually inhabits him, Set's imagination seizes upon stories and images, such as the story of Ursa Major, that most closely match those within his tribal memory (as Momaday defines it). Such images are for Set the key to knowledge and action, a fact Set realizes when he contemplates one of his finished paintings, "Venture Beyond

Time," and tries "to see more deeply into it" than he had seen, "to see what others could perhaps see more clearly than [he], what deepest part of [himself he] had imagined" (161).

The idea and image of the bear are so profoundly fixed in Set's psyche that, as a boy, he has no fear of "bee-wolves" (another name for bears). Moreover, when Set's paternal (Indian) family eventually contact him, the various pieces of his life as a "bear" begin to fall in place according to an ancient, established pattern.[65] Like Abel, Set is ill while he lives in the white world, and he grows well as he heeds the promptings of his imagination (and, of course, spirit and tribal memory). While he thinks and acts as a white man, Set describes himself as a piece on a checker board, an isolated, merely material pawn of some larger, vaguely sensed but unseen power; however, thinking and acting as an Indian, he rejects this view. He feels guided by spiritual vision onto a collectively meaningful path. On this path, many separate images come together to tell the story of a "complete" rather than a fragmented self. His paintings themselves, like Momaday's, bring forth images requiring contemplation and integration within his personality.

Set's efforts to discover and invent his Indian self as the bear reflect Momaday's own. Discussing the story of Devil's Tower and the Seven Sisters with Charles L. Woodard, Momaday explains: "probably in every generation there is a reincarnation of the bear—the boy bear. And I feel that I am such a reincarnation, and I am very curious about it. The way I deal with it, finally, is to write about it. . . . [The Kiowas] incorporated [Devil's Tower] into their experience by telling a story about it. And that is what I feel I must do about the boy bear." In *The Ancient Child*, he says, "I am writing about myself. . . . I'm not writing an autobiography, but I am imagining a story that proceeds out of my own experience of the bear power."[66]

By writing, drawing, and painting, Momaday has invented himself as the bear in response to an inner vision, an "idea" that he has about himself as an Indian.[67] In his latest novel, he suggests that this process of self-invention is similar to drawing and to producing a complete, fully-dimensional narrative. As metacommentary on the narrative process, his section titles in *The Ancient Child* are compositely a major clue to Momaday's thinking not only about the self, but also about narrative as an iconic, epistemic source of identity. These section titles ("Planes," "Lines," "Shapes," and "Shadows") have a number of referents in the text overall. First, they refer to the process of drawing and painting that so often preoccupies Set as a visual artist. Because Set views his own life partly as a series of images to be brought into focus and studied, we may also conclude that the four words refer to his gradual acquisition of a "complete," three-dimensional image or "idea of himself" (52). The novel ends with Set's vision of "Tsoai, the rock tree" (312), and the bear with whom he identifies. He sees definitive "shapes and shadows" (312) where earlier in his quest he had seen (and drawn) only "lines" and sketchy "impressions" (143). Momaday's pictorial terms suggest narrative itself as yet another iconic source of identity. Narrative, like images, materially embodies essence and shapes our sense of who we are. Indeed, one of Momaday's names for himself is "the Man Made of Words." Considering the "equation" of writing and drawing (and painting) that he explains to Woodard, he could as easily be called "The Man Made of Icons." Narratives, like other icons are, in effect, some of the outward "masks" that spirit, or "essence" dons. Lest we become too rigid as "icons," however, Momaday reminds us of the importance of the flexibility and motion embodied in nature when he concludes *The Ancient Child* with an image of Set running, and when he paints himself and other entities slightly blurred, as if in a state of endless transformation.

Varieties of "specular semiosis" and the notion of the iconicity of self are implied in the writings of other contemporary American Indian writers besides Momaday. Louise Erdrich's works, for instance, suggest that identity arises partly through iconic spatial relations to the land.[68] *Love Medicine* encodes character through syntagmatic chains of references to natural elements such as air, earth, fire, and water. June's, Lipsha's, and Nector's identities arise partly from their fated relationship to water. In the opening section of the book, June "walks on water," and in the end, Lipsha travels across water to his ancestral lands. Nector's life is a river, which sometimes rushes on, sometimes pools and is still, and sometimes takes a fateful change of course. When Nector feels the course of his life change, he feels "Time . . . rushing around [him] like water around a big wet rock. . . . Very quickly [he] would be smoothed away" (94). Marie Kashpaw's personality accrues through her relationship to fire. Her sadomasochistic feelings about Sister Leopolda include the desire to see the nun's heart "roast on a black stick" (45). Marie is burned with scalding water; her visions "blaze," and when she sees the old nun for the last time, she thinks to herself there is not enough left of Leopolda to serve as kindling for a small flame.

In *Tracks*, Fleur Pillager's identity derives from various references to "wolf teeth," to Misshepesshu, a fish-like creature in Lake Matchimanito, and other feral objects. And in *The Bingo Palace*, two powerful grandmothers (Zelda Kashpaw and Lulu Lamartine) manipulate Lipsha Morrissey and others, whose interior landscapes are as visible to them as a "map" that "springs up in blue light" on a medical machine (18). Like Momaday, Erdrich comprehends the iconicity of narrative itself, for she suggests that the construction of identity around visual phenomena is guided by cultural beliefs about such phenomena, beliefs that are inscribed in narrative. Chippewa beliefs as related in their traditional stories about death by water and fire, for example, frame her characters' and narrators' responses to these elements throughout her novels.

The Iconicity of Narrative

Such works by Momaday, Erdrich and others amount to a fictive project achieving a variety of results. First, they instruct readers in the semiotic construction of self and reality within cultural frames of reference, thus discouraging unquestioned, ethnocentric interpretations of text and world. Set's and Grey's bicultural self-envisioning, for instance, emphasizes the legitimacy and logic of both western and Indian modes of interpreting experience, and Erdrich's characters, cross-coded through references to elemental forces, suggest the common ground upon which all people attempt to make sense of self and world. Second, writers such as Momaday and Erdrich expand the reader's repertoire of what Sebeok calls "possible worlds" and the possible selves that might inhabit them. Momaday's Set, choosing Kiowa-Navajo alternatives, leaves behind western self and world, and Erdrich's Lulu and Zelda hint at whole dimensions of experience to which most people (especially non-Indians) are blind.

Third, these authors extend the parameters of the novel as a genre by attempting to broaden and deepen the sociolect of the average reader to contain detailed, accurate information about specific Indian people in place of stereotypes. In doing so, however, authors of cross-coded narratives frequently write in what social semioticians Hodge and Kress call a "modality of low affinity" with the dominant culture's definitions of self, reality and truth, even as they intentionally inscribe these dominant definitions in their texts.[69] "Modality" refers to the stance of any semiotic agent toward the "truths" or assumptions of a dominant group. The "modality" of an utterance or a discourse varies depending upon its implied stance toward the dominant "reality" — a consensus construction of the dominant group that is "never unmediated, never outside semiosis, always subject to competing forces in some semiotic process." [70] Thus, a "modality of high affinity" characterizes a statement in close or full agreement with the dominant reality, while "low affinity" characterizes a competing discourse. "Modality points to the social construction or contestation of knowledge-systems. . . . [It] is consequently one of the crucial indicators of political struggle" (122–23).

When Native American authors write in a modality of low affinity with the dominant culture, they endorse certain "Indian" views while they subtly undercut certain western views through a variety of discursive strategies. This feature of contemporary Native American writing defines its radically revisionary project. United in such a project, Indian writers become like Erdrich's Nanapush (the namesake of Nanabozho, the Chippewa trickster), who in *Tracks* reports how he frustrated the efforts of a Catholic priest to impose Euro-American reality on his people: "*I talked both languages* in streams that ran alongside each other, over every rock, around every obstacle. . . . I kept Father Damien listening all night. . . . Occasionally, he took in air, as if to add observations of his own, but I pushed him under with my words" (7; emphasis mine). Writers of cross-coded texts likewise "talk both languages," but they speak in "low affinity" with the dominant culture. Their works thus amount to an important destabilizing force within the literary mainstream — a creative, resistant force with an impact that is both political and aesthetic. Indeed, as Silko has proclaimed in an interview, "the most effective political statement I could make is my art work. I believe in subversion rather than straight-out confrontation." [71] Silko insists on the subversive power of storytelling to alter the world and its inhabitants by changing the "stories" that take "form in bone and muscle." [72]

Many cross-coded texts by Native American writers are perhaps destabilizing or "subversive" enough to disrupt and revise western notions of identity, alterity, and community. Furthermore, as these authors "invent" the Indian within the generic and ideological boundaries of the western aesthetic forms they have adopted, their texts radically revise these same forms. When Erdrich's Nanapush proclaims that he "pushed [the priest] under with . . . words,"[73] we should understand a subtextual message conveying Erdrich's strategy for placing the "Indian" material of her cross-coded text in a modality of low affinity with the "Euro-American" material. Moreover, Nanapush's statement is cast in a metaphor of drowning that points to the prevailing Chippewa ethos of Erdrich's narrative, as we have noted in Chapter One. In works by Erdrich and other contemporary Native American authors, "Indian" constructions of identity developed in one of the "two languages" of the cross-coded text challenge the "truth" and "reality" status of Euro-American models presented in the other "language."

In texts cross-coded with varieties of "western" and "Native American" realities, semic codes (devices for thematizing character, among other things)[74] from both cultural categories serve the narrative purpose of presenting an "Indian" self in a modality of low affinity with a "Euro-American" self. Erdrich's and Momaday's novels, Silko's *Ceremony*, Allen's *The Woman Who Owned the Shadows*, and Welch's *The Death of Jim Loney* (1979) are examples of cross-coded texts marked by similar narrative politics, though the particular models of identity emphasized in these novels vary. Erdrich is frequently concerned with conflicting models of spirituality, as are Momaday and Silko, who are also interested in western secular models of identity that have little or no counterparts in Indian societies. Allen focuses attention specifically upon female identity, and Welch concentrates intently upon models for male identity, especially as these are constructed within different (western versus Indian) temporal frames of reference.

As she "talks" the "two languages" (Euro-American and Chippewa), Erdrich deploys biblical references suggesting a Judeo-Christian ground for interpretation of her works. In this view, the self is a unique "soul" housed in a physical body that lives for some number of years of trial and tribulation, then dies. Freed of the body, the soul enters a realm separate from and invisible to that of the living. In *Love Medicine*, for example, chapter titles ("The World's Greatest Fisherman," "Saint Marie," "Flesh and Blood," "Crown of Thorns," and "Crossing the Water") suggest that the story will unfold within an intertextual framework of references to the Bible and, accordingly, within a Judeo-Christian, specifically Roman-Catholic, frame of reference defining self. The pattern of Christian references concerning Easter and resurrection suggests the same.

The opening scene of *Love Medicine* depicts the last hours of June Kashpaw's life on Easter weekend. During this time, June goes through a series of "rebirths" implying resurrection, and in the last sentences of this scene, she dies: "The pure and naked part of her went on. The snow fell deeper that Easter than it had in forty years, but June walked over it like water and came home" (6). Syntagmatic chains of references to Christianity that describe June's life and death indicate to the reader a clear interpretive framework: the reader assumes that June has gone "home" to a Christian heaven, and that the rest of the novel is likely to unfold against the same sociolectic backdrop. Chapter Two, which recounts Marie Lazarre's experience as a novice nun, reinforces this Christian interpretation.

In talking "two languages" in *Tracks*, Erdrich first invokes a Chippewa "medicine" [75] code as the apparently appropriate interpretive frame of reference. Events take on meaning within a framework of Chippewa beliefs about life, death, and mystical experiences. *Tracks* begins with the words of Nanapush addressed to "Granddaughter [Lulu], . . . the child of the invisible, the ones who disappeared when, along with the first bitter punishments of early winter, a new sickness swept down" (2). Nanapush finds Lulu in a cabin full of dead people. Because "Pukwan did not want to enter, fearing the unburied Pillager spirits might seize him by the throat and turn him windigo," Nanapush "touched each [one] . . . and wished each spirit a good journey on the three-day road, the old-time road" (3).

In subsequent chapters of *Love Medicine* and *Tracks*, however, codes antithetical to the ones initially invoked traverse the text. The cross-coded cosmologies are epistemologically, experientially, and teleologically different (indeed, Christianity is a religion, while Native American traditions are better described as sacred world views or ways of life).[76] In *Love Medicine*, June's posthumous "home" might not be a Christian heaven but instead the reservation, where her spirit (not quite the same as a Christian "soul") mingles with the living and carries out unfinished business. Competing with the syntagmatic chain of references to Christianity in *Love Medi-*

cine is a counter-chain of references to material and spiritual life which, in Chippewa as in most American Indian traditions, are not as distinctly separate as they are according to Christianity. While she lives, June inhabits an animistic universe in which machines and other inanimate things are endowed with spirit: a "pressurized hose" is "a live thing," and a car heater is "a pair of jaws, blasting heat" (3, 5). When she dies, her restless spirit does not depart for some separate "heaven," but lingers among the familiar things of the world to trouble at least one character, her husband Gordie, who perhaps goes insane or dies when June comes back to visit him in the shape of a wounded deer.

Likewise, despite its opening pages invoking a Chippewa cosmological scheme, *Tracks* is marked by conflicting codes of identity. No single character in the novel illustrates this conflict better than Pauline, a half-white and mixed-blood Indian (later to become Sister Leopolda in *Love Medicine*) to whom Nanapush refers as "an unknown mixture of ingredients" (39). Pauline wishes to be white, but despite her scorn for her Native American upbringing, she cannot quite escape her old ways of thinking about existence. As a character, she is herself a site of code conflict; she is "cross-coded" according to different models of identity. Part of her notion of good and evil, for example, derives from a non-Christian frame of reference rife with vivid, visual icons that she internalizes to represent "self." Twisted and deformed away from their Chippewa matrix and grafted into a Christian cosmology, such representations mark her sadomasochistic Christianity as marginal and aberrant, even within the conventions of martyrology. For example, according to Chippewa belief, Misshepesshu, the lake man, is a frightening but appeasable entity. When Pauline becomes a nun, she still believes in him, but she calls him Satan. Her distorted version of the Satanic lake monster is more horrible than either the Christian Satan, who is not appeasable but who cannot victimize the truly innocent, or the Chippewa monster, who can capture the innocent but who is appeasable. Pauline herself knows that her amalgam of religious views is unprecedented, and she defines herself boastfully as a unique sort of martyr. Recounting Christian narratives about the suffering of St. John of the Cross, St. Catherine, St. Cecelia, and St. Blaise, she says with pride: "Predictable shapes, these martyrdoms. Mine took a different form" (52).

In the open-ended question of June Kashpaw's fate, as well as in the warped theology of Pauline, lies a conflict between culturally constructed semic codes defining the self. June is depicted partially through references to Christian resurrection and partly through references to a set of Indian beliefs concerning the place of spirits among their families and tribes. Likewise Pauline/Leopolda's interpretation of experience is dual and irreconcilable, despite her grotesque assimilations. Both cosmological codes allow for a spiritual dimension of existence; however, the ways in which such a dimension is manifest according to each code, as well as the ways in which the individual relates to this dimension and the ultimate meanings and values associated with each code, lead to different conclusions about what constitutes a human self and about what kind of self is more ethically viable.

Pauline is Erdrich's grotesquely humorous example of failed bicultural construction of identity; however, Erdrich's novels contain other characters, such as Lipsha Morrissey in *Love Medicine* and Nanapush in *Tracks*, whose bicultural experience leads to the formation of more viable, if almost as conflicted, identities. Furthermore, their personalities underscore the missing ingredients in Pauline's own (especially compassion) and instate the Chippewa ethos of Erdrich's narrative that subtly "pushes under," or subordinates, the Euro-American alternative.

Lipsha resembles Pauline in some ways. Brought up Roman Catholic, he also bears the "healing touch" of Indian medicine. Like Pauline's, his beliefs frequently consist of a peculiar mixture of Christianity and traditional Chippewa views, though we learn in *The Bingo Palace* that he cannot speak or read Chippewa, a deficiency that leads to his demise. Reflecting his cultural ignorance, one of his biggest and most humorous mistakes in *Love Medicine* occurs when he sets out as a Chippewa to make a "love medicine" potion for Nector and Marie, but grows impatient and doubts his power, partly owing to his Euro-American beliefs. He buys some of the necessary ingredients at the grocery store, an action he later regrets when the love potion malfunctions. This episode epitomizes the comic dimension of Lipsha Morrissey, whose mistakes and shortcomings frequently result from humanitarian motives gone awry. Indeed, most of Lipsha's appearances throughout Erdrich's works are marked by events slipping slightly out of the control of this well-intentioned character. In every case, the implied authorial sympathies, like those of the reader, are aligned with Lipsha and other characters when their "Indian" ways of seeing and be-having come to the surface.

Like Lipsha, Nanapush is a compassionate character whose point of view in *Tracks* prevails over that of other characters, especially Pauline, an inveterate liar despite her professed Christianity. Rejecting his Jesuit education and upbringing in white society, Nanapush lives honestly as a Chippewa in the woods. Nanapush knows both worlds, as Lipsha and Pauline do. Like Lipsha, but unlike Pauline, he lives authentically, primarily according to values drawn or successfully adapted from his native culture. Lipsha and Nanapush adhere to a sacred world view that sharply contrasts with Pauline's lonely, punishing Christianity. In short, the values that are semiotically grafted onto characters such as Lipsha and Nanapush in Erdrich's texts underscore the "low affinity" of her discourse with Euro-American models of identity, which inevitably bring hardship or grief to characters who subscribe or attempt to subscribe to them.

Momaday's *House Made of Dawn* and Silko's *Ceremony* are similarly encoded. They resemble one another in cross-coding a primarily Navajo-Pueblo worldview with that of the dominant culture. As in Erdrich's works, this cross-coding produces competing notions of individual identity. Momaday and Silko, however, are less concerned with Christianity than with western secular concepts of self, particularly medical and social scientific models with which their characters contend. In both *Ceremony* and *House Made of Dawn*, a western, medical-psychological model of self stressing Euro-American "individualism" competes with Navajo-Pueblo relational models emphasizing community and broad, fundamental principles of spiritual "health" as a key to the workings of the universe.

Silko's Tayo is ill according to both western and Laguna-Pueblo standards. He suffers the physical and emotional ills of "battle fatigue," according to the army physicians. However, the Navajo description of his problems provided by Betonie is more complex. First, he suffers in general from the lack of proper, responsible relationship to his community, a relationship involving personal responsibility to fulfill the patterns for him set down in the sacred realm. Second, he has committed some specific transgressions against the Holy People, especially Reed Woman when he curses the rain. Third, he has been to war where he might have (he does not even know) killed the enemy without observing proper ritualistic behavior, and he has not been cleansed of this violence in a traditional Scalp Ceremony (which Betonie says no longer helps twentieth-century Indians, in any case).

Finally, Tayo's illness is one small part of a global sickness, the symptoms of which are world war and atomic weapons. Based on western concepts of self, however, the "white doctors had yelled at him—that he had to think only of himself, and not about the others, that he would never get well as long as he used words like 'we' and 'us.'"[77] Tayo's attempt in *Ceremony* to heal by the white doctors' methods fails because for Tayo, "medicine didn't work that way. His sickness was only part of something larger, and his cure would be found only in something great and inclusive of everything" (126). This cure begins with Tayo's visit to medicine men, proceeds with his vision quest through the Southwestern desert, and culminates (though it does not really end) with his return to the reservation to assume his preordained role as storyteller and artist of the sacred.

The white doctors "yell" at Tayo because he does not define himself "correctly" according to their psychological model of self. They see him as a particular "individual" with a specific disorder— "battle fatigue." Moreover, they view the source of the problem as likewise specific—particular battles fought in World War II. In Tayo's ceremony of healing, however, he discovers the source of his illness in the five-hundred year encounter of Native Americans and whites, and even more fundamentally, in a world gone mad with lust for power, iconically represented by the bomb crater at Trinity Site at White Sands, New Mexico, and by Hiroshima and Nagasaki. For such a world, the war is only one of many symptoms. Because it does not treat the cause of Tayo's sickness, the whites' "medicine drained memory out of his thin arms and replaced it with a twilight cloud behind his eyes" (15). For Tayo, to become a western "individual" is to achieve a form of nonbeing. Getting well means revising his identity according to relational models of the subjective, communal self that Betonie and others teach him.

The process and pattern of Tayo's rehabilitation are suggested through traditional Pueblo-Navajo chantways that are interwoven throughout the novel with improvised chantways detailing the historical specifics of Tayo's life. The first chantways recorded in the text are traditional—recounting, for example, the story of Hummingbird, who traveled between worlds to help The People when they were starving—but eventually, the chantways change and expand to allude to the contemporary world and to Tayo's life, specifically. This gradual but powerful infiltration of Tayo's reality with traditional Navajo-Pueblo views constitutes one way in which Silko, like Erdrich, endorses an "Indian" view of self. Native traditional stories, as an internalized part of his life, begin to reshape his sense of self and world. Both traditional and improvised chantways emphasize Tayo's relationship and personal responsibility to spirit beings and other people; they suggest Tayo's development of a self-definition alternative to the militaristic individualism that the white physicians encourage. Furthermore, Tayo's rehabilitation parallels the expansion of the traditional chantways to explain current events. As historical specifics are explained more and more within an Indian, rather than a Eurocentric, frame of reference, Tayo gradually understands "the order, structure, and the names of things,"[78] including ways to "name" himself as a self. He is integrated into what is for him a meaningful cosmic scheme and he begins to heal.

Abel's illness in Momaday's *House Made of Dawn* resembles Tayo's. He suffers from post-war stress, alcoholism, and from living out of harmony with the cosmic order. And like the cross-coded models of self informing Silko's Tayo and Erdrich's characters, the cultural "stories" comprising Momaday's Abel profoundly conflict. When Abel fights "snakes," for example, he acts as Monster Slayer in a way Euro-Americans cannot understand. As Benally and Tosamah explain, Abel is a "longhair"—a traditional Indian. His trial for the murder of Juan Reyes (a "snake") is absurd, for a Euro-American trial is irrelevant to a deed committed by a traditional Indian in a Native context. In Tosamah's words: "Can you *imagine* what went on at that trial? There was this longhair, see, cold sober, of sound mind, and the goddam judge looking on, and the prosecutor trying to talk sense to that poor degenerate Indian: 'Tell us about it, man. Give it to us straight.' 'Well, you [sic] honors, it was this way, see? I cut me up a little snake meat out there in the sand.'"[79] Confused by non-Indian models of selfhood by which he has attempted to live, Abel cannot at first explain even to himself why he has killed Juan Reyes; nor, as Monster Slayer, is he susceptible to "rehabilitation" by social workers and courts of law.

Throughout most of his life, Abel constructs himself haphazardly. Following neither Euro-American nor Pueblo models, he suspects a problem with his "frame of reference" (106), but he is too confused to pursue any line of thought. Not even in silence—"the older and better part of [Indian] custom still" (58)—can he find direction until he learns the stories that he needs to narrate himself into being. In so doing, he becomes "articulate" and thereby contrasts with Erdrich's Pauline, whose identity always consists of a tortured combination of the "two languages" through which she understands self and world. Ultimately, Abel's choices and his newfound powers of self-expression endorse an Indian "language" describing reality and personal identity; Momaday thus develops his novel in a modality of low affinity with the Euro-American alternatives that Abel rejects.

With few exceptions, Native American novels have focused primarily upon developmental crises of male characters, though in the process, nearly all of these novels suggest important, gynocentric values. For example, Tayo in *Ceremony,* and even Abel to some extent in *House Made of Dawn,* must learn to honor female forces in the universe as a part of their healing. One of the first Indian writers to trace a female self-transformational process is Paula Gunn Allen, whose *The Woman Who Owned the Shadows* explores lesbian feminist identity as it arises for her main character through the "two languages" of her Euro-American and Pueblo worlds.[80] Like its counterparts by Silko, Momaday, and Erdrich, this novel is cross-coded with various alternative narrative epistemes for identity.

Allen's protagonist, Ephanie, is a half-blood whose name itself implies a culturally fragmented self.[81] The name, "Ephanie," seems to her to consist of pieces of other words such as "epiphany" (with its Christian connotations) and of the white woman's name, "Stephanie." The name "stood before her like the emblem of a delphi that in this world could not exist."[82] (The allusion to Greek myth underscores the cross-coded nature of Ephanie's self.) Allen further emphasizes Ephanie's incoherent self-construction by narrating in sentence fragments, often marked by lack of cause-effect connectives. Indeed, a disjunctive series of states of being meet in Ephanie, a woman undergoing a cultural as well as a sexual identity crisis. Just as she herself is disconnected from a sustaining community, the disjunctive components of her life lack any clear frame of reference to bind them into a coherent life story, or Sebeokian "narrative schema."

Ephanie is torn between white and Indian models as well as between heterosexual and lesbian models for identity. She knows that even if she should choose to be "Indian," further difficulties await her. In the Indian stories of Grandmother Spider, Ephanie discovers a model for inventing herself as Laguna and lesbian, but fear of her incipient self emerges as a fear of spiders. Indians advise her to leave spiders alone, but Ephanie (behaving more like a white woman) vacuum-cleans them and their webs from her house. As an iconic site of various code-conflicts in *The Woman Who Owned the Shadows*, Spider provides clues to the process of cultural and gender identity-formation that Ephanie undergoes; Spider also becomes the device through which Allen develops the low modality relationship of her novel to the Euro-American and heterosexual "reality" that Ephanie repudiates.

As if to draw Ephanie into their own separate "webs" of reality, several different dominant groups compete to control the course of her self-transformation. Responding to Ephanie's psycho-spiritual disintegration, two different women's communities offer prescriptions for health. On the one hand, she seeks psychological counseling and joins a West Coast, 1970s-style women's "support-group." Ephanie also enlists the aid of urban Indian women, who invent themselves eclectically according to various Indian female models. In San Francisco, Ephanie comes under the well-intentioned control of Stephen, her Indian cousin, who teaches her about Native American life, but who wants to "bring her into a focus he could understand" (35). Resisting Stephen, Ephanie still lacks moorings; she "tries on" other people's lives without satisfaction (36). Finally, she breaks down. Her nonsensical speech reflects the welter of options she has "tried on" to no avail. Traditional Cheyenne, Arapaho, Navajo, and other stories swirl about in her mind, mingled with stories she has read: "the avenues of sensing that she wandered in had no counterpart in the books that walled her. They merely offered possibility by negation. . . . [S]he uttered strange sounds" (39). Struggling for words to explain her predicament, she speaks a jumble of Spanish and English: "thought can't hacer the impossible" (40).

One story emerges clearly in her mind, however. This story inaugurates Ephanie's return to health. Thinking of Hummingbird, who knew where to go to eat while all the rest of the world starved, Ephanie decides to leave the place where she starves. " 'I go back to

Shipap. To the mother' " (40), she declares, echoing Hummingbird. Gradually regaining her health, Ephanie realizes that personal power comes with deliberate choices in defining and inventing reality. Rejecting her white friend's well-intended but condescending ideas about Indians, she disagrees that Indians are powerless victims. "We are co-creators," she declares, suddenly comprehending the history of her people (159). Ephanie speaks to a spider in the corner and dreams herself into coherent existence as a member of the "Spider Medicine Society." This society consists of "double women, the women who never married, who held power like the Clanuncle, like the power of the priests, the medicine men" (211). Embracing her long "forgotten" and rejected Indian-lesbian identity, Ephanie "owns" the "shadows" of the Spider Woman that before only haunted her and made her ill.

During Ephanie's self-transformation, the story of the Little War Twins, Spider Woman's grandsons, serves her as an epistemic source of identity. Too long in the passive role of female, half-blood, and victim, Ephanie goes to "war" by fortifying herself with the tools of self-reconstruction. She acquires a will and changes her life. She struggles with words until (as for Tayo in *Ceremony*) all the "stories" come together at "Shipap. The Mother's home. The place of the one good heart" (190). Singing her own version of a Navajo song about the return to Navajoland after the Diné exile at Fort Sumner, Ephanie proclaims: "I am walking Alive / Where I am Beautiful / I am still Alive / In beauty Walking / I am Entering / Not alone" (213).[83] Like Betonie in *Ceremony*, Ephanie "makes changes" in the traditional stories and ways; no longer does she refuse to " 'shift and grow." [84] And like her Native American writer contemporaries, Allen underlines the "Indian" components of self that her protagonist chooses. Allen implies that the Indian ways are best because they are most closely aligned with nature, adaptability and health, specifically the health of a doubly marginalized female who is not only half-blood, but lesbian as well.

The crises of self and spirit that occur in these novels amount to an internal warfare, as Allen emphasizes through allusions to the War Twins. Ephanie begins to heal when she understands that "what is divided in two brings war" [85] and that such a battle nobly fought yields peace and wisdom. Thus the "warfare" of cross-coding in Allen's and other novels reminds us that for many Native Americans the term "war" may signify both positively and negatively. Like any challenge, a "war" is a trial and test of spirit as well as an effort to defeat an enemy. Indeed, the life of a "warrior" is not necessarily carried out in combat with a mortal adversary, but instead may be characterized by certain deliberately cultivated habits of mind. Such a conception of "war" and the "warrior" ethos informs many of James Welch's works, including *The Death of Jim Loney*.[86] In this novel, a Plains Indian warrior model of self competes with a western autobiographical model for ultimate control of the design of Jim's life. Jim "had been thinking of his life for a month. He had tried to think of all the little things that added up to a man sitting at a table drinking wine. But he couldn't connect the different parts of his life, or the various people who had entered and left it. Sometimes he felt like an amnesiac searching for the one event, the one person or moment, that would bring everything back and he would see the order in his life. . . . 'I will think of yesterday, last week, last year, until all my years are accounted for. Then I will look ahead and know where I'm going.'"[87]

Thus Welch's narrator portrays Jim's struggle to see his life, in western autobiographical form, as the coherent story of a stable self with clear origins and shaped by significant external and internal events taking place in linear time. In other words, Jim tries to see himself as an "individual." However, he soon finds that the facts of his life elude neat configuration; compounding his struggle is his lack (by both western and Indian standards) of clear family relationships. His Indian mother left when he was one year old, and his father, who left when Jim was about ten, has been absent for years. An orphan bereft of both western and Native models for identity, Jim suffers from nearly total "amnesia" about his origins and from a generally faulty memory of the past.

In addition to the autobiographical model of self that Jim struggles to fulfill, Welch's novel is also encoded with an alternative semiotic system of self-construction. This alternative system is derived from Native American Plains Indian tradition and departs altogether from the western autobiographical norm. It holds the promise of self-revelation, if only Jim can overcome his white man's resistance to promptings from the realm of spirit. Repeatedly, "dark birds" appear to Jim and beckon him out of a world where "In the past several years he had become something of a nonperson" (41). Unfortunately, instead of sharing his visions, as he sometimes wants to do (and as he must do according to the vision quest tradition),

Jim remains silent, alienated, and ill. One night with Rhea, his girlfriend, he "looked into the fire and he saw his dark bird. . . . And
he wanted her to see it too, but he knew she didn't. She had her
own thoughts. . . . He watched the bird getting smaller and he felt
bad. He had wanted to share this moment" (30).

Loney's dreams are also visited by a woman who tells him of her
lost son "out there" in the Little Rockies. Unfortunately, Jim deals
with dreams and visions as if he were white; they are unsharable evidence of his isolation and, even worse, mental instability. Supress-
ing his psychic intimations and ignoring his inner life (like Set in
the beginning of *The Ancient Child*), Jim paradoxically clings to and
rejects what little society he enjoys. He goes to a football game and
then abruptly leaves; he seeks out an old drinking buddy, but com-
plains he can no longer enjoy the man's company. Like Momaday's
Abel and Allen's Ephanie, Jim is both inarticulate and alienated.[88]
As long as he tries to make sense of his life "autobiographically" (acknowledging only those experiences unfolding within linear time
and material space), his life makes no sense. However, once he ac-
knowledges his dream-visions, life begins to assume a pattern.

Great critical controversy surrounds Welch's management of his
character, Jim Loney. Though Welch himself has said to Bill Bevis[89]
that we should see Jim's death at the end in a positive light, some
critics object to Jim's self-orchestrated suicide at the hands of the
law. However, if we see Jim as a warrior whose victory lies in design-
ing and choosing his own fate (much like the Plains warriors who
staked themselves to the ground in battle), we understand Jim's
choice of a model for self-construction that is simply very different
from the autobiographical one he struggles with early in the novel.
After a series of unfortunate events, Jim leaves a message with a
dog for Amos After Buffalo (a young boy who sympathizes with
Jim over the death of his dog, Swipesy): "You tell Amos that Jim
Loney passed through town while he was dreaming. Don't tell him
you saw me with a bottle and a gun. That wouldn't do. Give him
dreams. Tell him you saw me carrying a dog [Swipesy] and that I
was taking that dog to a higher ground. He will know."[90]

Jim's "dark bird" leads him to "higher ground," which for Jim
is death.[91] He joins the woman in his dreams, who seeks her son
"out there" in the Little Rockies where Jim chooses to die. The
two worlds evoked in this novel hold out to Jim two different "languages" for constructing an identity. Jim's chosen identity and des-

tiny lie in the Indian world of his spirit ancestors. Indeed, Welch implies that death is a viable choice for a man like Jim who cries for a dream [92] and who lives by the dream when it comes to him. Doubtless, Welch sees in Jim's suicide one form of fulfillment of his character's chosen fate—to be among tribal "family" at last.

Jim's choice raises many important questions about family as a context for constructing the self. His life, and especially his death, underscore the different ways in which western and Native American people understand kinship networks. Contemporary Native American authors frequently reject not only autobiographical formulations of identity, but other western patterns of family relationship and history as well. Erdrich's texts, for example, like Welch's *Jim Loney*, cross-code "Indian" models with western codes of individuation. Values associated with the western nuclear family are evoked in *Love Medicine*, especially in the arguments over the "real" status of Marie Kashpaw's biological children, as opposed to the outcast status of adoptees such as June (actually Marie's niece) and Lipsha (June's son). The idea that biological children are somehow superior or preferred over other children who belong in a nuclear family is a Western European, not a Native American, concept. On the contrary, the Native American "family" allows for various ties of kinship—including spiritual kinship and clan membership—joining the individuals living together in one house or, in Jim Loney's case, joining the individuals populating the same dreams and visions.

Erdrich's *Love Medicine* denies the significance of biological lineage, while *The Beet Queen* emphasizes the arbitrariness of ties between people. Just as Welch depicts the weak ties between Jim and his Euro-Americanized sister, Erdrich suggests that people who are biologically related are often much less central in each other's lives than the traditional family saga suggests. *The Beet Queen* concerns breakages in biological lines of kinship. Karl and Mary, abandoned by their mother, are raised separately from each other, as well as from their baby brother, who is kidnapped and raised as Jude Miller. Mary grows up with her aunt, who prefers Mary to her own daughter, Sita. Another character with a confusing lineage and pattern of relationships is Celestine James, a half-blood with a number of half-siblings. She becomes Mary's friend and Karl's wife, though Wallace Pfef, also Karl's lover, acts more like a husband to her. In *Tracks*, Nanapush calls Lulu "daughter" and "granddaughter," while she calls him "uncle," though Lulu is not directly kin to Nanapush at all. However, because Nanapush saved Lulu's mother, Fleur, from death, Fleur is a "daughter," and Lulu is thus a "granddaughter."

Erdrich's and Welch's texts deemphasize the importance of biological ties while emphasizing other, particularly spiritual, ties. The lives of Momaday's Abel and Silko's Tayo likewise illustrate the need for family kinship patterns alternative to the western norm; both characters learn how to belong to a community based on ties that are not biological. Abel's family, except for his grandfather, Francisco, are absent or "strange"—or both. To belong at home, Abel has to discover the designated patterns of his life that are metaphysically rather than biologically evident. Likewise, Tayo overcomes the stigma of being the outcast son of an absent white father and a drunken mother who brought shame to her Indian family. His aunt raises him, though she clearly prefers her own son, Rocky, a brother in spirit to Tayo, if in fact biologically only his cousin. Set in *The Ancient Child* also faces issues of biological lineage and heritage that, once clarified, also recede in importance to him by comparison with his spiritual lineage. All of these writers overdetermine Indian choices by showing how a self developed within the parameters of "something larger"[93] is more likely to create morally, ethically, and environmentally better "possible worlds."[94]

According to social semioticians Hodge and Kress, power is semiotically negotiated through consent or resistance to the dominant reality, which is upheld through the dominant forms of semiosis, or ways of making sense. The Native American writers I have focused on in this chapter not only withhold their "consent," but they actively articulate their "resistance" to certain Euro-American realities. To participate in reforming the "social definition of the real"[95] is a profound political act. The overt emphasis of these writers on the semiotic formation of self holds out a promise of liberation and escape from any model of self that becomes oppressive for whatever reason within any culture. We can, they insist, *re-sign* limited and destructive configurations of self and world.

Chapter Four
They All Sang as One: Refiguring Space-Time

> Jonnie Navajo began to chant in a sing-song voice . . . . All
> the medicine men sang that way. . . . Yes, they all sang as one,
> the melded voices drifting down . . . through time. . . . The
> present time and place were secondary to the song.[1]

As we have seen, western narrative frequently inhibits expression
of American Indian realities, but contemporary Indian authors are
adept in their strategies for expanding the semiotic range of western sign systems. Indeed, all semiotic forms are potentially subject to reimbrication of the sort we have considered in Chapters
Two and Three. Spatial and temporal codes inscribed within narrative forms constitute particularly significant challenges to Native
American and other ethnic writers in their endeavors to represent
worlds not in conformity with western material and mechanical
notions of space and time. "Numbers, time, inches, feet. All are
just ploys for cutting nature down to size" (221), says Lulu Lamartine in Erdrich's *Love Medicine* (221).

Contemporary Native American novelists have developed an impressive array of narrative techniques for criticizing and reforming
this tendency toward the reduction and commodification of nature
that they perceive at the core of western epistemology. These strategies range from the fairly straightforward treatment of the issue at
mimetic textual levels—for example, Welch's development of characters with troubling relationships to time in *The Death of Jim Loney*
and *Winter in the Blood* (1974)—to the structurally complex methods

of Erdrich, Momaday, Silko, and others who attempt to "re-form" the novel at subtler, semiosic levels to facilitate expression of the spatio-temporal norms of the Indian "Other." An overview of such methods that Welch, Hogan, Erdrich, Momaday, and Silko have devised provides an excellent background for a fuller discussion of spatio-temporal code revision in Walters's *Ghost Singer,* a stream-lined novel of grand proportions that has yet to receive due critical attention. Together with works by Momaday and Silko, Walters's *Ghost Singer* sets a standard for American Indian narrative envisioning an "Indian" reclamation and rehabitation of the Americas.

Crises of *Habitare*

Most contemporary Indian literature semiotically encodes a "crisis of *habitare,*" William Boelhower's term describing a "quest for a dwelling" in a place that, like the idealized America of the immigrant's dream, "does not exist" or, in the case of Native Americans, no longer exists.[2] At least as contemporary American Indian writers represent it, this "quest for a dwelling" involves complex relationships to space, time, and textuality that readers ideally must comprehend if these novels are to achieve their implied, world-transformative ends.[3]

Native Americans who are lost to themselves and dispossessed of home in space and time are frequent protagonists in the fiction of James Welch.[4] Aimless wanderers rather than purposeful travelers, his characters in *Winter in the Blood* and *The Death of Jim Loney* appear temporally disturbed; they struggle to feel at home in a world that seems progressively strange and hostile to them. Because his experiences resist containment within the Eurocentric telos of clock-time, the narrator in *Winter* appears almost obsessed with the passage of months and years. He constantly remarks his own or Mose's chronological age in a failed effort to force events into designated patterns, as we observed in Chapter Three. Welch's narrator marks time by recollecting vivid sights that form no chronological sequence and obey no particular causal logic; emotionally numb, he reviews his life as if it were a cinematic montage that makes no sense. He displays what Momaday calls an "emblematic" memory,[5] but he lacks the emotionally-directed, integrative capacity that for Momaday defines good "vision."

The narrator's feelings apparently return with the rain, however, as he tentatively muses upon a cyclic rather than a linear time-frame. His friendship with the traditional Yellow Calf helps the narrator break free from emotional paralysis by learning about his own Indian past. His assumption of traditional family responsibilities, especially attending to his grandmother's burial, likewise helps to reset his internal sense of "Indian" time. Though in the end he is still rather alienated from the world and himself, he has learned from the blind Yellow Calf that he ought to depend upon inner vision, which unfolds not according to mechanical time—Yellow Calf's calendar stops in 1936, when he goes blind[6]—but according to the implied cycles of nature (158). The narrator begins to respond to the ebb and flow of his feelings the way he responds to drought and rain on the land.[7]

While the narrator in *Winter in the Blood* fixates on mechanical time, Jim Loney seems dangerously oblivious to it. He never knows the date or the hour,[8] and he feels "like an amnesiac" (20) with no sense of any meaningful historical or personal past (91). Though the implications of Jim's suicide at the end of this novel are controversial, Jim's departure from this world into the spirit world might suggest his radical healing, as we have noted in Chapter Three. Breaking free of the material world, he connects with the spirits of ancestors who have inhabited his confused visions in life. In *Winter in the Blood* as well as in *The Death of Jim Loney*, Welch insists that traditional Native American spatio-temporal reality includes the past enfolded into the present. In death, Jim regains the tribal world that was lost to him in life, a world where spirits move between past and present with far less difficulty than incarnate beings are able to do. Ironically, in death Jim seems more thoroughly healed than *Winter*'s narrator in life, for the latter's regenerative journey is only tentatively begun at the close of the narrative, while Jim's is perhaps completed.

Spirit beings who likewise find the passage between then and now an easy one include the Hill People of Hogan's *Mean Spirit*. These spirit entities not only watch over the embodied, Osage inhabitants of the present world, but at the end of the novel they also escort them into another, timeless realm beyond history. Hogan represents Indian and Eurocentric temporal schemes through ostensibly casual references to macaws and parrots that fly south, on the one hand, and to a chiming clock on the other. These symbolic gestures mark the difference between ceremonial and linear temporal paradigms that, in turn, emphasize a seemingly unbridgable gap between Native and Euro-American cultures. Likewise, the medicine bundle that contains "the older world, wanting out"[9] exists at a liminal threshold between worlds that western industrial time does not acknowledge. At the conclusion of *Mean Spirit,* Hogan circumvents this epistemological constriction that is conventionally encoded in western narrative by having her characters "disappear," escorted by the Hill People into a realm beyond the bounds of written discourse.[10] Linearly narrated, historical time virtually collapses into mythical, ceremonial time and narrative silence, as we have previously observed in Chapter Two.

Eurocentric constraints on Native American spatio-temporal realities apparently command a great portion of Louise Erdrich's attention, as well. Within Erdrich's cross-coded texts, we see deft management of conflicting temporal paradigms as she attempts, at semiosic rather than mimetic levels of discourse, to evoke the semblance of "Indian" experience in her non-Native readers. Her works encode mechanical time as linear, incremental, and teleological, and as consisting of forward-moving, discretely measurable moments; some are "*moment*ous" and purposive, and thus command special status in memory. Moreover, in the western tradition of the novel, these momentous incidents build upon each other and contribute, as in *Bildüngsroman,* to character development and maturity. Erdrich draws upon these conventions and juxtaposes them with narrative approximations of ceremonial time. Consequently, her works expand the semiotic potential of narrative form, partially by drawing attention to the narrative construction of time itself.

By dating the chapters of *Love Medicine,* for example, Erdrich implies mechanical time. Owing to the prominent placement of these dates as chapter titles, they appear to have special significance marking a coherent series of privileged, momentous events in otherwise ordinary lives.[11] In the tradition of *Bildüngsroman,* the novel also appears to chronicle the history of various characters in a family. Moreover, the opening chapter begins at Easter, a holiday suggesting Christian teleology and thus a mechanical, linear-historical time code. However, as Paula Gunn Allen observes about Native American novels which attempt to unfold according to chronological time, linearity is often disrupted by flashbacks, lateral narrational pursuits, flights of free association, departures into "timeless" dimensions, and other indications of the failure of western chronological sequence to contain the full account.[12] Certainly there are many such narrative disruptions in *Love Medicine*, as if events, with their rippling effects backward and forward in time, exceed the forward-moving constraints of linear development. Indeed, Erdrich shows us through semiotic maneuverings what Welch and Hogan more overtly imply at the content level: "narration" frequently exceeds the conventional bounds of "story."[13]

By itself, such narrative management would not distinguish Erdrich's writing from modernist or postmodernist texts, likewise marked by temporal disjunction and subversion of traditional epistemological categories. However, Erdrich's narratives further resist mental efforts to re-order them according to Eurocentric norms: by cross-coding ceremonial time together with linear time, her works disrupt western conventional notions about what kinds of experience are "important." Here, with regard to what "matters," Erdrich strikes to the heart of the problem faced by Welch's protagonists in *Winter* and *Jim Loney*, as we have seen. Erdrich's technique resists the reader's acquired habits of mentally reorganizing textual data according to a linear model and of figuring out, despite narrative evasions, which are the pivotal events or developments in the story or in characters' lives. (A similar "confusion" of kinship lines further undermines the conventional reader's tendency to sort characters into "insider" and "outsider" categories inscribed in western family saga.[14])

Erdrich represents ceremonial time as cyclic rather than linear and as accretive rather than incremental; cyclic time also differently defines and distinguishes "momentous" and "ordinary" events.[15] One of the first cues to the presence of the ceremonial paradigm in *Love Medicine* is the chronological loop that the text makes, as if to satisfy both mechanical and ceremonial time schemes. The novel opens in 1981, loops back through the 40s, 50s, 60s, and 70s, returns to 1981, then proceeds to 1984. This organization suggests that the meanings of events and conditions in the present moment lie piecemeal in the endless round of time, not in a linear cause-and-effect progression of years.

Further emphasizing her point, throughout *Love Medicine* (and in her novels published subsequently), Erdrich develops a double-coded trope of fishing.[16] Nector Kashpaw's life is a river (a metaphor for cyclic, eternal return): it proceeds from a deep source, wanders the earth and once even changes course; finally, it returns to its source when Nector retreats behind the "smokescreen" of senility to "fish" for "deep thoughts" in "the middle of Lake Turcot" (208). On the one hand, the trope (within a network of biblical references) recalls Christ and his apostles as "fishermen" for the souls of the redeemed. Christ, who once inhabited historical time as a mortal man but who now resides in the spirit, will reel in his catch, so to speak, after the final Judgment at the end of time. Christ's apparent absence leads Lipsha to say that "Since the Old Testament, God's been deafening up on us" (194). Lipsha compares the Christian God to those of the Chippewa: "Our Gods aren't perfect . . . but at least they come around" (195). Nector's "fishing for deep thoughts," in other words, might yield more response from the gods of the Chippewa than from the Christian God.

Erdrich's trope of fishing also signifies within an alternative, Chippewa context in which the lake monster "fishes" for the fishermen on Lake Turcot and sometimes snatches people from their boats (194). Unlike Christ, the Chippewa lake monster materially inhabits both historical and eternal realms, and he collects his catch immediately. By double-coding the trope of fishing, Erdrich calls attention to the spatio-temporal barriers that separate the spiritual and material worlds of Christians and that deprive Christians of powerful spiritual experiences in the here and now as they await judgment in eternity. Lipsha remarks, for example, that in the Old Testament (before God went "deaf") "God used to raineth bread from clouds, smite the Phillipines [sic], sling fire down on red-light districts where people got stabbed. He even appeared in person every once in a while. God used to pay attention, is what I'm saying" (194). In *Tracks*, Erdrich pursues even further her point about the Christian God's retreat beyond spatio-temporal barriers. The lake monster's "fishing" and Fleur Pillager's repeated escapes expose the illusory nature of western epistemological categories that separate physical and metaphysical realms in spatio-temporal terms.

The Beet Queen (1986) unfolds more strictly than *Love Medicine* within mechanical time. The book opens in the 1930s and proceeds through the 1970s; the only fracture in chronology occurs with the placement of 1972 before 1971. However, this chronological unfolding overlies frequent narrational retreats into timeless and spiritual dimensions. Rather than characters who develop according to incremental life experiences occurring throughout the years, the characters' major stages of development consist of marked falls or deliverances from time. For example, the narrative is punctuated by metaphysical flights, as when Mary and Karl's mother, Adelaide, vanishes from their lives by flying away with a stunt pilot named Omar. For Mary, Adelaide is mythologized, frozen into an eternal moment of falling back out of the sky (recalling mother-figures in many Native American creation stories). The only time Mary ever corresponds with her mother again, she sends her a post-card with an "aerial view of Argus," as if to substantiate her vision of her mother still in the sky looking down at her. Chronology yields to timelessness again in Mary's trance vision and her subsequent formation of a spiritual tie with Celestine's baby, Mary's niece. As Mary "sees" the person the embryo will be, time speeds up and she watches an entire season elapse. Mary's prophetic dreams break down the notion that time flows sequentially in standard units, and they suggest simultaneity rather than linearity of time.

Tracks follows a similar cross-coded temporal development. Chronological events—the story*line*—contained between 1913 and 1924 exist in tension with narration, which (reminding us of the end of Hogan's *Mean Spirit*) collapses into mythical or ceremonial time. In the ceremonial tradition, which assumes fewer, different, and less absolute distinctions between "real" and "imaginary" events, *Tracks* interweaves storyline and dreamed events; consequently, the eleven years supposedly contained by the narrative constantly exceed their boundaries. Indeed, Nanapush declares that whites imposed their ideas of measurement and boundaries on the Chippewa, and he implies that the separation of experience into real and imagined events, of land into commodified tracts, and of time into past, present, and future, is part of an alien and oppressive worldview which, together with writing itself, amounts to the nearly total dispossession of Native American people of their place.

Certainly the majority of contemporary Native American writers, including Erdrich, are considerably indebted to N. Scott Momaday, the first Native American writer (and probably the first American writer) to devise semiotic strategies for such representation of conflicting spatio-temporal paradigms. His monumentally important novel, *House Made of Dawn*, established a model and precedent for the innovative fiction that would follow it over the next decades. In his autobiographical memoir, *The Way to Rainy Mountain* (1969), composed more or less concurrently with *House*, Momaday uses typeface variations and graphic placement on pages to emphasize oppositional discourses for telling essentially the same stories. Conventional U.S. historical accounts, traditional Kiowa stories, and pictorial representations invite the reader of *Rainy Mountain* to consider the different ways, both within and between cultures, that human beings have devised for keeping track of things. Eurocentric historical narrative juxtaposed with Kiowa emblematic fabulation amount to a narrational method that exhibits the semiotically complex techniques for encoding spatio-temporal paradigms in *House Made of Dawn*.

Momaday's sudden conflations of ceremonial and mechanical time schemes in *House* present a significant challenge for the reader. Direct and indirect allusions to Kiowa and Navajo-Pueblo cultural material signal the informed reader of narrative departures into nonwestern realities. These allusions have been impressively documented and explained by Susan Scarberry-García. Though she does not explore narrative technique, the wealth of explanatory information that she provides for the general reader of *House* certainly facilitates the study of Momaday's narrative strategies, and even those of other writers, such as Silko and Walters, who likewise draw upon Southwestern and Western Plains Indian cultural information in their works. Knowing, for example, that Abel shares brotherly relationships with other characters in the novel that replicate the model relationship between the Stricken Twins of Southwestern tribal lore enables Momaday's readers to understand the ceremonial implications of the goose hunting scene; in this scene, Abel and Vidal reenact in historical, present space-time the timeless, paradigmatic events recorded in the stories of Monster Slayer and Born for Water. This scene therefore takes place within a double time frame and bears important ramifications at the historical and ceremonial levels of *House*.

One of the most profoundly innovative Indian writers to appear shortly after Momaday published *House*, Silko manages the semiotic rearrangement of time and space in *Ceremony* in ways that probably establish her novel as the more literarily influential of the two, owing to its metatextually instructive features that we have already discussed at length in Chapter Two. We have likewise observed in Chapter One, concerning narrative power, how Silko in

Ceremony devises three large categories of discourse that encode atemporal, mythico-spiritual experience and temporal-historical experience. The different types of discourse that invoke different rules for their delivery and reception encourage the reader to learn how to "dwell" within the temporal realms of the text as defined by Silko's revisionary semiotic practice. An important dimension of the "crisis of *habitare*" encoded in *Ceremony* involves several kinds of material and non-material space: the public or federal space of the United States; the so-called "Indian" space of the "reservation"; the personal and psychological spaces of individual characters, including the space of the physical body; the "vertical" or metaphysical space that for Native Americans is both communal and personal; and finally, the space of the text itself—the ground on which Silko attempts her radical revision of the world.

On any typical road map of New Mexico, a reader may trace Tayo's journey as well as observe the ways in which federal space subsumes Native American space. On such a map, thin and thick lines representing county, state, and national thoroughfares connect small and large dots representing towns; in small letters appearing to lie "underneath" the more prominent lines, dots, and words one deciphers the names of reservations—Navajo, Jemez, Acoma, and so on. Silko likewise represents Euro-American space in cartographic terms as written or superimposed over Indian lands, and she regards Native American cultures as "buried under English words."[17]

In this novel, Euro-American space is encoded through references to high speed travel over interstate highways—artificial constructions marring the land and featuring billboards and road signs beckoning travelers onward incessantly toward a forever-postponed fulfillment of desire. Indeed, Tayo remarks of Rocky that he lived only for the future ever "since he first began to believe in the word 'someday' the way white people do'" (73). The road homogenizes United States space into redundant, syntagmatic chains of gas stations, billboards, and signposts urging the traveler onward to that "someday," the next concession, the next place. Towns are only intensified versions of the road with their railroad depots, restaurants, tourist traps, rodeo grounds, and city dumps full of broken glass and wrecked cars (117). While traveling, Tayo hitches a ride with a truck driver, who stops "at San Fidel to dump a load of diesel fuel. Tayo went inside the station. . . . The room smelled like rubber from the loops of fan belts hanging from the ceiling. Cases of motor oil were stacked in front of the counter; the cans had a dull oil film on them. . . . Above the desk, on a calendar, a smiling blond girl, in a baton twirler's shiny blue suit with white boots to her knees, had her arms flung around the neck of a palomino horse. She was holding a bottle of Coca-Cola in one hand. . . . [T]he horse's mane was bleached white, and there was no trace of dust on its coat. The hooves were waxed with dark polish, shining like metal. The woman's eyes and the display of her teeth made him remember the glassy eyes of the stuffed bobcat above the bar in Bibo" (153–54). Components in Silko's code of the highway, the humanly-made objects in the gas station (fuel, fanbelts, motor oil, Coca-Cola) are metonymic equivalents of automobiles and their drivers who stop merely to buy more commodities before moving on.

In contrast to the smelly and oily manufactured objects, the natural objects represented on the wall calendar are unnaturally clean. Horse and twirler alike are "bleached," "waxed," and free of the "dust" which "connect[s creatures] . . . to the earth" (104). The calendar depicts what Eco would call an American hyperreality—a space that does not (and cannot) materially exist'but which nevertheless orchestrates consumer desire.[18] Affected by this consumer culture, Tayo often "imagine[s] movie images of himself" in situations and settings more appealing than those of his mundane existence.[19]

Throughout *Ceremony*, Silko describes Euro-American space-time in terms of such hyperrealities.[20] She suggests that for the dominant culture, American space must become artificial—*re-presented* and commodified—to be valuable and that, consequently, experience of place is forever deferred into an imaginary realm which, according to advertisements, lies just ahead in the next moment, in the next purchase. The advertisement on the wall equates drinking Coca-Cola with living the idealized life depicted in the "American-girl-with-horse" scene. Likewise, when Tayo looks at the label on a Coors beer, he sees "the picture of the cascading spring on the bottle. He didn't know of any springs that big anywhere. . . . He drank the beer as if it were the tumbling ice-cold stream in the mountain canyon on the beer label."[21] Tayo is thus twice manipulated, first by the commodity—alcohol—the ruin of many Indian lives, and second by manipulative advertising, which distracts consumer attention away from the present moment into some forever deferred future (where we will need still more commodities to satisfy more manufactured desires).

Silko encodes Euro-American space and time through syntagms of the road, whether this is the literal highway or the "road" to the ideal future. Silko's representations emphasize restless, horizontal movement away from the implied emptiness of the here-and-now toward an elusive "someday" offered by culture in lieu of vertical space—a metaphysical dimension of existence making the present moment *meaning-full* and inhabitable. Her encoding of Native American paradigms, however, suggests her Indian characters' different relationship to time and place. Betonie, for example, has no doubts about his place in time and the landscape. When asked why he lives "so close" to the "filthy town" of Gallup, he replies, "this hogan was here first. . . . It is that town down there which is out of place. Not this old medicine man" (118). Aware of the relative ephemerality of Euro-American culture, Betonie remains in his long-held horizontal and vertical space. Later, Tayo's healing quest in the Southwestern desert teaches him the value of Betonie's way of being.[22] Home at Laguna and ready to tell his story, Tayo knows that "we came out of this land and we are hers" (255). Silko attributes contemplative stillness and connection to Indian people and juxtaposes these traits with Euro-American frenetic motion and alienation.[23]

Silko's various means of encoding Indian space include the references to the color blue that we have noted in Chapter Two. These references form a chain of associations revealing a Native American relationship to the earth and its inhabitants. Moreover, as the narrative develops, this associative chain generates a double sociolect, since "blueness" signifies within a Navajo as well as a Euro-American frame of reference, as we have seen.[24] In the Navajo-Pueblo cosmology informing this novel and thus comprising one part of its implied interpretive frame of reference, the color blue has a ritual use in sandpainting and occurs in chants that accompany various types of rituals. Just as the ritual of sandpainting is designed to reintegrate forces that are out of balance and to restore proper relationships between humanity and nature, *Ceremony* sets out to restore the proper equations between earth, femaleness, love, fertility, eternity, and health. References to the color blue are the key terms in such equations; blueness in ritual—an actual ritual or the "ceremony" of narrative—restores proper relationships to nature.

This double frame of reference generated through allusions to the color blue cues the non-Indian reader to the "Indian" code emphasizing eternity, stillness, and spiritual balance within ceremonial space-time that consists of geographical places with both horizontal and vertical dimensions. And whereas the syntagm of Euro-American space leads to the frenetic pursuit of an ever-elusive moment "just ahead" in time or down the road, the syntagm of Native space beckons the Indian and the non-Indian self to stillness within the present moment, within the immediate setting, and to reconnection with the past and the present rather than to flight toward an ever-receding future.

Two other kinds of Indian space that reward attention to Silko's encoding of them are the reservation and Tayo's Native American body. In *Ceremony*, both are sites of Euro-American violation of Native American sacred space. Just as roads, highways, and towns surround and even overlie the areas of the map marked "reservation," federal space in *Ceremony* semiotically obtrudes into land ostensibly "reserved" for the Indian. Paradoxically, Indian land is defined and managed by the U.S. government. In semiotic terms, the reservation is a prime example of what Hodge and Kress call an ideological complex—"a functionally related set of contradictory versions of the world, coercively imposed by one social group on another on behalf of its own distinctive interests or subversively offered by another social group in attempts at resistance in its own interests."[25]

Betonie's conversation with Tayo about Gallup reveals the profound ironies underlying the "set of contradictory versions of the world" that is the "reservation." The Gallup Ceremonial is an annual event. It is a ceremonial in name only, however, for it mostly involves the "Gallup merchants" making "a lot of money off the tourists."[26] White merchants exhibit and sell Indian cultural artifacts, and then the Indians return to the reservation, or to the " 'alleys between the bars' " in Gallup. Implying that Indian lands are little more than a place to store the Indians until they are needed in tourist season, Betonie tells Tayo that " 'this is where Gallup keeps Indians until Ceremonial time' " (117). A site of "contradictory versions of the world," the reservation is on the one hand, "reserved" as a space where Native American culture may flourish or at least prevail; on the other hand, as Betonie shows, the "reservation" is a place where Indians are held "in reserve"—suspended in time—until they may serve the economic interests of the dominant culture.

"Coercively imposed by" the U.S. government on Native Americans "on behalf of its own distinctive interests," the reservation is also a place where the Native Americans "attempt . . . resistance in [their] own interests," where Native Americans like Betonie attempt to preserve their culture against the incursions of the Other. Silko shows that Indians do not necessarily fare well on the reservation, but their fate at times seems even worse outside of this community. Whereas Betonie waits patiently in his hogan which "was here first," many off-reservation Navajos merely " 'dream . . . for wine, looking for it somewhere in the mud . . . crouching outside bars like cold flies stuck to the wall' " (107). Defined as federal space or as Indian space, the reservation shapes Native American behavior by defining it within a binary set of on- and off-reservation alternatives. One may be an Indian in "reserve" until Ceremonial time, or a displaced, "cold fly stuck to the wall."

As a half-blood, Tayo has been both. Part of his healing quest involves transcending the limits of vision imposed by cultural definitions of what it means to be white as well as what it means to be Indian; in other words, like Betonie he must choose deliberately how to live, how to dwell in the world. Once he is rehabilitated, Tayo's responsibility is to tell a new and radical story that will free whites and Indians alike from the unhealthy, spatio-temporal constraints imposed by the Euro-American "story." [27]

Distentio Animi

Exploring the intertwined subjects of time and narrative, Paul Ricoeur reminds us that St. Augustine "defines time as a distention of the soul, *distentio animi,* [that] consists in the permanent contrast between the unstable nature of the human present and the stability of the divine present which includes past, present, and future in the unity of a gaze." [28] In more secular terms, a certain fragmentation of consciousness results from the perceived "discordance" of "expectation, memory, and attention," or our senses of future, past, and present.[29] Developing his theory of narrative within the context of an Aristotelian-Augustinian dialectic on the nature of time, Ricoeur has explored in detail the homologous relationship between temporality (the phenomenal experience of time) and narrativity (semiotic efforts to make sense of that experience). In a discussion of fictional narratives "of time" as opposed to those "about time," Ricoeur declares that few fictional narratives "about time" exist: "All fictional narratives are 'tales of time' inasmuch as the structural transformations that affect the situations and characters take time. However, only a very few are 'tales about time' inasmuch as in them it is the very experience of time that is at stake in these structural transformations." Moreover, he contends, there "are varieties of temporal experience that only fiction can explore and they are offered to reading in order to refigure ordinary temporality."[30] Among the temporal experiences that narrative facilitates is a sense of the "primacy of concordance over discordance," or the impression of "temporal totality."[31]

Anna Lee Walters's *Ghost Singer* arguably ranks among the most profound of twentieth-century narratives "about time," though as we have seen, several contemporary American Indian narratives seem to fit into Ricoeur's exclusive category. Walters's characters' temporal experiences of their world serve as metatextual instruction for the reader about cultural constructions of time, but her world-transformative project also suggests her effort to "refigure ordinary temporality"—her effort to enhance her readers' ways of knowing and being in time outside of texts. As Wilbur Snake, an Ioway medicine man in *Ghost Singer*, tells Russell Tallman: " 'We're pitiful, sonny, we try to know the whole universe, but we set our minds when we're like pups and learn to see only certain things. . . . As pitiful as we human animals is, sonny, we got power. . . . Us peoples have to face ourselves sometimes. . . . Truth is facing ourselves, and seeing what we is, and swallowing the taste of it."[32] Like so many contemporary works by Native American authors that attempt to empower the audience by expanding our notions about reality, *Ghost Singer* challenges the reader to become a little less "pitiful." Walters's ceremonially constructed narrative semiotically conveys an alternative experience of temporality that the author apparently hopes her readers will adopt. Borrowing terms from Ricoeur, we might say that Walters offers us an expansive, semiotic "configuration" of time in her novel. A potential result of narrativity, or our "transfiguration" of her work into a virtual world, is the "refiguration" of our own temporal experience of the actual world.[33]

"Time is both what passes and flows away and . . . what endures and remains," says Ricoeur.[34] Few novels self-consciously capture this paradoxical feature of temporality better than *Ghost Singer*, and perhaps no other novel yet exists that specifically illustrates how the universally "cruel bite of time"[35] torments American Indian and Euro-American alike as they occupy different cultural worlds within the same geographical space. Indeed, Walters joins many of her Indian contemporaries in objecting to popular, romanticized views of tribal people as thoroughly at home in time. After all, as Momaday, Silko, Hogan and countless others show us, tribal people keep calendars and other records of the past, including detailed oral histories; they also develop prophecies, particularly in times of cultural crisis.[36] Both efforts (to preserve the past and to predict the future) point to a universally human angst regarding time. In *Ghost Singer*, however, Walters insists that western, mechanical time most intensifies the existential discomfort of *distentio animi* and blinds people to dimensions of the universe.

Ghost Singer illustrates how clock time merely "passes and flows away," discounting but not eradicating "what endures and remains." In this novel, white people continually monitor their wristwatches and schedules and hurry along, sometimes with no apparent reason. Their mechanistic vision of the world apparently aims to "make the mystery of . . . life into a tiny thing [that] don't mean nothing" (176), but the mystery endures in the form of an angry warrior's spirit inhabiting an attic room of the Smithsonian Natural History Building. This room is also filled with stolen tribal property, from ceremonial objects and medicine bundles to amputated body parts of Indians—the "trophies" of combat. In *Ghost Singer*, the past is present in these ghosts and artifacts, and it commands attention. Moreover, Walters's demand for immediate, responsible, extraliterary action on behalf of this present-past strikes the reader as forcefully as the ghost warrior strikes Donald Evans in the museum attic, as we shall see.[37]

A close look at Walters's semiotic configuration of time in *Ghost Singer* reveals much about the "transfigurative" act of reading, with its potentially world-altering, "refigurative" consequences. Sacred or "unitary" time is encoded in the novel together with mechanical time, a technique recalling other cross-coded texts by contemporary Indian authors. Like Erdrich, and with some of the same aims, Walters dates each chapter of her novel. The narrative opens with a preface concerning key historical events of June 1830, proceeds through thirty-three chapters taking place in 1968 and 1969, and ends with an epilogue recording events from the fall of 1976. A decelerating progression of chapters by date implies the weighty tug of history: the first three chapters are dated 1968, while the remaining thirty record events of 1969. These events (a proliferating series of suicides in the Smithsonian Museum of Natural History related to the stolen artifacts) are so directly connected to Jacksonian Era atrocities that the past appears actually to impede the forward flow of time that is measured by clocks and western-style calendars.

Moreover, even within this impeded flow of time (restated in a "whirlwind" trope to describe current events [42]), temporal eddies form as five chapters cover August of 1969, four chapters cover September, and eleven deal with October before the narrative briefly accelerates again with two and three chapters recording incidents in November and December, respectively. Overall, the chronological arrangement of the novel reinforces the thematic message that the consequences of slave-trading, desecration of the dead, and other past deeds of excessive violence against Native Americans in the early nineteenth century inform the present moment. Although the suicides propel the plot forward by generating in the reader the conventional expectations of an explanatory ending, the weight of the historical past registers more powerfully upon the reader as the timeline of the plot slows to a near halt. Furthermore, these counterforces in the text focus our attention upon the "traces" of the past that are present within a semiotically defined space—the museum—as we shall presently observe.

The chronological progression of the narrative from summer through early winter (preface through thirty-third chapter) likewise reinforces the attentive reader's impression of an impeded flow of time. In one of the final chapters, Wilbur and Anna Snake pray in their cabin on a " 'purty' " December day that makes Anna feel as if " 'someone just stopped time and froze everything in its place, even the sun. . . . Today the world is standing still,' " says Wilbur, and " 'old people knows this is a powerful thing.' " The " 'power to freeze the world, or to melt it in the summertime, is a holy thing' " (202–3). Walters "melts" her fictive world briefly in the epilogue, set in the fall of 1976. With the epilogue, the narrative takes us into a new year in the fall season when the world is not yet frozen, but still replete with signs of life. By ending her tale this way, Walters avoids "freezing" the material of her story into any conventional narrative closure. Indeed, the apparent aim of the novel is to cross the boundary of the world of the text and to carry out important semiotic work in the world of the reader whose mind has been opened to alternative modes of being in time.[38]

Instead of tying up "loose ends" in conventional mystery-writer's fashion,[39] Walters invites her reader to "participate,"[40] to connect the pieces of her story and to comprehend its call for world-transfigurative action. Like Wilbur Snake's ceremony in the museum attic, the "ceremony" of Walters's novel is interrupted. Its completion lies in the mind of the reader who has connected imaginatively with the world of Walters's text and who imaginatively creates an extratextual "future." Walters's advice to the Eurocentric reader is clear and recalls Wilbur Snake's advice to the noisy white woman, Elaine, in the museum during the ceremony: "Quiet," he warns her, for her nervous talk puts people at risk and reveals her cultural, metaphysical narrowmindedness (185, 187). Likewise, Russell Tallman eventually shouts at Donald Evans, "You have a fantastic opportunity here to learn something, something about yourself, and the world around you. At this moment it is possible to . . . learn some secrets of the universe. . . . Open up your mind and prepare to learn something" (211).

The "quiet," imaginative space where text and world intersect in an "open mind" compares to dreams. As LeClair teaches Wilbur, a dream recounted can change the future. Two dreams figure importantly in *Ghost Singer*, and both convey the same message concerning our partial control over eventuation. The first is Willie Begay's dream, which occurs as he lies in the hospital, sick from accidental contact with Navajo scalps and ears at the Smithsonian. In this dream, Willie walks through a canyon picking up Indian pottery fragments and other items scattered among the cliff dwellings. As he walks, anxiously stuffing his pockets, the cliff dwellings change into urban skyscrapers and high-rise apartments; as soon as he buries the things he has collected, however, the canyon resumes its former appearance. One infers from this dream that modern America is built upon a shattered and dishonored Indian world. Willie's responsible disposal of artifacts, recalling those in the Smithsonian, heals the past and dispels the white man's world that is built over ancestral lands, an action reminding us of a pan-tribal desire expressed through many Indian prophecies including those associated with the Ghost Dance.

The epilogue evokes the reader's memory of Willie's dream and reinforces the call for radical revision of the world. (Here, indeed, is a semiotic tactic for indicating the presentness of the past, as what we are currently reading evokes what we have read before.) In the epilogue, Willie visits Jonnie Navajo's grave near the cliff dwellings and worries that, someday, Jonnie's bones could become artifacts in a museum or in some trespasser's junk box. Human bones and broken pottery lie scattered throughout the area and underscore the legitimacy of his fears. Confronted with this last scene and recalling its connection to Willie's dream, the reader who has "picked up" the various fragments of Walters's narrative and "let all the bits and pieces f[a]ll into place" (158) understands his or her implied responsibility toward the past that is present in stories and in the historical "traces" of the past that lie in museum cases, drawers, and attics. This obligation involves restoring the "property" of Native peoples (a response to the past) and refraining from any further violence to Indian realities (a response to the future).

The second important dream in the novel reinforces Walters's point about responsible action, and it also emphasizes in particular the storytelling powers of "dreamers" such as Willie and Walters, herself. LeClair dreams of Wilbur's death by freezing. Troubled by this persistent dream, he visits Wilbur specifically to tell him about it. A few years later, when the dream begins to come true, Wilbur, LeClair, and Anna remember the story and thus fend off an otherwise almost certain death. Learning about medicine from LeClair throughout the years teaches Wilbur that the art of dreaming (while awake or asleep) is synonymous with the art of storytelling.

This equation of dreams, medicine power, and storytelling constitutes another of Walters's techniques for undercutting mechanical time. All three kinds of experience emphasize the present moment as a site of considerable power affecting both past and future in immediate, observable ways. Time does not merely "pass and flow away" in one direction, Walters insists; the impression of sacred time conveyed by *Ghost Singer* ameliorates the existential agony that clock time exaggerates. Walters suggests that mechanical time diminishes our sense of personal power when we assume that the past is beyond our control and thus outside the realm of our responsibility, and that the future is a clean slate where no ghostly messages from the past may appear. Indeed, the spectral handprint that suddenly appears on the wall of the museum attic is the mark of the past upon Donald Evans's potential future. It is a sign commanding his attention and action.

Another strategy for expanding the reader's understanding of the nature of time includes Walters's use of repetition. The "white yarn" (ix, xi, 11, 13) that holds back the hair of several generations of Red Lady's family appears in different contexts to remind us that Indians and non-Indians alike measure time by the succession of generations. The yarn signifies what "endures and remains" even as the generations "pass away." Red Lady's dress, worn by her in 1830 and Nasbah Navajo in 1969 reiterates this message. However, the stolen Indian artifacts in the Smithsonian most accentuate the enigmatical nature of time as both "passing" and "enduring." As plot-facilitating objects, they draw our attention back to the historical past that the novel encompasses and, simultaneously, they draw the reader forward through the story in the (disappointed) expectation of their appropriate treatment in the end. The most profound purpose served by the introduction of these artifacts into the narrative, however, is to invite the reader to ponder the "traces" of the past that are collected in museums and archives, to question the motivations of a society that "collects" such objects, and to investigate the nature of the museum itself as a semiotic construction.

In such "traces," we witness an "overlapping of the existential and the empirical," explains Ricoeur in a dialogue with Heidegger, Litré, Lévinas, and others on the ontology of historical documents and artifacts in *Time and Narrative*.[41] The "trace" tells us that someone or something "passed" by here before us and left its "mark." The "existential" dimension of the trace is suggested by this noted "passage," while the actual "mark" (the old document, the bones, the pottery) is "empirically" present. "This double allegiance of the trace," he argues, "constitutes the trace as the connection between two . . . perspectives on time. To the same extent that the trace marks the passage of an object or a quest in space, it is in calendar time and, beyond it, in astral time that the trace marks a passage" (120). In other words, the trace exists empirically within the present space and time as a "sign" reminding us of both empirical and existential realities of some other space, some other time. Two "times" meet in consciousness. Furthermore, Ricoeur argues, in effecting this intersection of times, the trace "disarranges some 'order' "; it intrudes into the present where it has effects (125). In *Ghost Singer*, these effects extend far beyond even what Ricoeur can apparently conceive and in the process, they corroborate his Heideggerian claims about the creative, originative power of the "thought experiments offered by literature."[42]

The "traces" in Walters's narrative are extremely intrusive into the lives of the characters within the text and, potentially, into the imaginative and actual life of the reader affected by the story. Contact with the objects makes characters physically, mentally, and spiritually sick, and thus directly connects the remote past with the immediate present in the form of illness. Indeed, the objects' "disarranging" power is overwhelming and even causes suicides, we are led to believe. However, prior to suicide, each of these characters falls into a state of *dis-ease* that could result in a profound change of consciousness (as it does for Willie). Before dying, both Jean Worley and Geoffrey Newsome have the "opportunity" to "learn some secrets of the universe."[43] Without knowing what she implies, even the closed-minded Elaine, Donald Evans's girlfriend, perceives the astonishing events in the attic as an opportunity: " 'I think the door is open, Donald,' she said." The "door is open" for the reader, as well. Like Donald Evans at the end of the novel whom Russell commands to "act responsibly" and accept his own personal power (211), we must decide what we will do.

Also like Donald, we are implored to ponder the motivations of a society that countenances such collections of artifacts as represented in *Ghost Singer*. As portrayed in the novel, the Smithsonian officials themselves have no clear, articulated idea about why the museum owns the offensive objects, nor about what they should do with them. The items are not on public display and museum officials prefer not to show them to Indians, whom they upset. Moreover, Walters asks us to consider the motives of those who first acquired the objects. The Navajo body parts, in particular, were collected as gruesome "trophies" during an epoch of Indian-hating, and other stolen objects were sold as curiosities, as the letter from "John," who wants a few dollars for the "junk" in his trunk, reveals (84). None of the items were gathered with the slightest pretense of their use in historical research (though this motive, too, remains questionable for Walters).[44]

Walters challenges those who argue that we effectively reconstruct history through the study of such "traces." First of all, the collection is almost an embarrassment to the museum, where it is hidden in the attic; second, and more importantly, we learn that even while such objects are uselessly preserved (and their implications ignored), rich sources of Indian history are dismissed by academic historians such as David Drake, who concludes that Jonnie has nothing of value to offer him by way of information about the Navajo. Like Jonnie, the "stories" in the objects held by the museum are available and "alive," but the white people cannot read them (not even when a ghost smashes a clock radio in the effort to get a white man's attention). Through this and other narrative gestures, Walters joins Thomas King in his comical short story, "Totem" (1993), by suggesting in this novel that the concept of the museum itself may point to Eurocentric blindness to the realities of the Other.

The museum (recalling the reservation, as Silko represents it in *Ceremony*) is a fascinating semiotic site inscribed with Eurocentric meanings and values, including the assumed meanings and values of historical "traces." Within the western "story" of the museum are housed a variety of things including those that tell the "stories" of other cultures. From these disparate materials, wrenched from their temporal and socio-cultural contexts, archaeologists, anthropologists, and other intellectuals produce "histories," which museum visitors receive. The museum as idea and construct implies that all contained inside it can somehow be organized and ordered into a seemingly coherent "story" such as "world history." Walters suggests, however, that these museum contents resemble the "mixed up" contents of spilled medicine bundles (27) from different tribes. They cannot be collectively understood within an alien society's artificially imposed epistemological frame. Such an effort might be compared to trying to produce one manuscript using words and sentences, helter-skelter, from many different languages.

Thomas King makes this same point in "Totem," a story about humming, singing, shouting, grunting, and generally noisy totem poles housed in the Southwest Alberta Art Gallery and Prairie Museum. The non-Native museum officials try hard to explain the weird phenomenon from within their own limited frames of reference, but they are defeated. They banish the poles to the basement and ignore them as if they were noisy traffic from the freeway. With Walters, King insists that the ceremonial and sacred items of nonwestern cultures cannot be forced into the "story" that museums tell, because the items "tell" of aspects of the universe that are traditionally inconceivable in the west. According to both authors, the museum is a site where radically different worlds come together and where the world of the Other may emerge to wreak havoc. Thus the historical "traces" in *Ghost Singer* and in "Totem" negate not only clock time, by insisting upon the immediate presentness of the past, but also clock time's corollary, "monumental" history,[45] by undermining the structures of "authority," such as the museum and historical narrative, which cannot apparently contain and control the very artifacts they attempt to incorporate.

In *Ghost Singer*, Walters presents us with a "temporal experience that only fiction can explore. . . . Only fiction . . . can explore and bring to language this divorce between worldviews and their irreconcilable perspectives on time, a divorce that undermines public time."[46] According to Ricoeur, reading effects "the mediation . . . between the fictive world of the text and the actual world of the reader. . . . It is by way of reading that literature returns to life, that is, to the practical and affective field of existence."[47] We might say that a narrative of the type that Walters produces in *Ghost Singer* gives us precisely the experience of time that Jean Worley so desperately cries for just prior to committing suicide. Terrorized by the events in the museum that she cannot understand, she tells her brother, David: "I need time. Time . . . . [ellipsis Walters's] I'll get it together. Time. That's all."[48] Walters's narrative art gives us the time that only storytelling can provide—time to "learn something . . . to . . . learn some secrets of the universe" or, at least, of the world of the Other (211).

Rehabitation

In their semiotic efforts to revise or reconstruct the world according to non-Eurocentric agendas, many American Indian authors create characters who do not feel "at home" even within the space of their own bodies. *House Made of Dawn, Ceremony, The Death of Jim Loney, Ghost Singer, The Woman Who Owned the Shadows,* and *The Ancient Child,* to name a few of the best-known works about ailing Indians, insist that rehabitation of the land (space) in the present (time) depends upon healing one's own body (a material space propelled through time).

Willie Begay, in *Ghost Singer*, in some ways resembles the museum where competing constructions of reality meet. His body—like Abel's in *House Made of Dawn*, Ephanie's in *The Woman Who Owned the Shadows* and Tayo's in *Ceremony*—becomes an object of competition between disparate constructions of reality, including notions of health and disease. These characters find themselves in hospitals and torn between recourse to the allopathic medicine of the white society or to the shamanic healing methods of tribal people. Tayo's experience in *Ceremony* is paradigmatic of the illness-and-healing pattern that many characters in contemporary Native American novels enact in their recovery from illness, which involves spatio-temporal disorientation, as well as physical and spiritual distress. Before assuming his responsibilities to land and tribe, Tayo must first reclaim the space of his own body that is (like the reservation and the museum), ambiguously encoded with white and Indian signs. As a half-blood, he must decide which half of himself to realize. Conflicting codifications of the space of Tayo's body include the white doctors' description of Tayo's illness versus the medicine men's description. (The same problem besets Walters's Willie Begay, who finds relief from symptoms in the hospital but who needs a Navajo ceremony to get at the essential cause of his sickness.) Underlying these different "medical" descriptions are profoundly different environmental conceptions of illness; according to the "Indian" model, disordered spatial relationships (to the land, to other people) and temporal relationships (to the past, where illness is frequently rooted) are the fundamental sources of disease. Tayo's recovery, like that of the protagonists of *House, Woman, Ghost Singer* and others, requires a struggle over the naming and meaning of illness and health, and over his ultimate definition of his body as Indian or white space.[49]

While Tayo lies ill in the veteran's hospital, the white doctors "yell" at him because he does not define himself "correctly," according to their psychological model of self. They see him as a particular "individual" with the specific symptoms of "battle fatigue." In the "ontological" tradition of western allopathic medicine, their aim is to respond to the symptoms and to make the disease disappear, not to speculate about possible metaphysical causes.[50] "[T]he Army doctors . . told [Grandma] and Robert that the cause of battle fatigue was a mystery, even to them,"[51] and that Tayo's recovery depend[ed] upon his forgetting about the war and the death he saw there (forgetting about the past and the foreign places), and thinking only of himself. Ku'oosh and Betonie, however, define Tayo's illness in a traditional "medicine" way which treats primarily causes, not symptoms. His sickness is a part of a larger pattern of historical events, including the less admirable features of western-style individualism, that " 'ha[ve] been going on for a long time' " (53). Tayo's innate sense of this fact is suggested in his recognition of similarities between the Asian features of the Japanese and those of American Indians, two groups possibly once occupying space and time as one people. Intuitively, Tayo knows that World War II is only one of many symptoms of global ill health. Because the Army doctors do not treat the cause of Tayo's sickness, their "medicine drained memory out of his thin arms and replaced it with a twilight cloud behind his eyes" (15). Tayo remains disoriented in time (his past is a blur) and space (he cannot see), and he is emotionally miserable and spiritually tormented as well.

To heal, Tayo must extend his reach beyond material space to sacred space, beyond clock time to ceremonial time. The reconnective pattern of his recovery suggests the regenerative purpose of Silko's ceremonial narrative. Various kinds of disorder, ranging from Tayo's disorderly conduct, to the Ck'oyo witches' destructive storytelling, to the disordering of atomic structure to produce cataclysmic explosions, define the essence of illness and degeneration. Efforts ranging from the various characters' sandpainting-like scratchings in the dirt (22), to Betonie's full-fledged medicine ritual in the desert, in part define healing as the sacred realignment or re-ordering of universal forces reconnecting material and metaphysical realms in a unitary space-time. Silko's novel insists that for American Indians, the "home" that was lost through colonization was as much "vertical" as "horizontal." That is to say, tribal people were reduced not merely to the constricted reservation (horizontal) space, but also to a world of shrunken metaphysical (vertical) dimensions.

Walters's point is the same in *Ghost Singer*. The ghost warrior in the museum attic smashes the clock radio in a symbolic effort to destroy the limited conception of time that denies his continued existence after the death of his physical body. Like the ghost who leaves fresh handprints, the artifacts exude a living "odor" and a debilitating force despite white society's reduction of them to merely empirical, dead-object status. Joining Silko and others, Walters thus insists that the phenomenal universe is spatio-temporally larger than western ideas of it. In particular, these writers explore the consequences of western notions of health and healing that cannot allow for the existence, much less the expression, of the spirit.

Over the past few years, evidence has begun to suggest that some allopathic medical practitioners now hear the voices of Native Americans and other nonwestern peoples on the subject of health. This evidence indicates that books like Silko's and Walter's do, in fact, affect the extratextual world, an issue which I will consider again at the end of the next chapter. The regenerative effects of storytelling, particularly for patients suffering from chronic conditions, are currently being investigated and reported in mainstream medical journals as well as in those associated more with "alternative" or "complementary" medicine.[52] Works by such well-known physician-writers as James J. Lynch, Arthur Kleinman, Carl Hammerschlag, and others are expanding the epistemological frame of allopathic medicine through investigations into the medicinal paradigms of other cultures. Lynch's work in cardiology, in particular, implies a semiotic dimension of healing.

Lynch has studied the ways in which nonwestern people experience illness, and particularly the ways in which they make sense of their experiences, from decline to recovery. Based on his research, Lynch concludes that mechanistic medicine is "deaf" to the patient's voice in ways that the healing practices of nonwestern cultures frequently are not. Consequently, at the Psychophysiological Clinic at the University of Maryland, Lynch specializes in the treatment of "dysfunctional human communication," particularly the types that he concludes may lead to or exacerbate cardiac problems. One stage of his therapy "centers on the social membrane as the nexus for teaching the patient about feelings and shared human experience"; Lynch also analyzes the "language which one uses to communicate emotional meaning to other people."[53] He has found that listening to the "stories" of cardiac patients, as well as exposing them to the "stories" of others, substantially reduces blood pressure and provides relief from other cardiovascular complaints.

Arthur Kleinman (psychiatrist and Professor of Anthropology at Harvard) arrives at similar conclusions in his book about "illness narratives." Both Kleinman and Lynch have fundamentally revised the "structures" within which they communicate with their patients about illness and health, and their revised structures re-situate both patient and healer with regard to a variety of space-time factors: "In the broader biopsychosocial model now making headway in primary care, disease is construed as the embodiment of the symbolic network linking body, self, and society . . . . In the biomedical model, the disease is an occluded coronary artery; in the biopsychosocial model, it is a dynamic dialectic between cardiovascular processes . . . psychological states . . . and environ-mental situations." [54]

These inroads in contemporary medicine partially result from what practitioners such as Lynch and others have learned from indigenous societies about the healing effects of oral communica-tion, particularly the construction of meanings about illness and health that may either empower both healer and patient, or "dis-able the healer and disempower the chronically ill." [55] Their mes-sage, like that of many contemporary Native American writers, is that "crises of *habitare*" take place in the human body, a complex nexus of time and space. Reductive conceptions of time and space within western thought are mirrored in reductive conceptions of illness and, particularly, of the mysterious process called "healing." Of such matters, I shall have more to say in the Epilogue.

That conventional medicine has taken a new direction from phy-sicians' studies of nonwestern cultures' storytelling practices tes-tifies to the accuracy of Ricoeur's statements about the "imbrica-tion of reality" by "lived stories." Ricoeur and many contemporary semioticians (particularly Eco, Scholes, Hodge, and Kress) insist upon the "dynamic circularity" between art and life and upon the ways in which "literature . . . can free us" from "narcissistic, egoistic, and stingy" philosophies.[56] Whatever the extent of con-temporary Native American writers' influence upon the "lived" reality of today's world, there is little doubt that their works com-prise a substantial portion of "American literature" from which they were almost totally absent only thirty years ago. If Native American literature has not yet "revised" the actual world, a mis-sion it seems to envision, it has certainly staked out for itself a significant textual space, a type of space where Indian storytellers have not been "at home" until quite recently. Moreover, the world-transformative message of much contemporary Indian writing is amplified through the number and types of intertextual connections that these narratives establish with one another as well as with non-Indian literary works. The refigurative power of contemporary Native American narrative cannot be fully comprehended outside of a discussion of the semiotic effects of intertextuality.

Chapter Five
All the Stories Fit Together: Intertextual Medicine Bundles and Twins

> He cried the relief he felt at finally seeing the pattern, the way all the stories fit together.[1]

Thomas King's collection of short stories, *One Good Story, That One*, graphically and verbally illustrates an intertextual principle: elements of story escape their textual bounds to spill over into life (as we have noted in previous chapters) and into other texts. King's Coyote—denizen of a vast number of American Indian stories including King's novel, *Green Grass, Running Water*—wanders through each of the works in the collection and even leaves "Coyote tracks," in the form of graphic images, throughout the white spaces in the text that conventionally separate one story from another. Louise Erdrich's novels are similarly linked together through many of the same characters' appearances from book to book. Furthermore, each of her novels provides important pieces of information that explain incidents or motivations of characters from companion volumes.

These and other modes of intertextuality unite contemporary Native American narratives with each other as well as with non-Indian fiction and nonfiction. This chapter explores the syncretic function of intertextuality as a mode of shaping Native American as well as mainstream literature and, by extension, the intertwined and living cultures that sustain both.[2] The kinds of intertextual relationships with which I concern myself in the following pages are best described metaphorically through concepts borrowed from Indian cultures: I will look at texts as "medicine bundles" and as "twins" to suggest how intertextuality serves the overall revisionary and regenerative purposes that are overtly declared by so much Native American writing. A few brief, prefatory remarks on intertextuality seem appropriate, however.

Memory and the Intertext

Structuralist-oriented semioticians including Tzvetan Todorov, Umberto Eco, Kaja Silverman, Michael Riffaterre, and others have written extensively on the subject of structural invariants (basic story patterns) common to certain kinds of narratives. Among numerous examples is the separation-and-return pattern uniting quest myths and literature. Riffaterre explains in meticulous detail how the variations on such invariants constitute originality on the part of an author who, necessarily, relies upon readers' previous encounters with invariants in other texts to guide their responses to the unique work at hand. Reading and interpreting texts, in other words, are largely functions of memory, or what Jonathan Culler calls acquired "literary competence" and Riffaterre calls our relative acquaintance with the "intertext." Having read three or four narratives by contemporary Indian writers (especially paradigmatic ones such as *Ceremony, House Made of Dawn,* or *Ghost Singer*), a reader begins to acquire an appropriate "competence" or memory and, doubtless, to recognize certain structural invariants uniting the texts that sometimes have no exact counterparts in western narrative. According to Riffaterre, "As readers progress through one or more novels, they come to realize that apparently unconnected and diverse representations or stories have relational and functional features in common that direct interpretation beyond what each instance authorizes. Therefore, these several representations and stories are now recognized as variants of structural invariants."[3] The "invariant," in fact, is only an inferred generalization held in memory—an abstract element against which we compare concrete "variants."

American Indian narratives concerned with the multi-faceted illness of liminal characters, or those dealing with certain contrasts between ordered, traditional Indian realities and a "cock-

eyed," unbalanced Euro-American world[4] embody "invariants,"
which become more and more recognizable to larger numbers
of readers as the canon of contemporary American Indian writing expands. Through an ever-expanding web of literary works,
including some that self-consciously manage intertextual connections, Native American authors introduce into mainstream society
many of the "authorless" but authoritative stories passed on to
them through oral tradition. At the same time, these writers fashion their own unique versions of traditional stories that conform
to the aesthetic criteria defining art within the dominant society.
Thus Native American narrative, with its multiply revisionary aims,
achieves its implied purpose: changing the mainstream audience
through a body of interconnected, marginal texts replete with instructions on how to read them, and changing the world by transforming its literary horizons.

My purpose in this chapter, however, is not to list the structural
invariants characterizing these narratives, nor to address the "variants" on these given patterns that constitute originality. Instead, I
mean to elaborate upon a few, more subtle intertextual phenomena
that are observable within contemporary Indian narratives and that
bear important political and ethical implications for the semiotically regenerated world implied in these texts. The body of works
by Native writers presents to the world at large an idea of tribal
people and realities that becomes part of a general intertext held
in memory and that influences the ways we read "textual" worlds
and produce "real" ones; this intertext also directs our attention to
questions about representations of the "real."

N. Scott Momaday has said that for him, being "an Indian" involves having a certain "idea" about himself. His autobiographical
works such as *The Way to Rainy Mountain* and *The Names* reveal the extent of his reading, including works by James Mooney and numerous ethnographic records,[5] as well as the extent of his knowledge
gleaned through personal contact with Native peoples. Both have
shaped his "idea" of himself. (Clearly, as we have noted in Chapter
Three, he also believes that an essential part of self exists that is not
a social construction.) Likewise, James Welch says he learned about
the Blackfeet and Gros Ventre partly by reading about them,[6] and
Linda Hogan remarks that reading other Indian writers led to insight into her own identity as a person and a writer.[7]

I do not mean to understate these writers' direct knowledge of their cultures. However, their comments on the role of language and reading suggest that they understand well the common semiotic action linking "life experience" with narrative production. To "make sense" for oneself of life's events is to construct narratives, sometimes based upon structures and ideas derived from other narratives.[8] Moreover, as previous chapters on identity and time reveal, the concepts, norms, and values encoded within such narrative constructions (implicit within the intertext) to a certain extent determine how we see the past and shape the future; thus, all intertextually extant stories bear considerable creative power within the present, lived moment.

Prior to the 1970s, very little single-authored, written Native American literature existed. A vast and conspicuous silence marked the absence of Native peoples' voices. The mainstream society's "idea" of matters "Indian" was limited, ethnocentric, and stereotypical indeed, and it remains so today. However, an ever-increasing volume of works by contemporary Native American authors now fills the silence (and many readers' memories) and shapes our intertextual "memories" at an astonishing pace. Each of these Indian authors is unique, with his or her own views and visions that do not always necessarily coalesce into any pan-tribal outlook for the future, nor a consensus opinion about the past, the present, or any other subject. (For instance, one of the first of these new voices was Momaday, whose works contribute to the "idea" of tribal peoples that prevails today even though his notions generate controversy among Native writers, some of whom object to Momaday's "idea" of himself as "Indian.")

However controversially, over the last twenty years mainstream society has witnessed an "invention" of "Indians" through Native-authored fictional and nonfictional works. The pastiche of ideas conveyed may or may not at any given time conform to the lived reality of any particular Native American individual. (The same is true of any textually generated "invention" of cultural identity—Italian, Irish, Jewish, etc.—conveyed through literature.) This fact alone, however, does not mitigate the power of texts to inform mainstream reality with new inventions of ethnic identity, which society understands as "real"; from this and other bases of knowledge we construct extratextual realities.[9]

The general study of semiotics has effectively exposed most of the naively assumed boundaries between "real" and "constructed" worlds by demonstrating how the "real" is itself always a construction. As Silverman proclaims, "reality" and "the symbolic order —the order of language, discourse, narrative—are so closely imbricated as to be virtually inseparable."[10] Robert Scholes likewise explains "that one context, made out of perceptual and experiential data held in common by author and audience, is always invoked by any fictional or mimetic context, whether 'realistic' or 'fantastic.' This 'real' context provides a background against which we perceive and measure any pseudo-experiential or fictional context presented to us."[11] Scholes reminds us that the " 'real' context is also a fiction, since it is based on past experience, no longer directly available." The memory of experience is not the same as experience itself; furthermore, he says, we must also distinguish our actual memories from "ideas we may acquire about things we have never experienced through our own perceptions. As memory grows fainter the events remembered lose their reality. But it is not until we try to reconstruct these fading events that fiction is generated. The passage of real experience into the past is not itself fictional, but all attempts to reconstruct are precisely that: fictions" (31–32).

With these thoughts in mind, we may understand how a body of literary works such as those we have been discussing throughout the present study may constitute an informational background, or intertext, shaping the "sense" we make of past and present experience, and especially the "sense" we make of other literature.

Texts as Medicine Bundles

In my discussion of Linda Hogan's narrative "power" and "solidarity" strategies in Chapter Two, I suggest that her novel, *Mean Spirit*, with its incipient, inner narrative in logonomic conflict with the outer narrative, might be viewed metaphorically as a "medicine bundle," for it contains a "world, wanting out" (138). This metaphor also facilitates a broader discussion of intertextuality. A medicine bundle is a bag or parcel containing different combinations of herbs and other plants, animal parts, and ritual or sacred objects. Its contents are semiotically and cabalistically significant to an individual's or a group's power, history, and identity. Some bundles are used or otherwise associated with certain ceremonies or with the recitation of stories at particular times of the year. No matter how old the bag, its full strength exists within the present moment (and often its power increases with age and use). Many medicine bundles are handled only by members of the societies who own them, carefully tend them, and pass them down through successive generations to others who inherit responsibility for them. An individual healer usually passes along his or her medicine bag to another healer, often a former apprentice.

Comparatively speaking, a text is likewise a "container" of powerful signs pertinent to individual and group history and identity, and passed along through the generations. Its power unfolds within the present moment of reading and, once read, a text resides in memory to shape our response to other texts and to experience. Furthermore, a text, like a medicine bag, over time accumulates "powers" or significance that it might not have carried at first. (A classical and noteworthy example of this accretive phenomenon is the well-documented tendency to read Milton through the Romantics. I have also suggested that those who have read widely among contemporary Native American works probably read newer authors through Silko and Momaday.) Like the objects contained within a medicine bundle, the sign action contained within a text may exert considerable transformative force, as we have noted throughout this study.

This considerable force includes the power that a narrative continues to exert once it has passed into memory and, especially, when its memory is invoked during the reading of other texts. According to Riffaterre, once read, a text seems to "return . . . from the written to the entirely unwritten. . . . [T]he telos of the literary text [seems] to spell out a story only as a rehearsal for an imaginary mnemonic possession of it." Somehow, the written text holds "within its fabric pockets of implicitly remembered, symbolic stories" that contain "the essence" of the narrative. While reading, we "store up indices of . . . significance, mementos of . . . important points, guidelines for the easy control of an understanding of [a narrative as a] fully developed complex."[12] These remembered "indices," "mementos" and "guidelines" also come into play when one work intertextually invokes another. Postmodern writer Jorge Luis Borges has aptly described this mnemonic phenomenon: if we have read Poe, or Dostoevsky or Shakespeare, we can never again read anything as though we had not read these writers.[13] Borges's insight especially applies when a text somehow awakens our memory of literary works through direct or indirect reference.

We may view Momaday's *House Made of Dawn*, Hogan's *Mean Spirit*, and Silko's *Almanac of the Dead* as textual "medicine bundles" that instruct us concerning the effects of reading upon reading, as well as upon material realities. *House* features a character, Father Olguin, who is preoccupied with the writings of his predecessor missionary, Fray Nicolás. These writings, re-presented in Momaday's text as an old journal, influence Father Olguin's change of heart toward his mission among the Indians. Fray Nicolás reflects back to him his own faults, especially his blinding ethnocentrism. Perhaps not just coincidentally, Linda Hogan's *Mean Spirit* also features a background character, another priest, who "turns Indian" as a result of insight into his own hypocrisy and "double tongue" (260).

In Hogan's character we see an intertextual link to *House* and to a wealth of nonfictional historical material such as captivity narratives that reside within the intertext sustaining both Hogan's and Momaday's individual works. Some of these captivity narratives tell the stories of the gradual conversion of white Christians to tolerance or adoption of Indian ways. However, Native American writers' representations of white people who "turn Indian" stand in revealing counterpoint to the old captivity narratives that tell the story from a Eurocentric perspective.[14] The intertextual links between Native-authored works such as Momaday's and Hogan's and, in turn, between these works and historical narratives of the dominant culture reveal that the literature of the Americas (and, ultimately, of the world) is all one fabric. "All the stories fit together," as Momaday and Silko overtly declare. Understanding the semiotic origins of social and political reform, the crafters of such intertextual connections also underscore their efforts to reinscribe the dominant discourse of U. S. society with indigenous peoples' stories, meanings, interpretive habits, and values.

Throughout *Mean Spirit*, for example, Hogan metatextually comments upon the power of writing as she weaves together her outer narrative and Michael's visionary *Book of Horse*. Her comments point to how Michael's writing-in-progress influences the world of the surrounding text and the text of the world within which Hogan's book resides. Early in the novel, we learn that "words" may be "a road out of pain and fear" (33). Michael Horse himself sees writing as a mode of exiting one reality and entering another. Indeed, "Horse felt . . . as if he could write away the appearances of things and take them all the way back down to the bare truth" (341). Near the end of Hogan's narrative, when we learn that Horse finishes *The Book of Horse*, we also see that the events prophesied in *The Book of Horse* begin to happen in the outer narrative. In the same way, in *House Made of Dawn*, Father Olguin's reading of the old journal affects his behavior as a character in the surrounding story. The intertextual links between the encapsulated narratives and the larger narrative surrounding each suggests a continuum of textual worlds in which semiosis precedes "reality."

Overall, the message of Momaday, Hogan, and other Indian authors is that storytelling (both oral and written) makes things happen, sometimes according to prophecies like those of Michael Horse, or according to other narrated dreams and visions. In Walters's *Ghost Singer*, we have observed (in Willie Begay's dream of the cliff dwellings) the author's hint that the restoration of the "old world" follows the telling of stories and dreams about the end of colonial dominance. Silko implies the same in her short narrative called "Storyteller" (1981), in which an old man passes on his shamanic storytelling responsibilities to a "granddaughter," as well as in both of her novels to date. Likewise embodying the same structural invariant concerning world-transformative, embedded texts that appears in *House*, *Mean Spirit*, and *Almanac of the Dead*, Vizenor's *Bearheart: The Heirship Chronicles* refers to a hidden "Bearheart" manuscript that partially constructs and finally resides in the "next world." These authors show us how a book may bridge worlds through the use of intertextual references establishing a potentially endless chain of literary interconnections. The connections established may extend even beyond the material boundaries of space and time.

Indeed, Michael Horse's divinatory textual "bridge," his *Book of Horse* in *Mean Spirit*, neither originates with nor is destined for most of the inhabitants of the historical world described in the framing narrative. Probably only transcribed by Michael from a spiritual source, *The Book of Horse* instructs its intended audience about how to live on the earth, but this audience appears to be the inhabitants of some completely transformed, future world: Horse writes that "the people will go out of their land. They, like the land, are wounded and hurt. They will go into the rocks and bluffs, the cities, and into the caves of the torn apart land. There will be fires. Some of them will be restored to the earth. Others will journey to another land and merge with other people. Some will learn a new way to live, the good way of the red earth. But a time will come again when all the people return and revere the earth and sing its praises" (362). The ending of *Mean Spirit* implies the imminent advent of this new phase of existence. With the Oklahoma landscape on fire behind them, several characters including Michael, with his book, follow the "good red road" that leads to the camp of the "Hill People" (traditional Osage spirit beings who have hidden from all but a chosen few the road that leads to their camp): "They looked back once and saw it all rising up in the reddened sky, the house, the barn, the broken string of lights, the life they had lived, nothing more than a distant burning" (375). *The Book of Horse* invokes Native prophecies about conflagrational fires[15] and about a post-conflagrational world of people "restored to the earth,"[16] people no longer constrained by the historical past recounted in the framing narrative. Hogan implies that texts compare to the bat medicine bundle that Michael Horse inherits from Sam Billy. Through Sam Billy, we learn that the bundle contains the power to "turn time around as if it were the steering wheel of [Michael's] roadster" (146). Release of the bat medicine in the present brings back the "time before time."[17] If, as Hogan's novel so profoundly intimates, texts may wield medicine power affecting the "real," then her novel-as-medicine-bundle likewise carries power to "turn time around."

As I have pointed out in an earlier chapter, Hogan's outer narrative virtually collapses into the prophetic, revisionary narrative of Horse. Horse and his projected readers, the inhabitants of a new world beyond time, disappear. The primary audience (Hogan's readers) remain, however, as does Hogan's story itself. Recalling Wilbur Snake's words to Elaine in *Ghost Singer*, Stace's interior monologue toward the end of *Mean Spirit* reminds us that "stories" teach us "that there [are] times when a person could do nothing but wait and be silent" (348). The intertext expands within the silence of the reader's memory to include novels by writers such as Momaday, Hogan, Vizenor, and Walters, whose works "return" to "the unwritten"[18] to shape our responses to other works and to connect us to other worlds, both extant worlds and potential realms of the future.

Recalling Momaday's and Hogan's layered, or "bundled," narratives, Silko's *Almanac of the Dead* presents us with a fragmented, ancient almanac as an inner narrative pitting its latent, world-making power against that of the outer narrative describing the world of the European "Destroyers." This latter world is home to drug dealers, kidnappers, murderers and other violent, antisocial offspring of European colonizers who resemble characters in Sterling's crime magazines, which he reads before the "old stories return to him." [19] Like Hogan, Silko teases the reader who is intrigued by a mysterious text promising to fill the gaps of history, but who never suspects how such a text as Silko's threatens to destabilize his or her own familiar reality. Though the guardians of the almanac never "complete" or even thoroughly decipher it, the manuscript contains semiotic codes that escape textual boundaries to affect the socio-political world represented in the outer layer of the novel. Silko's threat or promise (depending upon audience predisposition) at the end of the novel concerns the complete transformation of the Americas according to ancient prophecies heralding the disappearance of European influence. The power of the "secret clan" of blood and violence (the clan of Cortés and Montezuma) [20] wanes with the waxing of world-making powers of writing Indians who tell the "old stories" in new ways. In *Almanac of the Dead*, Silko insists that world-making and world-destroying power is ultimately semiosic, not material, and finally not even a matter of whose story is accurately recorded, but a matter of whose story, in the process of being told, shapes readers' responses.

As Yoeme's notebooks (and the almanac) are transcribed within Silko's novel, the world of the novel begins to reflect the world of the notebooks. (Here, Silko's narrative strategy recalls *Ceremony*, in which traditional lyric passages gradually begin to incorporate—become a version of—material historical events; in circular fashion, these events have also been shaped by traditional stories. The traditional lyrical passages are also intertextually linked to Silko's *Storyteller*, where they are joined together as a single work suggesting an interpretive context for the other works, especially "Storyteller," in the collection.) In *Almanac of the Dead*, we are presumably intended to view Silko's novel as a version or an instrument of the world-transformative almanac that her narrative encapsulates. All stories, she implies, exist together within a vast, intertextual network shaping reality. Even as we read about the almanac's prophecies, we see evidence of their accuracy in the tale proper, which in turn mirrors the social reality in which we live. Having read *Almanac*, for example, we cannot read of current Indian uprisings among Native peoples in Guatemala or in San Cristóbal de las Casas in the state of Chiapas, Mexico, without pondering Silko's astonishingly prophetic novel. We watch as world events seem to conform to Silko's story, just as her story reflects the shape of things intimated by Yoeme's notebooks.

Hogan and Silko portray "Indian" realities on the verge of eclipsing the dominant, or Eurocentric reality. The oppositional discourses (one narrative layer evoking a world pitted against the world described in the other narrative layer) characterizing both *Mean Spirit* and *Almanac of the Dead* semiotically embody the collision of Eurocentric and Indian worlds, and potentially renegotiate the rules by which we reconstruct the past and construct the future. Moreover, both authors insist, story gives birth to story. (As Silko says in *Ceremony*, stories come from the "belly" [2].[21]) Silko's message in all of her works is clear: as long as stories give birth to stories, the five-hundred-year "resistance"[22] goes on and, eventually, counter-colonial stories may "take form in bone and muscle."[23]

Textual "medicine bundles" such as Momaday's, Walters's, Hogan's, and Silko's teach us much about intertextual semiosis. However, stories-within-stories need not all originate with the same author. One text may draw another into its semiotic sphere merely through an author's deployment of allusions. Indeed, direct and indirect allusions probably constitute one of the most common, overt modes of intertextual linkage, in general. Riffaterre accounts for the semiotic action of allusions by describing them as "textual anomalies" or "ungrammaticalities" encountered within a work that a reader cannot decode without reference to a larger, extratextual field.[24] In *Bearheart*, for instance, Vizenor's barbs aimed at Sun Bear and Wabun, and at Carlos Castaneda make no sense at all to the reader unfamiliar with the activities and writings of these individuals. Vizenor's novel is rife with allusions. Likewise, Silko's, Allen's, and Momaday's references to Navajo-Pueblo stories in their works, Erdrich's references to Chippewa stories and to *Moby-Dick*, Welch's references to the grail romance and other American literature, King's allusions to Ishmael and other figures in *Green Grass*, and Hogan's allusions to the Bible in *Mean Spirit* all depend upon the reader's close acquaintance with extratextual sources.[25]

Artfully deployed, such allusions are usually double-vectored. The encapsulated text affects our interpretation of the text at hand, and vice-versa. For example, when Erdrich mentions *Moby-Dick* in *Love Medicine*, an attentive reader sees beyond Nector's comparison of himself to the mad captain[26] to Erdrich's implied commentary upon philosophical issues raised in Melville's American classic. Although Erdrich suggests that life is maddening for all human beings universally, Nector's madness has collective roots and tribal definition; Ahab's personal hell, on the other hand, is defined individualistically in Greek heroic and Old Testament terms, and seems to concern only him and an apparently malevolent God (though others are affected by Ahab's megalomania). Thus, Erdrich subtly situates her own text in dialogue with its literary precursor. Certainly, a complex variety of sign actions occur as Melville's biblically nuanced "fisherman" story becomes a mainstream point of reference for Erdrich's own cross-coded but likewise biblically allusive story of spiritual and material "fishers" of souls. In the same way as our memory of Melville's romance informs our reading of *Love Medicine*, our experience of Erdrich's revisionary "American" narrative potentially causes us to reconsider Euro-American dialectics on deity, nature, individualism, U. S. cultural identity, and other subjects that arise within mainstream works from nineteenth-century America. Erdrich suggests ways of seeing the world that originate with America's indigenous peoples and that are different from those views implied in the Transcendentalist and Anti-Transcendentalist argument implicit within *Moby-Dick*.

Thomas King's *Green Grass, Running Water*, however, probably best illustrates the maximum effects an author may achieve through a cross-culturally allusive work. Like Erdrich through her reference to *Moby-Dick*, King suggests through numerous allusions that Euro-American and Indian stories "fit together" in dialogue. King, however, conducts a more sustained and self-conscious meditation upon the human condition with regard to "making sense." According to King, no particular story or version of reality is "true." Human beings are united merely through their inveterate penchant for making up stories, most of which go wrong and create worlds in need of "fixing up." Through intertextual allusion, King suggests that an overarching, mythical matrix (or one story) unites us all; this Story features Semiotic Man and Woman (and Animal), inept raconteurs who cannot put together a satisfactory account.

In King's novel, four "old Indian" storytellers join Coyote in an effort to begin the "story" of humanity over again and this time, "get it right." After one of many cyclic escapes from a mental institution (perhaps a comic allusion to Vizenor's obsessive semioticians inhabiting the "Word Wards" in *Bearheart*), they assume the names of Ishmael, Hawkeye, The Lone Ranger, and Robinson Crusoe from American and British literary and popular culture classics. Throughout his works, King portrays Indian people similarly imbricated or informed by odd versions of western myths and stories (of the biblical "Ahdamn," for instance) and white people telling distorted versions of Indian stories (through the Lone Ranger's sidekick, Tonto, for example). By giving his "old Indians" non-Indian names from mainstream literature, and by "mixing up" stories, King implies that Native and non-Native stories and realities are inextricably intertwined. With Vizenor, he believes that Indians and non-Indians alike (together with "culture") are semiotic constructions—"inventions" constantly under revision through sign action based on a vast, multicultural intertext.

Through Indian characters named Ishmael, Hawkeye, the Lone Ranger, and Robinson Crusoe, moreover, King provides his readers with an important lesson in semiotics. Within their respective, original stories, each of these characters enjoys the companionship of a "native" Other: Ishmael and Queequeg, Hawkeye and Chingachgook, the Lone Ranger and Tonto, and Robinson Crusoe and Friday. From the vast array of western literary works available, King has fashioned an intertextual network of stories rich in subtextual messages about the relationship of European peoples to indigenous cultures throughout the world. *Moby-Dick*, the Leatherstocking Tales, "The Lone Ranger," and *Robinson Crusoe* introduce the shadowy, indigenous Other in ways that imply the white man's dependence upon an indigenous man who feels "at home" in the world and who helps the non-native stranger in times of difficulty. The "stories" of the Other, particularly the sidekick's life-saving stories of "reality" in a strange land, inform those of the dominant society. Though the indigenous sidekicks of Ishmael and the others do not appear in King's novel, they are drawn by memory into the reading experience. Their absence-presence generated within the intertext brilliantly limns the semiotic process through which Euro-Americans create selves and worlds in connection with the subordinated, silenced Other who, nevertheless, plays a fundamental role in the overall elaboration of "reality."

A final, comic twist is evident when we recall that King's Ishmael, Hawkeye, Lone Ranger, and Robinson Crusoe are really "four old Indians" with aliases. King thus reminds us through his development of these and other mythical characters that all people are "natives" of earth who assume names and who discover and invent themselves within "stories." Melville's Ishmael links *Moby-Dick* to the Bible, which informs his "constructed" story as an outcast. The name "Ishmael" also links King's novel through Melville's to the Bible, which necessarily becomes a significant portion of the vast intertext informing the story that King's Ishmael constructs. The name of Ishmael thus conjures a series of botched stories which humans have made and from which they dream of escape, followed by new beginnings. As a textual "medicine bundle," King's *Green Grass, Running Water* contains strategically managed, encapsulated references to a variety of works and the "worlds" they conjure. He reminds his readers of the dream that drew the colonizers ("natives" of other lands) to the so-called "New World" in the first place—a world that many now dream of escaping—and he confronts Native and non-Native American alike with the responsibilities that accrue to semiotic beings whose dreams may not be universally shared.

A few final remarks on an intertextually self-conscious passage from Momaday's *The Ancient Child* appropriately sum up my discussion of textual "medicine bundles." This passage from Momaday's novel corroborates King's points about intertextuality and humorously illustrates the mutual imbrication of "reality" and "the symbolic order—the order of language, discourse, narrative,"[27] including the imbrication of the dominant discourse with the signs of the Other, and vice-versa. In *The Ancient Child*, a young Navajo woman named Grey is an indiscriminate, naive reader and viewer of art. She models herself after pieces of art such as the Indian dolls she has seen in museums; and when she writes in her journal, she describes herself based on a hodgepodge of popular fictional conventions, including Cooperesque descriptions of Indian women typical of the Westerns that she reads:

I *am* a bonny lass. I have enjoyed eighteen wondrous summers, all of them in the vastness of the wilderness, which is my incomparable element. I am tall and limber and well formed. My mind is clear. I am as trim and graceful as a doe, and I am free of the strictures of "civilization," so-called. I have dark, lustrous hair, gathered becomingly behind my shell-like ears, sparkling green eyes, an aquiline nose, a small, shapely, delicate mouth like a Cupid's bow, and a whole, symmetrical, and lovely face. My profile is comely and well defined, classical. My skin is olive and translucent, and my bearing is graceful and dignified. My unpretentious attire is altogether appropriate. It consists of a chamois sheath, with leggings beautifully made by hand, and a tunic, woven of wolf's hair, similar to garments worn by kings and queens of yore. My small alabaster feet are encased in tiny moccasins, elaborately decorated with bright beads, and a string of iridescent shells encircles my long, slender, curved, unblemished throat. (18–19)

Through Grey's clichéd imagery, Momaday alludes to an array of mainstream texts (both verbal and visual) that have structured her perceptions. Her writing calls attention to an unavoidable intertextuality that unites all stories within the "one story," a frame of reference that no writer can escape and that itself cannot escape cross-culturalization. Moreover, through Grey's writing, Momaday parodies his own, for like Grey's, his identity, knowledge, beliefs, ideas, and images are inherited from, and shaped by, western as well as American Indian art. Momaday apparently joins King, Vizenor, and other contemporary Native American writers who appreciate the irony involved in their "authentic" speech on behalf of Native peoples.

Texts as Twins

Twins, usually pairs of male warriors, are important figures throughout traditional Native American tribal literature as well as within the contemporary written literature that so heavily draws upon traditional stories.[28] We encounter twins or their equivalent in Momaday's *House Made of Dawn* (in pairs of brothers, especially Abel and Vidal, but also in Abel's implied, brotherly relationship to several male characters, including Ben Benally), *Mean Spirit* (Moses and Ruth), *Ceremony* (Tayo and his cousin Rocky) and Allen's *The Woman Who Owned the Shadows* (where Ephanie learns the stories of male and female twins and uses them to heal her own divided consciousness).[29] As a semiotic phenomenon, twins in tribal cultures express the larger unity of opposing forces. Together, twins constitute "complete" entities bound by mutually interdependent but opposite abilities and qualities.

The Navajo Monster Slayer and Born for Water, for example, complement one another as Elder Brother and Younger Brother, the former aggressive and active, the latter passive and compliant. Twins sometimes switch roles, however, and when one is absent, the other assumes all or part of his brother's identity. Twin females also

express such dual or complementary forces. In some traditional stories, for example, Changing Woman (mother of warrior twins) has a destructive opposite. "Twins" provide an apt metaphor to describe the intertextual relationship between two different pairs of novels: Silko's *Ceremony* and *Almanac of the Dead* and Welch's *Winter in the Blood* and *The Death of Jim Loney.*
Having read both novels by Silko, a reader naturally tends to compare them because they are written by the same author. However, these two books strike most readers as somehow profoundly different from one another even though they share some of the same concerns.[30] Silko's novels share much more than thematic concerns, however, for each is encoded in ways that may evoke the reader's memory of the other (provided a reader has read both books). Riffaterre explains that texts frequently cue readers to important intertextual connections by causing a "doubletake" or "recognition of syllepsis."[31] In Riffaterre's usage, "syllepsis" refers to the appearance of a sign that evokes meanings in the immediate context, but that also evokes the reader's memory of another context in which the sign has other meanings. The reader dwells in the intertext while negotiating these meanings, whether the negotiation results in reconciling implications, considering paradox or contradiction, or otherwise adjusting interpretations based on extratextual factors.

For example, the word "Destroyers" in Silko's novels provides an example of this type of syllepsis. In *Ceremony*, the "Destroyers" are a group of witches from diverse cultures; in *Almanac of the Dead*, the "Destroyers" are the collective of criminals, drug dealers, corrupt politicians, and other vicious characters (indigenous and Euro-American, alike) comprising a financially powerful but immoral social class. Silko's use of the word "Destroyers" in both novels makes each novel the "remembered"—what Riffaterre calls the "unwritten"—context for the interpretation of the other. Silko means for us to see that the witches and the corrupt humans are manifestations of the same force within a "larger pattern" suggested by interconnected texts. On the basis of this intertextually stimulated insight, we might next recall the "Gussucks" (white oil riggers in Alaska) in "Storyteller," the white doctors in "Lullaby," the policemen in "Tony's Story," or even move beyond the corpus of Silko's works to the Indian and non-Indian equivalents of the Destroyers in novels by other American Indians. A "larger" story of the oppression of Native Americans resides in the intertext and amounts to one of the structural invariants uniting American Indian writings.

Ceremony and *Almanac of the Dead* are related as "twins" in other ways, as well. Their differences suggest how Silko perhaps expects us to see them as complementary: whereas *Ceremony* is short and lyrical, *Almanac* is long and discursive; in *Ceremony*, we see spiritual forces acting through Tayo to repair the world, while in *Almanac* we are confronted with a world on the brink of total dissolution; and where *Ceremony* holds out the promise of cultural bridging and a peace "offering," *Almanac* is uncompromising and combative, commanding the reader to decide whether he or she in real life is a Destroyer or the opposite. Together, the two novels make a complete statement concerning the oppositional forces of creation and destruction composing the universe. Sometimes, she insists, we have a choice about which force we are aligned with, and sometimes not. In *Almanac of the Dead*, we obtain a close-up view of destructive forces more gently described in *Ceremony*, but *Almanac* also contains important messages for seekers of healing and social harmony. In *Ceremony*, we have a chance to become more intimately acquainted with constructive powers that might help us write the story of an inhabitable world, though in the novel we also note Silko's unambiguously confrontational acts of resistance. Silko's warning is clear in both novels and echoes loudly in intertextual space: all people, not just whites, are "trailed" by the "possibility of becoming" one of the Destroyers.[32] Her "twins" play different roles, but in each novel, the other is incipiently present and evokes its companion. Consequently, though the "larger" or whole story is told only through the interconnected stories linking the two novels, each novel carries out its revisionary work in ways different from its "twin." Such revisionary work recalls the different responsibilities of Elder and Younger Brother in restoring the world to balance and harmony. Each brother interacts with and affects the world in his own way, just as each of Silko's novels may reach slightly different types of audiences, one responsive to abrupt confrontation and the other more amenable to gentle instruction.

Another pair of novels, James Welch's *The Death of Jim Loney* and *Winter in the Blood* are, like Silko's narratives, advantageously compared as "twins." Welch's narratives intertextually evoke one another and invite comparative readings. Their ambiguous and much-debated endings, in particular, are illuminated in the inter-text they generate between them. Moreover, two avenues of Welch's thought in these texts suggest his self-conscious concern with the sort of intertextuality that links these novels: first, his overt interest in memory and, second, his concern with how spirits and visions function in relation to collective and individual memory, defined as a vast "intertext" between material and nonmaterial realities where the power of writing and storytelling perhaps originates.

In Chapter Four we have observed the different relationships to time portrayed through Welch's protagonists that instruct us about the role of memory as Welch envisions it. In *Winter in the Blood*, the time-obsessed narrator's cinematic memory serves him in "real" life the way the intertext serves a reader. Frequently, his retrieval of important information about his immediate experience depends upon stimulation of his thoughts by a story or a movie. For in-stance, he sees a Randolph Scott movie and shortly thereafter re-calls events leading up to and including the death of his brother, Mose, in an accident. The narrator's depressive condition results partially from gaps in memory and from his inability to put all the "stories" of his life together. His ignorance of his family and tribal history (compounded by his mother's lies) constitutes an empty mental space impeding the connection of stories and memories as a meaningful context for his own existence. Finally, however, the narrator learns enough from his grandmother and from Yellow Calf (late discovered to be his grandfather) to put together a satis-factory story. Although some critics consider his newfound sense of himself at the end of the novel as Welch's cynical statement on the cobbled nature of contemporary Indian identity,[33] closer scrutiny of the narrator in light of Welch's implied, "intertextual" theory of memory suggests otherwise.

For *Winter*'s narrator, memory is always "more real than experi-ence" (22). Consequently, possession of adequate information to fill the gaps in his memory amounts to his first, more or less co-herent, meaningful contact with "reality." Welch hints that his nar-rator's full rehabilitation begins with his meeting with Yellow Calf, who tells him stories and who instructs him about how to live in time: " 'When one is blind . . . and old, he no longer follows the cycles of the years. He knows each season in its place because he can feel it, but time becomes a procession. Time feeds upon itself and grows fat.' A mosquito took shelter in the hollow of his cheek, but he didn't notice. He had attained that distance. 'To an old dog like myself, the only cycle begins with birth and ends in death. This is the only cycle I know" (157–58). In the end, the narrator's feelings and a sense of integration within reality awaken with the spring rain.[34] Though as a young man, he is not yet beyond noting the "cycles of the years," like Yellow Calf, he now *feels* their comings and goings. These aroused feelings signify the beginnings (in "spring") of a meaningful life within a formerly numb and confused man. We understand that the narrator now possesses knowledge sufficient to allow him to grow old like Yellow Calf within a context of personal and tribal "memories" that may guide his passage by providing an interpretive ground for experience.

Both *Winter in the Blood* and *Jim Loney* encode the structural invariant pattern of the ailing Indian, whose psycho-spiritual and sometimes physical malaise results from ignorance of tribal identity and a consequent lack of a firm, epistemological frame of reference (a story) for making sense of self and experience. For this and other reasons, a reading of one novel generates memories of the other, if we have read both. When we meet Jim, an "amnesiac" who never keeps account of days and weeks, we may recall his opposite "brother" in *Winter* who is obsessed with time and with probing his own memory. Thus, the two protagonists are "twins" in their expression of dual tendencies. One young man learns of his history while the other does not; one recovers human feelings, whereas the other sinks further into despair and death. The narrator in *Winter* undergoes a kind of rebirth through knowledge in the end, while Jim commits suicide by deliberately allowing himself to be shot. In life, Jim never manages, like his "brother" in the other novel, to piece together a coherent, life-sustaining story.

The tantalizingly ambiguous ending of *Jim Loney* has generated much controversy; critics debate the meaning of Jim's suicide, as we have noted in a previous chapter. Careful observation of the intertextual relationship between this novel and *Winter*, however, makes sense of Jim's suicide in ways that a reading of *Jim Loney* alone does not. In *Winter*, as we have seen, Welch emphasizes the importance of coherent memory, the "intertext" affording perspective upon current events. Although Jim never acquires the sort of informational context that the narrator in the other novel acquires, Welch invites the reader to consider a fascinating alternative with which Jim does, perhaps, connect in the end. Spirits and visions in

Jim Loney provide Jim with a link to his ancestral past that, unlike the present, makes coherent sense should he chose to explore it; moreover, these ghostly and totemic visitations amount to "stories" (an intertext) linking the material world that Jim abandons and the spiritual realm toward which his visions of his mother seem to beckon him.

Throughout the novel, a "dark bird" periodically appears to Jim.[35] Since Rhea and others do not see it, the bird is doubtless Jim's power animal sent from the realm of dreams and spirits to offer him its protective guidance. Though to the end, Jim remains too ignorant and lethargic to heed the bird, he seems to understand that it links him to something beyond himself. In one passage late in the novel, the narrator equates this "dark bird" with the memories that Jim cannot piece together into his own story: "Loney closed his eyes . . . . He was tired and his mind was full of flickering images, of scenes just past and scenes a long time past. He stood with his eyes closed and tried to black out the images, but they kept coming like dark birds, one following another, in and out of his mind, simple memories of trivial times. But they brought me here, he thought, to this place, to this time. Presently, he opened his eyes and the birds were gone, and he turned and entered the canyon" (168). In the canyon, Jim meets his totemic, dark bird one last time before he dies. As he dies, the bird disappears into the distance, possibly escorting Jim's spirit into a world where he will be more at home and where, at last, things might "make sense." Furthermore, Welch's syntagmatic equation of a world-linking, spirit-bird with bird-like, yet disconnected memories intertextually recalls the ending of *Winter in the Blood*, where the narrator revives through semiotic reconnection. Perhaps Jim's rehabilitation through reconnection also occurs, not in this material dimension but in the spiritual realm of his ancestors. Perhaps Welch in *The Death of Jim Loney* has not, after all, succumbed to the idea of the Indian as "vanished" and as having no place in the contemporary world, as some critics have suggested in response to Jim's suicide. On the contrary, Welch's "twinned" novels might be seen as representing two different avenues of healing.

Part One of *Jim Loney* opens with a biblical allusion to Isaiah —a prophetic book warning that things are frequently not what they seem—that possibly corroborates the latter interpretation. Jim ponders the prophet's advice in Isaiah 2:22 to turn away from life, "from the man in whose nostrils is breath, for of what account is he?" (1). While breath is in Jim's nostrils, he certainly remains unable to account for himself, especially to give an account of himself in a coherent story. The rest of the passage from Isaiah, not quoted but intertextually implicit ("unwritten" and remembered) within Welch's text declares, further, that "in the last days, the Lord's house will be established in the top of mountains." Jim's suicide occurs among mountains, but in a canyon atop a "rocky outcropping" from where he sees into a lower "valley" (174). Situating Jim in death so ambiguously with regard to Isaiah's prophecy about the mountain tops, Welch leaves us to decide whether Jim's dark bird "climbs" with or without his freed spirit "to a distant place" (179). Furthermore, we are left to ponder the gap between Isaiah's disparaging attitude toward the "breath" in the nostrils and the opposite, pan-tribal conception of the sacredness of the breath that Jim, as an Indian, would share. However, hints in the narrative suggest that Jim "climbs" with the bird. After he has decided to die, Jim meets Amos After Buffalo's dog in the street. He tells the dog to deliver a message to Amos: Jim "passed through town" carrying his own dead dog, Swipesy. "Tell him you saw me carrying a dog and that I was taking that dog to a higher ground" (167). Moreover, as a Blackfeet male who disappears from the world, Jim reminds us of Earthboy,[36] a model for the regenerated narrator in *Winter in the Blood*. Welch's subtly articulated intertextual resonances keep before us the distinct possibility that Jim has, indeed, found "higher ground," and that Isaiah's warning about mere appearances is well-heeded by a reader inclined to read Welch's signs too hastily.

Syncretism

As I have remarked in a previous chapter, an ostensibly bleak, prophetic comment on the fate of apparently "vanishing" American Indian people such as Jim Loney and others occurs at the end of Erdrich's *Tracks*. At first seeming merely to lament the fate of her own conquered people, Erdrich declares through Nanapush that the Chippewa now amount to nothing more than a "tribe of file cabinets and triplicates, a tribe of single-space documents, directives, policy. A tribe of pressed trees. A tribe of chicken-scratch that can be scattered by a wind" (225). Previously, I pointed to the subtle message conveyed by these apparently cynical words. *Tracks* and other post-colonial, ethnosemiotically resistant works such as those we have considered throughout this study are books made of "pressed trees." As these books proliferate in number, their collective "tribal" power creates new audiences with revised reading practices. These once extremely marginalized writers are forging bonds of solidarity with ever-increasing numbers of readers whose facility with marginal texts necessarily redefines the "mainstream" art of the late twentieth century. Native American authors and the "language of their leaves" [37] expand the intertext and re-form memory which, in turn, informs our habitual reading practices.

According to Hodge and Kress, "the context of semiosis is itself organized as a series of texts, with meanings assigned to categories of participants and relationships. . . . The [semiotic] behaviour of the participants is constrained by logonomic systems which operate through messages about their identity and relationships, signifying status, power, and solidarity. . . . Where a semiotic exchange does not involve direct contact by all participants [as in written discourse], producers are likely to include instructions specifying producers, receivers and contexts into the form of their text. . . . The set of messages which organizes a particular semiotic exchange will imply a generalized version of social relations." [38] In this chapter, we have considered how Native American authors articulate a version of social relations characterized by solidarity that is achieved through intertextual links. The "semiotic behavior of the participants" in their endeavors will, presumably, change in a number of ways conducive not merely to adequate reception, or "readings," of all kinds of American Indian "texts," but also to better production agendas at both semiosic and "real" levels. In other words, these Native American writers attempt a kind of "literary intervention" [39] into contemporary reality predicated upon the world-making behavior that they have fostered in their audiences.

Can such a scheme truly be fulfilled? Is literary intervention of this sort actually possible? After all, says semiotician Robert Hodge, "literature's record in changing the world is not exactly impressive. This is unsurprising, since its typical function from the point of view of any ruling group is precisely to allow the expression of critique and aspiration in a safe form. The linchpin in systems of control of literary meaning is the modality apparatus that pre-assigns a low modality to literary texts as a general category, although . . . there are different modalities assigned to different

genres and to different aspects of individual texts. This apparatus is enforced through reading regimes which become taken-for-
granted strategies for both writers and readers, the contract that
bonds them into a consensus community." [40] But this arrangement
is never entirely stable," Hodge insists, "since it is a compromise
between the interests of the dominant [who] confirm the dominant
order and the interests of many others, including writers, [who]
oppose it. The balance can always shift, and the truths contained
by literary texts can suddenly have a new effectivity, becoming part
of a process that mobilizes people and mounts a powerful challenge to 'reality' itself" (166). I have suggested *how* this balance can
be shifted through certain semiotic features of texts, through the
mobilizing process activated within the audience-participants, and
through mutually reinforcing messages that reside in the intertext
that guides our reading.

When we make these broad claims about projected reader-
response, we are wise to pause to think carefully about the actual
readership in whom such responses are purported to occur. "Up to
a point," says Hodge, "we can describe the contexts and roles constructed by the text, but this process quickly loses any explanatory
power unless we try to label the actual participants" (8). I believe
that contemporary Native American writers are especially capable
of galvanizing reader-response with world-altering power mainly
because the actual audience for their work is so diverse, so replete
with readers with different reading practices, some of which have
been shaped, in turn, by other Native American art. We have seen
how individual works such as Silko's *Ceremony*, for example, deliberately address multiple audiences and particularly tutor the non-
Indian audience in the semiotic practices of the Other. Trinh T.
Minh-ha refers to this and other radically revisionary writing strategies of marginalized cultures as a way of "beating the master at his
own game," and Inés Hernández-Ávila writes persuasively about
how American Indian writers have, in some ways, made an alien discourse their own. [41] Consequently, self-authorizing, non-dominant
voices speak from within structures (such as the novel) of the dominant society, without having to speak exclusively through the Eurocentric perspectives traditionally encoded within these structures.
Moreover, year by year, the audience for American Indian literature widens to include readers from a variety of ethnic backgrounds
for whom Eurocentric interpretive strategies are themselves the

strategies of the Other. It seems quite obvious to me that contemporary Native American writers have, indeed, "intervened." I agree with Christopher Norris when he argues (against Derrida, DeMan, Bhaskar, and Fish) that a text can do something besides corroborate the consensus, that "language [can] muster an effective resistance to the workings of [the dominant] ideology."[42] New interpretive communities are formed when large numbers of readers change their interpretive habits; and when great numbers of writers begin to write for these alternative communities, there exists a much greater chance that "truths contained by literary texts can suddenly have a new effectivity, becoming part of a process that mobilizes people and mounts a powerful challenge to 'reality' itself."[43]

Michael Riffaterre describes the intertext as the "unconscious" of the text, not the mental unconscious of the author or reader that is "accessible to psychoanalysis," but a textual unconscious accessible to "semanalysis" and commanding sophisticated mnemonic processes.[44] This textual "unconscious," or intertext, recalls Victor Turner's descriptions of the ritual, liminal space where ceremonial art fulfills its transformative purpose, and Philip Wheelwright's concept of the "indefinable coalescence of things in mythic perspective."[45] Wheelwright, Turner and Riffaterre all understand one function of myth to be the unification of storyteller and audience, a unification that both precedes and precipitates change. Wheelwright's notion of "trans-subjectivity" (34), like Turner's notion of the ritual powers of art and Riffaterre's idea of what takes place in the intertext, is especially pertinent to the implied purpose behind much of today's Native American writing. Wheelwright argues that poets and artists expand areas of "shared mentality" between people. The regenerative and world-transformative "chicken-scratch" of contemporary Native American writers, united in an ever-expanding intertextual web, may one day enlarge the collective human imagination beyond any of our previously conceived limits.

Epilogue
All We Have Are Stories: Semiosis and Regeneration

> I will tell you something about stories,
> [he said]
> They aren't just entertainment.
> Don't be fooled.
> They are all we have, you see,
> all we have to fight off
> illness and death.[1]

A quick glance at a dictionary reveals the common root of the words *regenerate* and *genre*: both derive from the Latin, *generare*. To "generate" is "to produce, or bring into being," while to belong to a "genre" is to be of a certain form or "genus" produced; to "*re*generate" is to *bring back* into being, or to revive, renew, remake. An implicit theory of semiotic "regeneration" and, so to speak, "re-genre-ation" has guided my investigation of contemporary American Indian literary works throughout this study. As I have shown, and as many Native American authors declare outright, Indian literature frequently includes a ritual or ceremonial dimension aimed at the psycho-spiritual regeneration of the audience. Moreover, I have discussed contemporary Native American narrative as a cross-cultural site replete with lessons for the attentive reader about semiotic practices involved in the ongoing production, or regeneration, of culture in its experiential as well as its textual forms.

I have also suggested that during the later years of the twentieth century, the grounds for cross-cultural communication between Indians and non-Indians have become especially fertile, and in my opening chapters I have credited certain postmodern trends with facilitating the mainstream reader's understanding of Native texts. I would now like to broaden my discussion to speculate about the role that Native American and other ethnic literature seems to play within mainstream culture at the present time. Besides answering the sometimes monotonic, facile demands for "diversity" that we hear so frequently today, the literature of the Other seems to fill an emptiness in mainstream culture. Indeed, Native American authors and numerous mainstream social analysts repeatedly diagnose the present age as spiritually bereft.

Anticipating the turn-of-the-century, a large portion of the dominant American society desperately invokes the old American Dream mythology, even as the poor, the homeless, the "post-Boomer" generation, and otherwise seemingly disfranchised sectors declare their alienation almost beyond remedy. Society's leaders call for imaginative, radically innovative solutions to human problems, both domestic and global. Some among them argue that the time has come for western cultures to reconsider the world views of nonwestern peoples whose communal and environmental practices suddenly appear as attractive alternatives to contemporary greed and ecological destruction. Hence, the appeal in recent years of various nonwestern and "marginal" literatures, and the values and worldviews they imply. Hence, also, the romanticization and cultural appropriation of indigenous peoples that so many contemporary Native Americans resent. First they stole our lands, say many American Indians, and now they want our lifeways and spiritual practices.

Perhaps a less cynical view of recent developments is possible. As I have suggested in the Prologue, along with postmodernism, some dovetailing trends in western aesthetics and science have created an auspicious environment for the development of "regenerative" texts that I have focused upon in this study. Indeed, much recent increasingly centrist discourse on the physician's "art" affords a fascinating intertextual background for a discussion of contemporary Native American storytelling.

Native American Medicine and Art

We have noted that a conception of art as ritual, specifically as a ritual of healing, underlies many contemporary works of literature by Native Americans. For example, as various critics have explained and as we have observed, Leslie Marmon Silko's *Ceremony* is not merely *about* a ceremony—it *is* a ceremony. The story is not merely *about* a healing—it is meant to *be* a healing. Accordingly, this novel, like the Navajo cosmology perfusing it, is formally meticulous; as a ceremony, it is carefully designed to change the participants (both author and reader) and, ultimately, the world, which Silko apparently views to be, like art, a partly divine, partly human creation in a participatory universe. Drawing on Laguna Pueblo and Navajo cosmology together with United States history, *Ceremony* accounts for the disastrous condition of the post-nuclear, contemporary world by exposing humanity's destructive "story," a semiosic matrix within which human beings define reality and shape destiny. Only a new story, the author insists, can repair the world by altering its currently "monstrous design."[2]

As a "ceremony" aimed at a general rather than at an exclusively Indian audience, Silko's novel, like Walters's *Ghost Singer* and others, invites us to think carefully about two "stories" or "realities" existing within the United States—that of Euro-American culture and that of indigenous Americans. She warns us to avoid a disastrous future by revising both "stories" before it is too late. As Silko and her contemporaries portray it, the world created by the Euro-American is in critical transition. A society plagued by violence, poverty, racial conflict, and a deteriorating natural environment—to name only a few problems of an excessively materialistic culture—may continue on its present course until, as Momaday fears, "the human species is doomed."[3] Other, less grim possibilities exist, however, and these alternatives interest many American Indian authors, whose bicultural experience has shown them the best, and the worst, of both "worlds."

Insistence on an immediate relationship between art and the health of individuals and collectives perhaps most emphatically distinguishes American Indian writers from their mainstream Euro-American counterparts. This perceived relationship arises from ontological, epistemological, and axiological grounds significantly different from those underlying conventional western thought about art and scientific healing. Whereas western society has for centuries privileged rationalism while distinguishing it from, and devaluing, "subjective" knowledge, Native American thought is frequently "psychic and mystical."[4] Unfortunately, however, such words as "psychic" and "mystical" barely suffice, for they are western terms tainted by long association with irrationalism and by their negatively dualistic relationship to "reason" and "logic." Moreover, because Native American tribal societies are not typically characterized by western-style dualisms, such terms as "psychic" and "mystical" may, if we are not careful, import non-Indian perspectives into Native world views. Through the "ceremony" of art and rooted in the belief that "stories" are "all we have to fight off / illness and death,"[5] American Indian works remind all, but especially non-Indian, readers that human choices and creative power can either destroy or enhance life as we know it. Indeed, Silko directs a large portion of her own creative energy to instructing the non-Indian reader of her book in some important alternative ways of thinking about contemporary problems.

In their didactic pursuits, Silko and others take advantage of synergistic developments in science and art that have to some extent created conditions for the emergence of a non-Indian audience receptive to the form and content of their work, with its central philosophy of "medicine" and its emphasis on the role of consciousness in material creation.[6] As we shall presently see, "alternative" western medicine and Native American "medicine" are philosophically comparable because both are anti-reductionist and anti-mechanistic. Like shamans, holistic practitioners treat the "whole" person, who (regardless of doctors' or patients' religious beliefs) is assumed to consist of more than mere flesh to be healed. Both kinds of medicine not only reject the idea of the body as a machine, but they also insist on the role of mind — thoughts, emotions and attitudes — in health and disease.

Ceremonial maintenance of proper relationships between humanity and the universe is an aspect of "medicine," a complex worldview incorporating what Beck, Walters, and Francisco have identified as the six general or "pan-Indian" concepts that underlie most Native American tribal belief systems:

1. A belief in or knowledge of unseen powers, or what some people call The Great Mystery.
2. Knowledge that all things in the universe are dependent on each other.
3. [A belief that p]ersonal worship reinforces the bond between the individual, the community, and the great powers. Worship is a personal commitment to the sources of life.

4. [A belief that s]acred traditions and persons knowledgeable in sacred traditions are responsible for teaching *morals* and *ethics*.

5. [A reliance upon] trained practitioners who have been given names such as medicine men, priests, shamans, caciques, and other names. These individuals also have titles given them by *The People* which differ from tribe to tribe. These individuals are responsible for specialized, perhaps secret knowledge. They help pass knowledge and sacred practices from generation to generation, storing what they know in their memories.

6. A belief that humor is a necessary part of the sacred. And a belief that human beings are often weak—we are not gods—and our weakness leads us to do foolish things; therefore clowns and similar figures are needed to show us how we act and why.[7]

American Indian verbal art frequently serves tribally specific varieties of the communal and ceremonial ends suggested in this list.[8] In traditional oral and, most recently, in written works, the regenerative or healing purpose of Native American storytelling remains constant: A theory of health based on the harmonious interdependence of "all things in the universe" and a belief in the ceremonial power of aesthetic forms to restore or maintain personal and communal well-being underlie much of American Indian song, prayer, and storytelling.[9]

As Beck, Walters, and Francisco proclaim, most tribal belief systems acknowledge an "unseen" or spiritual force pervading the material universe, where individual and collective well-being depends upon morally and ethically responsible actions of conscious entities. Another pan-Indian concept is the idea of "balance" in the universe, an idea suggested in Beck's statement about "all things in the universe [being] dependent on each other" (8). The Cherokee cosmological model, for example, depicts the Middle World, the human realm, precariously situated between a chaotic "lower" world and the "Sky Vault," the lower world's opposite. The responsibility for maintaining harmony between these two realms falls to inhabitants of the Middle World. Navajo cosmology likewise depicts a universe in which the order decreed by the Holy People, or *Diyin Diné'e*, must be carefully maintained in the human world. In nearly all Native American cosmologies, the universe responds to human will expressed for good or evil purposes through words and actions, especially through their combination in ritual, including ritual art.[10]

With words, a storyteller can change peoples' ways of seeing, understanding, and behaving, so she potentially wields powerful "medicine."[11] Obviously, such a storyteller bears a profound, moral responsibility to the audience, since what is said (or written) may have a direct, immediate impact upon the "balance" of the universe. As Silko demonstrates in *Ceremony*, a "story"—a semiotic matrix shaping belief and action—may cause or cure all manner of ills, from the physical illness of an individual, to the psycho-spiritual malaise of a culture, to the environmental deterioration of the earth. Storytelling, as "ceremonial literature serves to re-direct private emotion and integrate the energy generated by emotion within a cosmic framework."[12] In other words, ritual art both makes and remakes the world and is thus a fundamental aspect of the "medicine" worldview.

In addition to its emphasis on psycho-spiritual matters, Indian "medicine" incorporates a version of *physic*, the western science (also commonly called an "art") of healing the body. However, Native American healing recalls modern scientific medicine much less than it harkens back to ancient and medieval medical practices based on a spiritual foundation. Prior to the triumph of scientific medicine, which Foucault places sometime during the late eighteenth century, the western physician treated a body and a spirit that responded to physical *and* metaphysical forces. Such a physician often considered "invisible" or unobservable spiritual causes behind the overt symptoms of disease; moreover, the medieval and Renaissance physician, still working in the alchemical tradition, took for granted an *anima mundi*—a world-soul infused with the divine breath or Logos.[13]

Indian "medicine" presupposes a similar relationship of spirit, matter, and language. Most Native American traditions regard the breath as sacred. So are words formed from the breath and stories formed from words. Thus, Indian "medicine" resonates with some, though certainly not all, aspects of Judeo-Christian tradition that underlie pre-scientific western medicine. Indeed, in *House Made of Dawn*, and in an interview, Momaday observes similarities between Native American metaphysics and biblical concepts of Logos in the Gospel of John.[14] (Momaday also suggests in this novel that such similarities have enabled the Native American church to incorporate Christian components more readily.) However, Momaday thinks that despite their words and good intentions, Christians seem tragically detached from their God, the vital source of their words. Momaday and other Indian authors show that for tribal peoples, the "invisible" realm of spirit is not a remote "heaven" on the far side of an ontological divide from the "visible" material realm.[15] On the contrary, like the medieval alchemists and some contemporary "alternative" physicians, many Native Americans believe that spirit is immanent in material forms and that ailments of the spirit inevitably precede ailments of the flesh. For them, healing must address spirit and body, in that order. Therefore, as well-meaning western physicians attempting to treat Indians have often learned, "medicine" directed merely at the body often fails.[16]

Owing to an assumed, direct link between language and spirit, and to the powerful role of words in shaping individual and collective experience of "reality," language for Native Americans is a kind of "medicine." Momaday who calls himself "a man made of words," claims, reminiscent of Heidegger, that "naming confers being" and that "words are original and originative."[17] Moreover, Momaday's statement recalls the Navajo concept of poesis that he introduces through the "Nightchant" passages in *House Made of Dawn*, when he emphasizes the great regenerative power that resides in the formal arrangement of words (and images) as art. Abel's recovery occurs partly owing to his own and his friends' ceremonial singing and storytelling addressed to his tormented spirit.

Besides Navajo "singing," sandpainting is another aesthetic form that combines verbal and visual signs in an aesthetic ceremony aimed at transforming the universe. In Silko's *Ceremony*, a sandpainting occupies the narrative and moral center of the text. As an icon of "medicine," it does not merely "stand for" or illustrate but, instead, embodies Navajo therapeutic principles.[18] Betonie's sandpainting begins the process of Tayo's recovery from post-war trauma and from his even more significant, self-inflicted malady that results from cursing the rain and otherwise failing to learn and fulfill his designated purpose in society. Tayo's vision quest for rehabilitation culminates at Trinity Site, humanity's destructive "sandpainting" in the form of an atomic bomb crater, a collectively self-inflicted "wound" and a profound offense against nature. Tayo's and humanity's "cure" depends upon the ceremonial revision of this nuclear "story"; the cure begins with Tayo's acceptance of his healer's role in Pueblo society as embodiment and teller of a new "story."

An important component of many contemporary Native American works, this idea that storytelling and health are aligned is frequently developed in connection with a radical critique of the west and its dismissal of Native wisdom. Like the Ghost Dance of the late nineteenth century, these critical works of art often register powerfully as warnings of doom, as when Linda Hogan, in *Mean Spirit*, and Silko, in *Almanac of the Dead*, forecast the imminent downfall of Euro-American society. In Hogan's novel, Joe Billy "talk[s] about toppling worlds. 'The Indian world is on a collision course with the white world,' Billy said" (13). His bat medicine bundle moves ominously beneath his hand as a sign of the " 'older world, wanting out' " (138). Silko's *Almanac of the Dead* concludes with a main character remembering the "old story" that foretells the disappearance of all things European from the Americas (760). Anna Lee Walters's *Ghost Singer* likewise equates the illness of those involved in the appropriation and misuse of sacred Indian artifacts with the greed of an acquisitive western mentality.

Native American "medicine" and art are thus aligned in their social and political aims. As I have argued, some knowledge of this alignment is necessary for anyone who would participate fully as a reader of these texts. Though a non-Indian reader learns much about Indian worldviews simply through the act of reading such narratives, I believe that it is the existence of analogous worldviews in the contemporary western reader's frame of reference that best explains how he or she may so successfully expand this frame to include Native American material.

Western Aesthetics and Science

From the perspective of empirical science, the idea that an aesthetic construction, or "story," can heal is illogical. Nevertheless, throughout western history and especially today, various types of relationships between art and health are consistently acknowledged, if not always satisfactorily explained or widely accepted. At least since the time of Plato, western aesthetic theory has entertained questions about the diverse effects—from morally deleterious to psychologically therapeutic—of art on its audience. Some of the generally recognized versions of this critical dialogue include Platonic statements on the dangers of poetry to the body politic, Aristotelian statements on the benefits of catharsis, classical rhetoricians' remarks on the affective powers of discourse,

Jungian arguments about the balancing and restorative powers of art, Burkean statements on "literature as prescription for living," Marxist proclamations about the politically reformative capacities of storytelling, and even some of the current "subjective" theories of reader-response developed by psychoanalytically-oriented critics such as Holland and Bleich.

These critical perspectives share pre-modern origins in the same traditions that underlie western medicine, which has never entirely freed itself as a science from its origins in mysticism, ritual, and art.[19] Despite at least three centuries of efforts to establish itself on purely empirical grounds, modern medicine has yet to explain scientifically all the phenomena of healing. Particularly vexing are questions about the effects of the patient's attitudes and beliefs upon the healing process, effects that few among even the most conservative in the medical establishment altogether deny.[20]

Indeed, though they are often grouped indiscriminately as "alternative" or "holistic medicine," an array of unorthodox medical theories and practices have recently gained more acceptance within the orthodox medical community than ever before in modern history. The term "complementary" medicine was fairly recently coined because so many physicians holding credentials in allopathic medicine are now willing to "complement" their practices with therapies they have learned outside of establishment medical institutions. As of 1998, fifty-three American medical schools— including those at Dartmouth, Johns Hopkins, the University of Pennsylvania, Stanford, the University of California at Irvine, Yale, Georgetown, and Columbia—have incorporated training in alternative therapies into their curricula.[21] Many of these therapies are contemporary varieties of ancient—including nonwestern— practices such as herbalism, homeopathy, acupuncture, and other non-mechanistic approaches to healing. From "logotherapy" to "visualization," treatments for a range of ills from hypertension to cancer, "holistic" or "complementary" practices assume direct or indirect connections between mental processes (especially language and mental imagery) and health.[22] Recent accounts by physicians interested in the relationship between health and human symbolic behavior include James J. Lynch's studies of the effects of language on the cardiovascular system, Arthur Kleinman's studies of patients' narratives about their illness, Andrew Weil's prescriptions for "optimal" health, Carl A. Hammerschlag's investigations of shamanic healing, and Deepak Chopra's integration of allo-pathic endocrinology and Ayurvedic medicine, to mention only a few. Bibliographies of works in complementary medicine and medical anthropology conducted since the 1960s often fill many pages. Attracting special attention during the 1980's and 1990's is the subject of "medical conversation" or dialogue between doctor and patient.[23]

Lynch, for example, notes "the unique relationship" between a patient's dialogue and "the cardiovascular system" (178): "I began to recognize . . . a common social membrane which centrally af-fected [a patient's] body. Just as the uterine environment surrounds the individual fetus, and as the heat shielded metal surrounds the astronaut's capsule, so too it occurred to me that a social mem-brane surrounds each human being, simultaneously separating one from and connecting one to the rest of one's living world. While ad-mittedly odd in terms of the usual concept of a membrane, never-theless the notion of a social membrane did help my colleagues and me to conceive of how a person's external world meshes with the internal world of physiology to influence human blood pres-sure, as well as to understand why the cardiovascular system is so responsive to human speech." [24] Lynch's expanded repertoire of therapeutic methods comes partially from knowledge acquired in China, where he studied ancient Chinese medical theory and prac-tice, as well as the ways in which ill people endow their sufferings with meaning. Another physician, Larry Dossey, relates what he learned about healing from *curanderas* on the Texas-Mexican bor-der; he also studies the apparent power of prayer and hands-on healing techniques to affect the course of serious illness in some patients. Finally, Chopra recalls his first days as a young physician trained in the U.S. but practicing in India; he reports that "any-thing" can be "medicine" if the patient is so predisposed.

Galvanizing studies such as Lynch's and others is a problem as ancient as medicine itself, yet undispelled by even the most awe-inspiring advances in medical technology: how to account for sub-jective factors involved in healing and in being healed. According to these physicians, between physician and patient there is an inter-subjective relationship; together they command nothing less than the transformation of self and world.

Like shaman and subject, physician and patient must share some mutual attitudes, as well as some common beliefs about reality,

especially the design and purpose of the doctor-patient interaction.[25] Thus, their shared or different cultural identity often affects healing. Lynch and other physicians, including Kleinman and
Levy, report their difficulties in practicing western medicine on
Third World and other nonwestern patients, whose understanding of sickness and health often does not derive from the scientific
model. Despite "magic bullets" and "miracle" drugs, their patients
frequently languish until treatment incorporates healing methods
consistent with the patients' cultural beliefs. Often, these non-
scientific treatments consist of elaborate rituals that are primarily
religious and aesthetic in nature and that feature profound linguistic components.

Contemporary writer-physician Richard Selzer, who says his love
of medicine originated in a love of medical language, eloquently
describes the mystical and aesthetic dimensions of healing when
he compares himself as physician to his "brother shaman"[26]: "At
the age of ten . . . I first became aware of the rich alliterative language of medicine. . . . It should not . . . come as a surprise, then,
that one day I would . . . try to interpret the human body and
those who tend it, in the keenest language [I] could find. . . . Why
should [a surgeon] write? . . . It is to search for some meaning in
the ritual of surgery. . . . [I]t is the exact location of the soul that I
am after. . . . I have caught glimpses of it in the body diseased. If
only I could tell it. . . . [I am] a hierophant . . . . So shall I make
of my fingers, words; of my scalpel, a sentence; of the body of my
patient, a story."[27] According to Selzer, "surgery and writing are
more alike than they are different. In surgery, it is the body that is
being opened up and put back together. In writing, it is the whole
world that is taken in for repairs, then put back in working order,
piece by piece" (9). Corroborating Selzer's and Lynch's insights is
Stanley Burnshaw, who writes that "the sources of an artist's vision
involve aspects of biological responses and processes of accumula-
tion and release to which no investigation has yet found access."[28]

Thus we may reasonably conclude from the examples of Lynch,
Selzer, and other physicians who have pondered the aesthetic and
linguistic dimensions of healing that western scientific thought,
despite its positivistic bent, nevertheless contains some significant
analogs to the Native American understanding of art as ritual
"medicine." These analogs are a fundamental part of what we bring
to the experience of reading, since reading, like healing, always

occurs within a complex "network of [personal, social and linguistic] circumstances"[29]—in other words, within an intertext on which we rely to decode specific texts. Especially today, the average reader is bombarded with popular notions about holistic health, even if he or she knows little to nothing about the art-as-therapy tradition in the west, or about the mystical origins of modern medicine. From the point of view of semiotics, we may observe that such messages "encode" the audience with ideas about connections between a healthy mind and a healthy body, and between the thoughts we hold (and express through words and images) and the way we feel. During approximately the last twenty years, the groundswell of interest in holistic medicine—together with a revival of interest in unorthodox spiritual practices that sometimes accompany it[30]—has affected the knowledge and behavior of the general public and medical professionals alike. Such a revival of ancient ideas in new form has occurred simultaneously with a virtual renaissance in studies of Native American and other indigenous peoples. From the convergence of such cultural trends emerges a fortuitous context within which the non-Indian reader may understand much of Native American philosophy and literature (particularly as these are invented through contemporary, written works).

In this study, I make no claims about the scientific validity of any particular type of holistic medicine. I mean only to emphasize that a store of common knowledge and interest in such subjects exists in the public at large, and that as one part of the average reader's sociolect—the reservoir of general, extra-textual information within which particular literary works become meaningful—this store of knowledge contributes to our understanding, or successful decoding, of Native American texts. Overall, such developments have perhaps contributed (along with other movements such as feminism) to the rise of an audience receptive to Native American literature. In these social changes, we might also observe what Felix Cohen calls the ongoing "Americanization of the White Man, the transformation of the hungry, fearful, intolerant men that came to these shores with Columbus and John Smith."[31] I have tried to show how contemporary Native American narrative directs considerable energy toward such transformational ends. As one student of post-colonial literature has said, "A characteristic of [the literature of the] dominated is an inevitable tendency toward subversion, and a study of the subversive strategies

employed by post-colonial writers would reveal both the configurations of domination and the imaginative and creative responses
to this condition."[32] Adding to our collective knowledge of such
"configurations" and "responses" has been the motive behind my
performance as a reader in this study.

Notes

Prologue: A Universe Perfused with Signs

1. Linda Hogan, *Mean Spirit* (New York: Ivy Books, 1990), 39.
2. Ibid., 138.
3. Michael J. Fischer, "Ethnicity and the Post-Modern Arts of Memory," in *Writing Culture: The Poetics and Politics of Ethnography*, ed. James Clifford and George E. Marcus (Berkeley: University of California Press, 1986), 195.
4. Werner Sollors, "Introduction: The Invention of Ethnicity," in *The Invention of Ethnicity*, ed. Werner Sollors (New York: Oxford University Press, 1989), ix.
5. For Momaday's remark, see Charles L. Woodard, *Ancestral Voice: Conversations with N. Scott Momaday* (Lincoln: University of Nebraska Press, 1989), 88. Vizenor's comment occurs in "Trickster Discourse: Comic Holotropes and Language Games," in *Narrative Chance: Postmodern Discourse on Native American Indian Literatures*, ed. Gerald Vizenor (Albuquerque: University of New Mexico Press, 1989), 189. On the effects of language and naming, see also Carter Revard, "Traditional Osage Naming Ceremonies: Entering the Circle of Being," in *Recovering the Word: Essays on Native American Literature*, ed. Brian Swann and Arnold Krupat (Berkeley: University of California Press, 1987), 446–66; and Linda Hogan, "Who Puts Together," in *Studies in American Indian Literature: Critical Essays and Course Designs*, ed. Paula Gunn Allen (New York: Modern Language Association, 1983), 169–77.
6. Robert Scholes, *Protocols of Reading* (New Haven, Conn.: Yale University Press, 1989), 10.
7. Thomas A. Sebeok, *American Signatures: Semiotic Inquiry and Method* (Norman: University of Oklahoma Press, 1991), 128.
8. Ibid.
9. Ibid. On Wheeler's notion of a participatory universe, see also chapter 19 in Martin Gardner's *Order and Surprise* (Buffalo, N.Y.: Prometheus Books, 1983).
10. See Laura Coltelli's interview with Silko in Coltelli's *Winged Words:*

American Indian Writers Speak (Lincoln: University of Nebraska Press, 1990), 138.

11. The *American Indian Quarterly* 20 (Summer/Fall 1996) is devoted to the subject of Native spirituality and the difficulties involved in its cross-cultural communication, whether through art, religion, or other means. See Lee Irwin's introduction—"Themes in Native American Spirituality"—on pages 309–26 of this issue.

12. Scholes, *Protocols*, 9–10. Peter Rabinowitz is also insightful about how literature effects certain kinds of transformations through intertextual and other semiotic features. See *Before Reading: Narrative Conventions and the Politics of Interpretation* (Ithaca, N.Y.: Cornell University Press, 1987).

13. Victor Turner, *The Anthropology of Performance* (New York: Division of Performing Arts Journal, Inc., 1988), 80.

14. See for instance Elaine Jahner, "Allies in the Word Wars: Vizenor's Uses of Contemporary Critical Theory," *Studies in American Indian Literatures* 9 (Summer 1985): 64–69; and "Metalanguages," in Vizenor's *Narrative Chance*, 155–85; Arnold Krupat, "An Approach to Native American Texts," *Critical Inquiry* 9 (March 1982): 323–28; and "Identity and Difference in the Criticism of Native American Literature," *Diacritics* 13 (Summer 1983): 2–13; Patricia Linton, "The 'Person' in Postmodern Fiction: Gibson, LeGuin, and Vizenor," *Studies in American Indian Literatures* 5 (Fall 1993): 3–11; Susan Pérez-Castillo, "Postmodernism, Native American Literature and the Real: The Silko-Erdrich Controversy," *Massachusetts Review* 32 (Summer 1991): 285–94; Nancy J. Peterson, "History, Postmodernism, and Louise Erdrich's *Tracks*," *PMLA* 109 (October 1994): 982–94; and Gerald Vizenor, "A Postmodern Introduction" and "Trickster Discourse," in *Narrative Chance*, 3–16, 187–211.

15. The tribal affiliations of the writers included in this study are as follows: Paula Gunn Allen (Laguna Pueblo/Lakota), Robert Conley (Cherokee), Louise Erdrich (Chippewa), Linda Hogan (Chickasaw), Thomas King (Cherokee), N. Scott Momaday (Kiowa), Leslie Marmon Silko (Laguna Pueblo), Anna Lee Walters (Pawnee/Otoe-Missouria), Gerald Vizenor (Chippewa), and James Welch (Blackfeet/Gros Ventre).

16. See Andrew Wiget, "Telling the Tale: A Performance Analysis of a Hopi Coyote Story," in Swann and Krupat, *Recovering the Word*, 297–387.

17. See Hayden White's book by this title, *The Content of the Form: Narrative Discourse and Historical Representation* (Baltimore: Johns Hopkins University Press, 1987).

18. Robert Scholes, *Semiotics and Interpretation* (New Haven, Conn.: Yale University Press, 1982), 60.

Chapter One: Acts of Deliverance: Narration and Power

1. Linda Hogan, *Mean Spirit*, 341.

2. Tzvetan Todorov, *The Conquest of America: The Question of the Other*, trans. Richard Howard (New York: Harper Torchbooks, 1984), 53.

3. Robert Hodge and Gunther Kress, *Social Semiotics* (Ithaca, N.Y.: Cornell University Press, 1988), 45.

4. The objections of Arnold Krupat—see his *Ethnocriticism: Ethnography, History, Literature* (Berkeley: University of California Press, 1990)—and others to Todorov's western bias in this study are duly noted. Whatever Todorov's attitude might be regarding the relative cultural superiority and inferiority of these two groups, however, I believe that he has identified a key "difference" between them that allowed for the Europeans' otherwise rather unaccountable advantage. Furthermore, the fact that Cortés was able rhetorically to manipulate the Aztecs based on his knowledge of their prophecies is not proof of their intellectual "inferiority." Indeed, European Christians (like many other cultural groups) have throughout history also been manipulated by powerful figures appealing to various claims of their faith. On the subject of Spanish semiotic manipulation of Indians, see also Laura E. Donaldson, "Noah Meets Old Coyote, or Singing in the Rain: Intertextuality in Thomas King's *Green Grass, Running Water*," *Studies in American Indian Literatures* 7 (Summer 1995): 27–43.

5. For example, the Alabama and Coushatta of East Texas were among the most tolerant, congenial of tribes and they were nearly exterminated, whereas some of the fiercer, warrior tribes of the plains endured better. For a thorough discussion of the similar fates of resistant as well as cooperative tribes, see Angie Debo, *A History of the Indians of the United States* (Norman: University of Oklahoma Press, 1970).

6. Raymond Friday Locke, *The Book of the Navajo* (Los Angeles: Mankind, 1992), 406.

7. Anna Lee Walters, *Ghost Singer* (Flagstaff, Ariz.: Northland Press, 1988), 110.

8. Todorov, *Conquest*, 97.

9. See Gayatri Chakravorty Spivak's remarks in "Imperialism and Sexual Difference," *Oxford Literary Review* 8 (1986): 225–48; and in *In Other Worlds: Essays in Cultural Politics* (New York: Methuen, 1987), particularly throughout chapters 8–11. See Jane Gallop, *Around 1981* (New York: Routledge, 1992), especially pages 231–39. See Vizenor's comments in his "Introduction," *Native American Literature: A Brief Introduction and Anthology*, ed. Gerald Vizenor (New York: HarperCollins, 1995), 1–15.

10. On environmentalism as post-colonial "ritual" of community in Native American literature, see Christopher Norden, "Ecological Restoration as Post-Colonial Ritual of Community in Three Native American Novels," *Studies in American Indian Literatures* 6 (Winter 1994): 94–106.

11. Eva McKay, "We Are Here," in *Our Bit of Truth: An Anthology of Canadian Native Literature*, ed. Agnes Grant (Winnipeg: Pemmican, 1990), 347.

12. Todorov, *Conquest*, 97.

13. Thomas King, *Green Grass, Running Water* (Toronto: HarperCollins, 1993), 104.

14. Walters, *Ghost Singer*, 68, 69.

15. An intricately detailed discussion of these terms appears in Hodge and Kress, *Social Semiotics*. See especially pages 39–59.

16. Ibid., 40.

17. On ethnic diversity and semiotic instability, see William Boelhower's arguments throughout his *Through a Glass Darkly: Ethnic Semiosis in American Literature* (New York: Oxford University Press, 1987). I disagree here with Louis Owens, who implies in his *Other Destinies: Understanding the American Indian Novel* (Norman: University of Oklahoma Press, 1992), 18, that the "monologic authority" of the mainstream culture thoroughly excludes the subversive voice.

18. For a fascinating discussion of an early American case of semiotic power management by a Native American, see Laura Murray, " 'Pray Sir, Consider a Little': Rituals of Subordination and Strategies of Resistance in the Letters of Hezekiah Calvin and David Fowler to Eleazar Wheelock, 1764–1768," *Studies in American Indian Literatures* 4 (Summer/Fall 1992): 48–74.

19. These works unfold in a "modality of low affinity" with mainstream culture, a phrase that Hodge and Kress (*Social Semiotics*, 130–35) use to define a work that resists and rejects dominant "truths" and "realities" by playing the role of a marginalized semiotic agent with limited but disruptive power.

20. Though specifically conceived within a western intellectual tradition, these semiotic concepts of "solidarity" and "power" are, arguably, non-culture-specific, and perhaps even non-species-specific. Social organization of even the most primitive sort observed in nonhuman animals involves "signs" of dominance and submission. Expressions of solidarity and power might in fact be evolutionary developments of nonlinguistic semiotic capacities that exist within nonhuman animals, such as the sign action characterizing predator-prey relations. See for example Sebeok's chapters on zoosemiotics in *American Signatures*, 147–73; and Paul Shepard's arguments throughout his *Thinking Animals: Animals and the Development of Human Intelligence* (New York: Viking, 1978). Thus to discuss Native American works in terms of such power relations is not to commit the error of interpreting them through *inappropriately* western critical categories. And in any case, as I have previously remarked, contemporary Native American narrative is inscribed with western power politics from the moment it assumes written, not to mention published, form, for such is the nature or the "content of the form."

21. See Roland Barthes arguments in general, but in particular throughout *The Semiotic Challenge*, trans. Richard Howard (New York: Hill and Wang, 1988); and Michel Foucault's essay, "What Is an Author?" in *Language, Counter-Memory, Practice: Selected Essays and Interviews*, ed. Donald F. Bouchard (Ithaca, N.Y.: Cornell University Press, 1977), 113–38.

22. Wallace Martin, *Recent Theories of Narrative* (Ithaca, N.Y.: Cornell University Press, 1986), 77.

23. Rabinowitz in *Before Reading*, especially in chapters 1 and 6, and Martin in *Recent Theories* (especially 156–72) provide excellent syntheses of Freudian, Barthesian, and a variety of postmodern arguments concerning the situation of the reader as a kind of "victim."

24. On the use of oral strategies by Indian writers, see Larry Evers,

"Cycles of Appreciation," in Allen, *Studies*, 23–32; "Words and Place: A Reading of *House Made of Dawn*," *Western American Literature* 11 (Winter 1977): 297–320; James Flavin, "The Novel as Performance: Communication in Louise Erdrich's *Tracks*," *Studies in American Indian Literature* 3 (Summer 1991): 1–12; Bernard A. Hirsch, " 'The Telling Which Continues': Oral Tradition and the Written Word in Leslie Marmon Silko's *Storyteller*," *American Indian Quarterly* 12 (Winter 1988): 1–26; Hogan, "Who Puts Together," in Allen *Studies*, 169–77; many works by Dell Hymes including "Breakthrough into Performance," in *Folklore: Performance and Communication*, ed. Dan Ben-Amos and Kenneth S. Goldstein (The Hague: Mouton, 1975), 11–74; "Discovering Oral Performance and Measured Verse in American Indian Narrative," *New Literary History* 8 (Spring 1977): 431–57; Elaine Jahner, "Indian Literature and Critical Responsibility," *Studies in American Indian Literatures* 5 (Summer 1993): 7–12; "Metalanguages," in *Narrative Chance*, 155–85; Arnold Krupat, "An Approach"; and "Post-Structuralism and Oral Literature," in Swann and Krupat, *Recovering the Word*, 113–28; Owens, *Other Destinies*; A. Lavonne Brown Ruoff, "Gerald Vizenor: Compassionate Trickster," *Studies in American Indian Literatures* 5 (Summer 1993): 39–45; James Ruppert, *Mediation in Contemporary Native American Fiction* (Norman: University of Oklahoma Press, 1995); Susan Scarberry-García, *Landmarks of Healing: A Study of House Made of Dawn* (Albuquerque: University of New Mexico Press, 1990); Vizenor, "Trickster Discourse"; and Wiget, "Telling the Tale."

25. See my "The Semiotics of Dwelling in Leslie Marmon Silko's *Ceremony*." *American Journal of Semiotics* 9, 3 (1992): 219–40.

26. Wiget, "Telling," 321–32.

27. Walter Benjamin's essay on the storyteller, particularly his discussions of how the shift from listening to solitary reading bore many social implications, makes fascinating reading in connection with contemporary Native American oral strategies and their designs on mainstream realities. See "The Storyteller: Reflections on the Works of Nikolai Leskov," in *Illuminations*, ed. Hannah Arendt, trans. Harry Zohn (New York: Harcourt, Brace, Jovanovich, 1968), 83–109.

28. Leslie Marmon Silko, *Ceremony* (New York: Penguin, 1977), 121.

29. Victor Turner, *The Anthropology*, 8.

30. Obviously, oral tradition lies behind western literature. Traditional western narrative reflects origins in oral forms such as epic, for example. As Benjamin, Bakhtin, and Foucault among others have shown, the written text contains a vestigial orality. Thus we may see that oral codes are implicit within such narrative and render it open to revisions based on oral agendas. Indeed, the "loneliness" of the reader in a text-based society may be a factor in the development of postmodernism (for postmodern forms often play on the western-defined, isolated, voyeuristic roles of the reader) and in the apparent receptivity of the postmodern audience to ethnic literature, as I have argued.

31. See Scarberry-García, *Landmarks*, 8.

32. See "Metalanguages," in Vizenor, *Narrative Chance*, 163.

33. Silko, *Ceremony*, 204.

34. Hodge and Kress, *Social Semiotics*, 6.

35. There are, of course, a few earlier Indian writers such as D'Arcy McNickle and others whose narrative techniques are of considerable interest. However, these writers were never widely read in their day and had to be "rediscovered," in effect, following the post-1960s rise of interest in Native American writing.

36. The "sociolect" refers to that nebulously defined body of extratextual information and meanings that a reader brings to bear when he or she interprets a text. Though one reader's "sociolect" might be a little different from another's, basically, our shared knowledge of such matters as a particular language, connotations of words and phrases, literary and other types of conventions, etc., make up a common background of information necessary to the interpretation of any text. By contrast, the "idiolect" refers to the particular meanings generated by a particular text which we negotiate in our overall interpretation of that text. For an expanded discussion of these terms and critical exposition based on their use, see Michael Riffaterre, *Text Production* (New York: Columbia University Press, 1983).

37. See my discussion of oppositional discourses in Silko's *Ceremony* in "Semiotics of Dwelling."

38. Interesting to note is that all of these options have been exercised by critics over the years. Many critical studies explicating cultural and contextual backgrounds of the novel exist, including most recently Scarberry-García's *Landmarks*. In the early 1970s, as non-Native literary scholars struggled admirably but often misguidedly to respond to Momaday's novel, a few such as Matthias Schubnell in *N. Scott Momaday: The Cultural and Literary Background* (Norman: University of Oklahoma Press, 1985), Alan Velie in *Four American Indian Literary Masters: N. Scott Momaday, James Welch, Leslie Marmon Silko, Gerald Vizenor* (Norman: University of Oklahoma Press, 1982), and Kenneth Lincoln in *Native American Renaissance* (Berkeley: University of California Press, 1983) somewhat overly imposed western frames of reference. Many other critics, feeling unequal to the task, avoided commentary, as revealed by a glance at the *MLA International Bibliography*, which cites few books and articles on *House* until recently.

39. N. Scott Momaday, *House Made of Dawn* (New York: Harper and Row, 1968), 210. Another priest character who gradually "converts" to Indian views and ways appears in Hogan's *Mean Spirit*; see Andrea Musher, "Showdown at Sorrow Cave: Bat Medicine and the Spirit of Resistance in *Mean Spirit*," *Studies in American Indian Literatures* 6 (Fall 1994): 23–36, for a discussion of Father Dunne's cross-cultural function.

40. See Nora Barry, "The Bear's Son Folk Tale in *When Legends Die* and *House Made of Dawn*," *Western American Literature* 12 (Fall 1978): 275–87; and Scarberry-García, *Landmarks*.

41. On Silko's reader, see also Michael Hobbs, "Living In-Between: Tayo as Radical Reader in Leslie Marmon Silko's *Ceremony*," *Western American Literature* 28 (Winter 1994): 301–12; Mary F. Sheldon, "Reaching For a Universal Audience: The Artistry of Leslie Marmon Silko and James Welch," in *Contemporary Native American Cultural Issues: Proceedings from the Native*

American Studies Conference at Lake Superior State University, October 16–17, 1987, ed. Thomas E. Schirer (Sault Ste. Marie, Mich.: Lake Superior State University Press, 1988), 114–24; and Jim Ruppert, "The Reader's Lessons in *Ceremony*," *Arizona Quarterly* 44 (Spring 1988): 78–85.

42. Silko, *Ceremony*, 255.

43. Hodge and Kress, *Social Semiotics*, 4.

44. Hayden White is especially thought provoking on the subject of the paradoxical distinctions we make between what is "true" and what is "imaginary" content in verbal representation. See especially the first chapter of *The Content of the Form*. Though White does not employ Hodge and Kress's concept of logonomic systems, his discussion emphasizes the fact that different agendas of reception (activated in the reader by the form of a work) to a great extent determine what we think of as "history" versus "myth," even though the two contents are often carried in similar forms. On the subject of how the illusion of truth is semiotically created and sustained in fiction, see also Michael Riffaterre, *Fictional Truth* (Baltimore: Johns Hopkins University Press, 1990).

45. See Paula Gunn Allen's remarks in *The Sacred Hoop: Recovering the Feminine in American Indian Traditions* (Boston: Beacon Press, 1986), 68–69 and throughout.

46. On the power of imagination, see Silko's "Landscape, History, and the Pueblo Imagination," *Antaeus* 57 (Autumn 1986): 83–94.

47. Silko, *Ceremony*, 2.

48. For more on traditional sources informing Momaday's and Silko's novels, see the following: Paula Gunn Allen, "Bringing Home the Fact: Tradition and Continuity in the Imagination," in Swann and Krupat, *Recovering the Word*, 563–79; *The Sacred Hoop*; and *Studies*; Nora Barry, "The Bear's Son"; Robert C. Bell, "Circular Design in *Ceremony*," *American Indian Quarterly* 5 (Winter 1979): 47–62; Robert L. Berner, "Trying To Be Round: Three American Indian Novels," *World Literature Today* 58 (August 1984): 341–44; William Bevis, "Native American Novels: Homing In," in Swann and Krupat, *Recovering the Word*, 580–620; Mary Chapman, " 'The Belly of This Story': Storytelling and Symbolic Birth in Native American Fiction," *Studies in American Indian Literatures* 7 (Summer 1995): 3–16; Evers, "Words and Place"; Valerie Harvey, "Navajo Sandpainting in *Ceremony*," in *Critical Perspectives on Native American Fiction*, ed. Richard F. Fleck. 2nd ed. (Boulder, Colo.: Passeggieta Press, 1997), 256–59; Elaine Jahner, "An Act of Attention: Event Structure in *Ceremony*," *American Indian Quarterly* 5 (Winter 1979): 37–46; Carol Mitchell, "*Ceremony* As Ritual," *American Indian Quarterly* 5 (Winter 1979): 27–35; Robert M. Nelson, *Place and Vision: The Function of Landscape in Native American Fiction* (New York: Peter Lang, 1995); "Snake and Eagle: Abel's Disease and the Landscape of *House Made of Dawn*," *Studies in American Indian Literatures* 1 (Summer 1989): 1–20; B. A. St. Andrews, "Healing the Witchery: Medicine in Silko's *Ceremony*," *Arizona Quarterly* 44 (Spring 1988): 86–94; Susan J. Scarberry, "Memory as Medicine: The Power of Recollection in *Ceremony*," *American Indian Quarterly* 5 (Winter 1979): 19–26; Scarberry-García, *Landmarks of Healing*; Matthias

Schubnell, *N. Scott Momaday*; and Edith Swan, "Healing Via the Sunrise Cycle in Silko's *Ceremony*," *American Indian Quarterly* 12 (Fall 1988): 313–28; "Laguna Symbolic Geography and Silko's *Ceremony*," *American Indian Quarterly* 12 (Summer 1988): 229–49.

49. N. Scott Momaday, *The Ancient Child* (New York: Harper, 1989), 120.

50. Set's rejection of modernist tenets probably reflects Momaday's reaction to his own mainstream literary education. He and Yvor Winters (Momaday's mentor and friend) might easily have debated the idea of art as surrender to mystery and to an implicit, if not always easily perceived, universal order, as opposed to art as "resistance" to chaos. Though he agrees with Winters about the moral dimensions of art, Momaday sees the "equation" between aesthetics and morality in terms quite different from Winters. For Momaday, morality is revealed, explored, and maintained, not willfully or existentially imposed (as Winters believes), through the creative process. Indeed, as Abel's misbehavior in *House Made of Dawn* suggests, the misguided individual will, with its egocentric designs, is frequently a destructive force. Unlike Winters and the Anglo-American formalists with whom Winters was uneasily aligned over the issue of morality, Momaday does not see literary works as merely self-referential "verbal icons" shored up against the ruin of life in a meaningless universe. On the contrary, he sees art as potentially immanent with truth, meaning, and order—intrinsic properties of what he apparently believes to be an overall aesthetically perfect Creation. As such, works of art are also a means of personal and social guidance and transformation. Consequently, the artist must necessarily be a responsible agent of change. On Set and art in *The Ancient Child*, see also Kenneth Roemer, "Ancient Children at Play—Lyric, Petroglyphic, and Ceremonial," in Fleck, *Critical Perspectives*, 99–113; Marie M. Schein, "Alienation and Art in *The Ancient Child*," *Studies in American Indian Literatures* 2 (Winter 1990): 11–14; and Matthias Schubnell, "Locke Setman, Emil Nolde and the Search for Expression in N. Scott Momaday's *The Ancient Child*," *American Indian Quarterly* 18 (Fall 1994): 469–80.

51. King, *Green Grass*, 123.

52. Gerald Vizenor, "Feral Lasers," in *Landfill Meditation: Crossblood Stories* (Hanover, N.H.: University Press of New England, 1991), 11–21.

53. Thomas King, "A Seat in the Garden," in *One Good Story, That One* (Toronto: HarperCollins, 1993), 81–94.

54. Boelhower, *Through a Glass*, 37–38.

55. See Boelhower (Ibid., 23, 33) on the "costructured interpretation" required of the reader of ethnic literature.

56. On Erdrich's use of the oral tradition, see also Joni Adamson Clark, "Why Bears Are Good to Think and Theory Doesn't Have to Be Murder: Transformation and Oral Tradition in Louise Erdrich's *Tracks*," *Studies in American Indian Literatures* 4 (Spring 1992): 28–48.

57. Louise Erdrich, *Tracks* (New York: Henry Holt, 1988), 1.

58. For an admirably lucid and insightful examination of the ethnic writer's management of the reader's interpretive position vis-à-vis the text, see Vévé Clark, "Developing Diaspora Literacy and *Marasa* Conscious-

ness," in *Comparative American Identities: Race, Sex, and Nationality in the Modern Text*, ed. Hortense Spillers (New York: Routledge, 1991), 40–61.

59. Louise Erdrich, *The Bingo Palace* (New York: HarperCollins, 1994), 3.

60. See Wiget, "Telling the Tale," 321–25, on iconic gestures in oral performance.

61. For a discussion of racial and gender concerns implied in the shifting power relations between Pauline and Nanapush, see Daniel Cornell, "Woman Looking: Revis(ion)ing Pauline's Subject Position in Louise Erdrich's *Tracks*, "*Studies in American Indian Literatures* 4 (Spring 1992): 49–64; on Pauline and Nanapush's spiritual conflict, see Michelle R. Hessler, "Catholic Nuns and Ojibwa Shamans: Pauline and Fleur in Louise Erdrich's *Tracks*," *Wicazo Sa Review* 11 (Spring 1995): 40–45; for a discussion of point of view as affected by Pauline, see Victoria Walker, "A Note on Perspective in *Tracks*," *Studies in American Indian Literatures* 3 (Winter 1991): 37–40.

62. Erdrich, *Tracks*, 39.

63. On Erdrich's reader, see also Barbara L. Pittman, "Cross-Cultural Reading and Generic Transformation: The Chronotope of the Road in Erdrich's *Love Medicine*," *American Literature* 67 (December 1995): 777–92.

64. Several of Erdrich's characters remark that drowning is a death no Chippewa can survive. Their belief is that the drowned victim cannot begin the afterlife journey to the Land of Souls. On Chippewa beliefs about death, see Basil Johnston, *Ojibway Ceremonies* (Lincoln: University of Nebraska Press, 1982). Other discussions of Native traditions informing Erdrich include J. A. Clark, "Why Bears Are Good"; Susan Stanford Friedman, "Identity Politics, Syncretism, Catholicism and Anishinabe Religion in Louise Erdrich's *Tracks*," *Religion and Literature* 26 (March 1994): 107–33; Hessler, "Catholic Nuns"; Jennifer Sergi, "Storytelling: Tradition and Preservation in Louise Erdrich's *Tracks*," *World Literature Today* 66 (May 1992): 279–82; and Annette Van Dyke, "Questions of the Spirit: Bloodlines in Louise Erdrich's Chippewa Landscape," *Studies in American Indian Literatures* 4 (Spring 1992): 15–27.

65. Erdrich, *Tracks*, 7.

66. On Nanapush as Erdrich's authorial voice, see Sharon Manybeads Bowers, "Louise Erdrich as Nanapush," in *New Perspectives on Women and Comedy*, ed. Regina Barreca (Philadelphia: Gordon and Breach, 1995), 135–41.

67. Erdrich, *Tracks*, 39.

68. Erving Goffman, *Frame Analysis: An Essay on the Organization of Experience* (Cambridge, Mass.: Harvard University Press, 1974), 364–68; Wiget, "Telling the Tale," 312.

69. On the cultural and symbolic status of the half-blood figure, see William J. Scheick, *The Half-Blood: A Cultural Symbol in 19th-Century American Fiction* (Lexington: University Press of Kentucky, 1979).

70. Concerning Erdrich's dialogue on colonialism, see also Gloria Bird, "Searching for Evidence of Colonialism at Work: A Reading of Louise Erdrich's *Tracks*," *Wicazo Sa Review* 8 (Fall 1992): 40–47.

71. Erdrich, *Tracks*, 185.

72. Wiget in "Telling the Tale" explains this kinesic dimension of oral performance. See also remarks throughout Boelhower's *Through a Glass* on the kinesic role of signs in literature, both oral and written.

73. See Jahner's remarks in "Metalanguages," 163, and in "Indian Literature" on narrator authority and responsibility in oral literature and in written texts by Native American writers (especially N. Scott Momaday) that derive from oral literature.

74. Erdrich, *Tracks*, 34.

75. Ibid., 7.

76. Erdrich, *The Bingo Palace*, 145.

77. Royal B. Hassrick, *The Sioux: Life and Customs of a Warrior Society* (Norman: University of Oklahoma Press, 1964), 96.

78. On the relative openness of postmodern forms to nonwestern material, see Allen, *The Sacred Hoop*; Bill Ashcroft, Gareth Griffiths and Helen Tiffin, *The Empire Writes Back* (London: Routledge, 1989); Krupat, *Ethnocriticism* and "Post-Structuralism and Oral Literature"; Trinh T. Minh-ha, "Not You/Like You: Post-Colonial Women and the Interlocking Questions of Identity and Difference," in *Making Face/Making Soul/Haciendo Caras: Creative and Critical Perspectives by Women of Color*, ed. Gloria Anzaldúa (San Francisco: Aunt Lute Foundation, 1990), 371–75; and Gerald Vizenor, "A Postmodern Introduction" and "Trickster Discourse."

79. On creating the listener, see Momaday in "The Man Made of Words," in *Indian Voices: The First Convocation of American Indian Scholars* (San Francisco: Indian Historian Press, 1970), 49–62; and Momaday's comments to Charles L. Woodard in *Ancestral Voice*, 113.

80. Barthes, *The Semiotic Challenge*, 147.

81. For cogent analyses of Native versus non-Native audience issues, see Inés Hernández-Ávila, "Mediations of the Spirit: Native American Religious Traditions and the Ethics of Representation," *American Indian Quarterly* 20 (Summer/Fall 1996): 329–52; and "Relocations upon Relocations: Home, Language, and Native American Women's Writings," *American Indian Quarterly* 19 (Fall 1995): 491–507.

82. Native audiences assume moral and ethical responsibilities, while mainstream, postmodern audiences assume a more exclusively intellectual range of responsibilities for knowing literary conventions, etc.

83. Hodge and Kress, *Social Semiotics*, 249.

84. King, *Green Grass*, 109.

85. Hodge and Kress, *Social Semiotics*, 6.

Chapter Two: Imagining the Stories: Narrativity and Solidarity

1. Gerald Vizenor, *Landfill Meditation*, 4.

2. See Momaday in "The Man Made of Words"; and Momaday's comments to Charles L. Woodard in *Ancestral Voice*, 113.

3. Robert Hodge and Gunther Kress, *Social Semiotics*, 111.

4. For two different critical angles on this argument, see Jon Hauss, "Real Stories: Memory, Violence, and Enjoyment in Gerald Vizenor's *Bear-*

heart," *Literature and Psychology* 41 (Winter 1995): 1-16; and Chris LaLonde, "The Ceded Landscape of Gerald Vizenor's Fiction," *Studies in American Indian Literatures* 9 (Spring 1997): 16-32.

5. Hodge and Kress, *Social Semiotics*, 39.

6. On this subject of deliberate efforts at social reform on the part of Indian authors, critical attention has focused primarily on Vizenor. For a Foucauldian analysis of Vizenor's management of discursive power to effect social change, see Juana María Rodríguez, "Gerald Vizenor's Shadow Plays: Narrative Mediations and Multiplicities of Power," *Studies in American Indian Literatures* 5 (Fall 1993): 23-30. For analyses of Vizenor's nonfiction narrative strategies of political advocacy, see also Irene Gonzales, "Textual Stimulation: Gerald Vizenor's Use of Law in Advocacy Literature," *Studies in American Indian Literatures* 5 (Fall 1993): 31-42; and Winona Stevenson, "Suppressive Narrator and Multiple Narratees in Gerald Vizenor's 'Thomas White Hawk,'" *Studies in American Indian Literatures* 5 (Fall 1993): 36-42. And on Vizenor's postmodernist, deconstructive strategies, see Barry Laga, who perceives in Vizenor a muted idealism about the possibilities of social reform: "Gerald Vizenor and His *Heirs of Columbus*," *American Indian Quarterly* 18 (Winter 1994): 71-86.

7. On ritual and ceremony in *Ceremony*, see also Carol Mitchell, "*Ceremony* as Ritual"; Robert C. Bell, "Circular Design"; St. Andrews, "Healing the Witchery"; and Swan, "Healing Via the Sunrise Cycle"; and "Laguna Symbolic Geography."

8. On Navajo and Pueblo medicine and ceremony, see Carl A. Hammerschlag, *The Dancing Healers: A Doctor's Journey of Healing with Native Americans* (San Francisco: Harper and Row, 1988); Stephen J. Kunitz, *Disease, Change, and the Role of Medicine: The Navajo Experience* (Berkeley: University of California Press, 1983); and Gladys A. Reichard, *Navaho Religion: A Study of Symbolism* (Princeton, N.J.: Princeton University Press, 1950). On the symbolic meanings of directions and colors, etc., informing Silko's novel, see Swan, "Healing," and "Laguna"; Valerie Harvey, "Navajo Sandpainting"; and Kathleen Manley, "Leslie Marmon Silko's Use of Color in *Ceremony*," *Southern Folklore* 46, 2 (1989): 133-46.

9. Silko, *Ceremony*, 234.

10. The average or implied "reader" I discuss may or may not be literally Euro-American. As reader-response theorists have demonstrated repeatedly, there are many actual readers, but the hypothetical reader is always a theoretical construct, to some extent. Unless I specify otherwise, the assumed "reader" to whom I refer is someone who has, in general, internalized the dominant culture's conventional strategies of reading and producing meaning from novels, no matter what his or her ethnic identity might be. I believe Silko's text is directed primarily toward such a reader, who may most benefit from acquiring some non-Eurocentric perspectives.

11. See Umberto Eco on how readers draw inferences from fictional texts: *The Role of the Reader: Explorations in the Semiotics of Texts* (Bloomington: Indiana University Press, 1979), especially 20-22.

12. On feminist values in Silko's *Ceremony*, see Helen Jaskoski, "Thinking Woman's Children and the Bomb," in *The Nightmare Considered: Critical*

Essays on Nuclear War Literature, ed. Nancy Anisfield (Bowling Green, Oh.: Bowling Green State University Popular Press, 1991), 159–76.

13. Louise Erdrich, *Love Medicine* (Toronto: Bantam, 1984), 73.

14. Ibid., 94.

15. Turner, *The Anthropology,* 103.

16. Momaday, *House Made of Dawn,* 210.

17. Riffaterre, *Fictional,* 4.

18. On metacritical devices in Native American literature, see also Hobbs, "Living In-Between"; and Elaine Jahner, "Metalanguages."

19. Thomas King, *Green Grass,* 293.

20. Riffaterre, *Fictional,* 5.

21. Hodge and Kress, *Social Semiotics,* 109.

22. Early critical responses to *House* by non-Native critics sometimes overemphasize the contextual relevance of Greek myth and canonical modernist literature. See for example Lincoln in *Native American Renaissance* and Schubnell in *N. Scott Momaday.* Though Momaday's novel does, indeed, invite such responses, the overall pertinence of myth and modernism is profoundly shaped by the overriding "Indian" content and ethos. The "outsider" reader is, consequently, potentially ill-equipped to participate.

23. Arnold Krupat discusses this passage in "Post-Structuralism and Oral Literature," in Swann and Krupat, *Recovering the Word,* 113–28. He argues that the concern with clear, fixed, and stable meanings of signifiers is not a part of oral tradition, but has arisen since Native Americans have shifted to written literature. Oral storytellers, he claims, basically assumed that such meanings were "at least possible" (117). The need to insist or to argue the point, says Krupat, arises when storytellers shift to a western form during the post-structuralist era. Krupat's claim supports my general argument, along similar lines, that contemporary Native American writers are beginning to claim new textual "territory" and thus to transform the novel as well as many of their traditional ways of telling stories.

24. Silko, *Ceremony,* 132–33.

25. Sebeok, *American Signatures,* 128.

26. On Hogan's agenda of social reform and healing in *Mean Spirit,* see Anna Carew-Miller, "Caretaking and the Work of the Text in Linda Hogan's *Mean Spirit,*" *Studies in American Indian Literatures* 6 (Fall 1994): 37–48.

27. Linda Hogan, *Mean Spirit,* 138.

28. Hodge and Kress, *Social Semiotics,* 42.

29. Walters, *Ghost Singer,* 199.

30. On *Ghost Singer* as historical mystery, see Melissa J. Fiesta, "Solving Mysteries of Culture and Self: Anita and Naspah in Anna Lee Walters's *Ghost Singer,*" *American Indian Quarterly* 17 (Summer 1993): 370–78.

31. Walters, *Ghost Singer,* 173.

32. Eco, *The Role of the Reader,* 67.

33. Boris Eichenbaum, "The Theory of the Formal Method," in *Russian Formalist Criticism: Four Essays,* ed. and trans. Lee T. Lemon and Marion Reis (Lincoln: University of Nebraska Press, 1965), 99–139.

34. Eco, *The Role of the Reader,* 87.

35. I have described many of the obstacles encountered by the non-

Native reader. The Native reader, however (perhaps with the exception of academically-inclined Native readers such as those who write novels), will likely encounter some of the same obstacles, particularly those arising from tribal differences. The fact that the written text is a non-Native form might also present difficulties for some Native readers. My point is, of course, that culturally cross-coded texts present challenges of various types to all readers.

36. Silko, *Ceremony*, 246.

37. In Coltelli, *Winged Words*, 161.

38. See Louis Owens' review of this novel's publication history and reception in " 'Ecstatic Strategies': Gerald Vizenor's *Darkness in St. Louis Bearheart*," in *Narrative Chance*, 141–53; and "Introduction," *Studies in American Indian Literatures* 9 (Spring 1997): 1–2.

39. See, for instance, Nora Barry, "Chance and Ritual: The Gambler in the Texts of Gerald Vizenor," *Studies in American Indian Literatures* 5 (Fall 1993): 13–22.

40. Gerald Vizenor, *Bearheart: The Heirship Chronicles* (Minneapolis: University of Minnesota Press, 1990), 130.

41. Hauss, "Real Stories," 11, 12.

42. We might perhaps see Vizenor's resistance here in the same way that Barry Laga understands it to exist in another Vizenor work, *The Heirs of Columbus*: "the very presence" of the book constitutes " 'discourse' where we once had silence"—see Laga, "Gerald Vizenor," 84. The implications of deconstructive acts must always remain problematic, and perhaps we must always see Vizenor's "destructive" project in terms of the "larger story" of reconstructive contemporary Native American literature. On Vizenor and compassion, see also Ruoff, "Gerald Vizenor."

43. Woodard, *Ancestral Voice*, 165.

44. Coltelli, *Winged Words*, 162.

45. Eco, *The Role of the Reader*, 87.

46. King, *Green Grass*, 293.

47. As noted in E. H. Gombrich, *Art and Illusion: A Study in the Psychology of Pictorial Representation* (Princeton, N.J.: Princeton University Press, 1960), 5.

48. On water imagery in Erdrich, see also Marianne Barnett, "Dreamstuff: Erdrich's *Love Medicine*," *North Dakota Quarterly* 56 (Winter 1988): 82–96.

49. Erdrich, *Tracks*, 92.

50. Ibid., 23.

Chapter Three: Re-Signing the Self: Models of Identity and Community

1. Paula Gunn Allen, *The Woman Who Owned the Shadows* (San Francisco: Spinsters/Aunt Lute, 1983), 4.

2. On identity formation and transformation in Native American literature, see also Allen, "A Stranger in My Own Life: Alienation in American Indian Prose and Poetry," *MELUS* 7 (Summer 1980): 3–19; Peggy V. Beck,

Anna Lee Walters, and Nia Francisco, *The Sacred: Ways of Knowledge, Sources of Life* (Tsaile, Ariz.: Navajo Community College Press, 1992); and Jana Sequoya-Magdaleno, "Telling the *Differance*: Representations of Identity in the Discourse of Indianness," in *The Ethnic Canon: Histories, Institutions, and Interventions,* ed. David Palumbo-Liu (Minneapolis: University of Minnesota Press, 1995), 88–116.

3. On identity and motion in Welch, see John Purdy, " 'He Was Going Along': Motion in the Novels of James Welch," *American Indian Quarterly* 14 (Spring 1990): 133–45. On motion and King's *Green Grass,* see William J. Scheick, "Grace and Gall," *Canadian Literature* 138 (Autumn 1993): 155–56. Types of stillness are also valued and attributed to "Indians" by some Native writers, as I will remark in Chapter Four. It is important to note the difference between this contemplative, focused quietude as opposed to "rigidity."

4. King, *Green Grass,* 159.

5. Silko, *Ceremony,* 126.

6. Andrew Wiget, "*American Indian Literature: An Anthology,*" *Studies in American Indian Literatures* 4 (Summer/Fall 1992): 216.

7. A post-structuralist (Derridean) term not to be confused with "structure." While "structure" refers to form, "structuration" refers to an unavoidable phenomenon concerning the way in which unperceived structures shape our creative enterprises as well as our critical investigations and interpretive responses to perceived structures and contents. Thus, our efforts to detail what is "western" and what is "nonwestern" are to some extent limited by our preconditioned ways of thinking. Though there is no absolute escape from such a hermeneutical dilemma, awareness of the predicament lends insight to our investigations.

8. Hartmut Lutz, *Contemporary Challenges: Conversations with Canadian Native Authors* (Saskatoon: Fifth House, 1991), 40.

9. Coltelli, *Winged Words,* 161.

10. However, as DeKoven's study of modernism and Boelhower's study of ethnosemiosis advantageously remind us, the most thoroughly Anglo-European (and Anglo-American) canonical texts are neither intrinsically nor intertextually homogeneous in their inscription or endorsement of Western norms, points of view, or values. See Marianne DeKoven, *Rich and Strange: Gender, History, Modernism* (Princeton, N.J.: Princeton University Press, 1991), and Boelhower, *Through a Glass.*

11. Robert Hodge and Gunther Kress, *Social Semiotics,* 123.

12. See Christopher Norris's *Derrida* (Cambridge, Mass.: Harvard University Press, 1987), and *What's Wrong with Postmodernism: Critical Theory and the Ends of Philosophy* (Baltimore: Johns Hopkins University Press, 1990).

13. For a variety of Indian people's discussions of both favorable and unfavorable aspects of Pan-Indian identity that results from generalizations about Native Americans, see Beck, *The Sacred,* and Coltelli, *Winged Words.*

14. Coltelli, *Winged Words,* 172. Vizenor's argument with anthropologists might not include Victor Turner, whose interests, like Vizenor's, lie in the semiotic self-transformation of cultures.

15. Momaday, *House Made of Dawn,* 92–94. See also Beck—*The Sacred,*

8–who explains that in contrast to western propensities to discuss and analyze thought, Native American traditions frequently involve prohibitions
on discussion, especially discussions of the sacred.
16. Tosamah is a priest of the sun in the Native American Church. Perhaps owing to the Euro-American and Christian influences, he talks a
great deal himself.
17. Momaday, *House*, 93.
18. Walters, *Ghost Singer*, 185.
19. Erdrich, *Tracks*, 39.
20. Western concepts of "individuality" that are associated with the rise
and development of the novel and that fundamentally contrast with some
Native American notions of self are a product of western philosophical
discourse dating from the Renaissance and the eighteenth century. Contemporary western notions of personal identity originate primarily with
Locke, Hume, Berkeley, and other Enlightenment philosophers. Their
successors in philosophy, theology, psychology, and even biology continue
to ponder equations of personal identity with body, mind, and spirit; they
argue over whether the self is a unified essence, a dualism, a recorder of
random impressions, or (after structuralism) a product of semiosis. For
discussions of self (including the ethnic self) that have influenced the
present study, see Vévé Clark, "Developing Diaspora Literacy"; Martin,
Recent Theories, especially pages 76–78; Kaja Silverman, *The Subject of Semiotics* (New York: Oxford University Press, 1983); Arnold Weinstein, *Fictions
of the Self, 1550–1800* (Princeton, N.J.: Princeton University Press, 1981);
White, *The Content of the Form*; and Launcelot Whyte, *The Unconscious Before Freud* (New York: Basic Books, 1960). Michel Foucault in *The Order of
Things: An Archaeology of the Human Sciences* (New York: Pantheon, 1971) argues that the construction of self and Other is inextricably linked with the
construction of culture through signifying practices.
21. Tribal peoples cannot be described as "foundationalists" or "essen-
tialists" in the western tradition; however, most of the authors (with the
exception of Vizenor) adhere to undeniable claims of truth. Hence, almost
none of them "qualify" as postmodernists.
22. Sebeok's work in zoosemiotics is extensive. He believes that in the
future, the field of zoosemiotics will expose historically proclaimed boundaries between humans and other animals, and even between animal and
non-animal, as erroneous. See *American Signatures*, 160. He believes that
discovery of the true differences between human and nonhuman animals hinges upon a thorough, even neurobiological understanding of sign
action. Nonhuman animals, he argues, have consciousness but no "self,"
and they display sign action but not "language," whereas human beings
have both consciousness and "self" and display both sign action and language. Sebeok's studies are devoted to investigations of such significant
differences, for not until we know more in these areas are we able to speak
confidently about what constitutes a "self."
23. This theory would seem to imply that a person blind from birth
would have no self. Indeed, herein lies a blind spot, so to speak, in Sebeok's
thinking. A remedy might lie in the work of Oliver Sacks, whose studies of

modes of perception and communication in blind and deaf people suggest that spatial icons exist in forms we do not generally anticipate. Sacks finds that the world of the blind is constructed of non-visual icons formulated through alternative senses. Sacks also explains the sophisticated spatial features of American Sign Language. See his *An Anthropologist on Mars: Seven Paradoxical Tales* (New York: Knopf, 1995) and *Seeing Voices: A Journey into the World of the Deaf* (Berkeley: University of California Press, 1989).

24. Thomas A. Sebeok, "The Semiotic Self Revisited," in *Sign, Self, and Society*, ed. Benjamin Lee and Greg Urban (Berlin: Mouton de Gruyter, 1989), xi.

25. Sebeok, *American Signatures*, 13. On the "umwelt" and Sebeok's debt to Jakob von Uexküll in formulating his notions of the semiotic self, see also his "The Semiotic Self," and *The Sign and Its Masters*, 2nd ed. (Lanham, Md.: University Press of America, 1989).

26. Sebeok, *American Signatures*, 101–2.

27. Silverman, *The Subject*, 126.

28. Neurophysiologist Walter J. Freeman argues controversially against materialist and cognitive theories to support a concept of mind and self similar to Sebeok's. Freeman contends that "mind" is the accretive result of purposive behavior and the consequences of said behavior. Perceptions and future actions are predicated upon what is learned from interactions between mind and society. We know ourselves as a result of interactions with the world, including but not limited to sign actions. See *Societies of Brains* (Hillsdale, N.J.: Laurence Erlbaum, 1995).

29. Sebeok, *American Signatures*, 102.

30. See also Beck, *The Sacred*, chapters 5, 8, and 9, on the subject of the formation of Indian identity in connection with ritualistic elements of social interaction.

31. On the subject of Abel's misbehavior, see Scarberry-García, *Landmarks*, 45.

32. For more on the "double woman" figure in Native American culture, see Janet Catherine Berlo, "Dreaming of Double Woman: The Ambivalent Role of the Female Artist in North American Indian Myth," *American Indian Quarterly* 17 (Winter 1993): 31–43. Likewise informative on the role of the homosexual male in Southwestern Native cultures is Will Roscoe in *The Zuni Man-Woman* (Albuquerque: University of New Mexico Press, 1991).

33. Momaday, *House*, 170.

34. Scarberry-García, *Landmarks*, 12.

35. Charles L. Woodard, *Ancestral Voice*, 55.

36. For more on land, identity, and aesthetics, see also Paula Gunn Allen, "The Psychological Landscape of *Ceremony*," *American Indian Quarterly* 5 (Winter 1979): 7–12; *The Sacred Hoop*; Richard F. Fleck, "Sacred Land in the Writings of Momaday, Welch and Silko," in Schirer's *Contemporary Native American Cultural Issues*, 125–33; Reyes García, "Senses of Place in *Ceremony*," *MELUS* 10 (Winter 1983): 37–48; Nelson, *Place and Vision*; and "Snake and Eagle"; Rock Point Community School, *Between Sacred Mountains: Navajo Stories and Lessons from the Land*, ed. Sam and Janet Bingham

(Tucson: Sun Tracks and University of Arizona Press, 1982); and Frederick Turner, *Spirit of Place: The Making of an American Literary Landscape* (San Francisco: Sierra Club, 1989).

37. On Kiowas and Kiowa traditions, especially the pictorial calendar tradition so important to Momaday, see Mildred P. Mayhall, *The Kiowas* (Norman: University of Oklahoma Press, 1971), and James Mooney, *Calendar History of the Kiowa Indians* (Washington, D.C.: Smithsonian Institution Press, 1979). Momaday's traditional Indian knowledge, however, is quite eclectic and not limited to Kiowa material. Plains traditions as well as Southwestern Pueblo lore inform his works. See also Matthias Schubnell, who discusses the influence on *The Ancient Child* of German expressionist artist, Emil Nolde, in "Locke Setman, Emil Nolde." Schubnell sees Nolde as a kind of prototype for Momaday's main character, Set. On the role of petroglyphs in *The Ancient Child*, see also Roemer, "Ancient Children."

38. On the visual orientation of Native American cultures see also Lee Irwin, "Dreams, Theory, and Culture: The Plains Vision Quest Paradigm," *American Indian Quarterly* 18 (Spring 1994): 229–45.

39. For a discussion of Kiowa animal and other types of icons, see Mayhall, *The Kiowas*; Mooney, *Calendar History*; A. Irving Hollowell, "Bear Ceremonialism in the Northern Hemisphere," *American Anthropologist* 28 (March 1926): 1–175; and Hamilton A. Tyler, *Pueblo Animals and Myths* (Norman: University of Oklahoma Press, 1975). More generally, a fascinating body of literature exists on animals as iconic shapers of human mind and identity. See for example John Berger, "Why Look at Animals?" in *About Looking* (New York: Pantheon, 1980), 1–26; Shepard, *Thinking Animals*; and Paul Shepard and Barry Sanders, *The Sacred Paw: The Bear in Nature, Myth, and Literature* (New York: Viking, 1985). On animals in Erdrich, see Joni Adamson Clark, "Why Bears Are Good." On animals in Silko, see Susan Blumenthal, "Spotted Cattle and Deer: Spirit Guides and Symbols of Endurance and Healing in *Ceremony*," *American Indian Quarterly* 14 (Fall 1990): 367–77.

40. Momaday's theory of a collective "racial memory" resembles Jung's. However, Momaday calls this "racial memory" a "genetic" phenomenon in his interview with Woodard in *Ancestral Voice*, 20. On the subject of Native American art and memory, see also Scarberry, "Memory as Medicine."

41. Woodard, *Ancestral Voice*, 170.

42. Douglas Cardinal and Jeanette Armstrong, *The Native Creative Process* (Penticton, British Columbia: Theytus, 1991), 58.

43. See Allen, *The Sacred Hoop*; Blumenthal, "Spotted Cattle"; Carol Mitchell, "*Ceremony* as Ritual"; St. Andrews, "Healing the Witchery"; and Edith Swan, "Healing" and "Laguna."

44. Woodard, *Ancestral Voice*, 200–201.

45. Obviously, there are important differences in this regard between ceremonial and non-ceremonial art, as Paula Gunn Allen explains in *The Sacred Hoop*, 72–75.

46. Woodard, *Ancestral Voice*, 206.

47. N. Scott Momaday refers to the "one story" in *The Ancient Child* (216),

and in his interview with Louis Owens—"N. Scott Momaday," in *This Is About Vision: Interviews with Southwestern Writers*, ed. William Balassi (Albuquerque: University of New Mexico Press, 1989), 141–53.

48. On singers and healers and ceremonial design, see Beck, *The Sacred*, especially chapter 3; and Reichard, *Navaho Religion*.

49. Momaday, *House*, 43.

50. Momaday, *The Ancient Child*, 134.

51. See "Squaw Dance," "Shaman," "Anthracite," and the self-portraits in Woodard, *Ancestral Voice*, 122, 87, 65, 19, 184.

52. Ibid., 173.

53. On diegetic order and the reader's impulse, see also Scholes, *Semiotics and Interpretation*, 75–76.

54. Scarberry-García in *Landmarks* identifies and explains the traditional sources of Momaday's stories and images in *House Made of Dawn*. She also explains important interconnections among the various parts of the text that are drawn from these sources. See also Hogan, "Who Puts Together."

55. Momaday insists throughout his works on the importance of having an overall, specific "idea" of oneself. See for instance *The Ancient Child* (52), his essay "The Man Made of Words," and his remarks throughout Woodard's *Ancestral Voice*.

56. Momaday, *House*, 96, 119, 212.

57. See Reichard, *Navajo* on flood and emergence.

58. Woodard, *Ancestral Voice*, 163, 165.

59. This "universalist" claim situates Momaday among the Panofskyans in their argument that iconological themes fall into only a few categories found throughout history and cultures. See Giulio Carlo Argan, "Ideology and Iconology," in *The Language of Images*, ed. W. J. T. Mitchell (Chicago: University of Chicago Press, 1980), 15–23; and Erwin Panofsky, *Meaning in the Visual Arts: Papers in and on Art History* (Garden City, N.Y.: Doubleday Anchor, 1955).

60. Woodard, *Ancestral Voice*, 13.

61. Momaday, *Ancient Child*, 132. Leslie Silko also sees writing and drawing as equivalents, as she explains in *Yellow Woman and a Beauty of the Spirit: Essays on Native American Life Today* (New York: Touchstone, 1996), 167.

62. Woodard, *Ancestral Voice*, 152.

63. Ibid., 19.

64. Ibid., 184.

65. On the subject of Navajo and Pueblo cosmological patterns established by the Holy People, see Beck, *The Sacred*.

66. Woodard, *Ancestral*, 13, 15.

67. In his essay, "The Man Made of Words," Momaday claims that "an Indian is an idea which a given man has of himself" (49). He could easily substitute the word "image" for "idea." On the iconic meanings of "bear" (and Set-Angya, Tsoai-talee, etc.) that Momaday appropriates from Kiowa and other Indian cultures, see Mooney, *Calendar History*. Momaday comments on the Kiowa history of Devil's Tower in Bettye Givens' "A *MELUS* Interview: N. Scott Momaday—A Slant of Light," *MELUS* 12 (Spring 1985): 79–87. On Momaday's use of the bear in his works, see also Scarberry-

García, *Landmarks*, and Barry, "The Bear's Son." Shepard and Sanders, *The Sacred Paw*, are also enlightening on the subject of bear myths in literature.

68. On Erdrich and identity, see also Claire Crabtree, "Salvific Oneness and the Fragmented Self in Louise Erdrich's *Love Medicine*," in Schirer's *Contemporary Native American Cultural Issues*, 49–56; Jeanne Smith, "Transpersonal Selfhood: The Boundaries of Identity in Louise Erdrich's *Love Medicine*," *Studies in American Indian Literatures* 3 (Winter 1991): 13–26; Jeanne Rosier Smith, *Writing Tricksters: Mythic Gambols in American Ethnic Literature* (Berkeley: University of California Press, 1997), 71–110; and Van Dyke, "Questions of the Spirit."

69. *Social Semiotics*, 123, 264.

70. Ibid., 122.

71. Coltelli, *Winged Words*, 147.

72. Silko, *Ceremony*, 226.

73. Erdrich, *Tracks*, 7.

74. On semiotic codes, see Barthes, *The Semiotic Challenge*; and Silverman, *The Subject of Semiotics*.

75. In an earlier article on Erdrich I use the word "shamanic," knowing of course that this is an Asian term which is nevertheless applied generally to Native American "medicine" practices. Each tribe has its own name for "medicine" person, but there is no satisfactory pan-tribal term other than "medicine" as used here.

76. Beck, *The Sacred*, 6.

77. Silko, *Ceremony*, 125.

78. Beck, *The Sacred*, 11.

79. Momaday, *House*, 149.

80. For remarks about Allen's own identity formation, see her essay, "A Stranger."

81. See also Renae Bredin, "'Becoming Minor': Reading *The Woman Who Owned the Shadows*," *Studies in American Indian Literatures* 6 (Winter 1994): 36–50; and Vanessa Holford, "Re-Membering Ephanie: A Woman's Re-Creation of Self in Paula Gunn Allen's *The Woman Who Owned the Shadows*," *Studies in American Indian Literatures* 6 (Spring 1994): 99–113.

82. Allen, *Woman*, 32.

83. The novel opens—"Shinasha Shinasha / Shinasha La de ho zho la / He ye He ne ya / A ly A ly Ko ny sha / A ly A ly Ko ny sha" (I am Walking, Alive / Where I am is beautiful / I am still alive, / Walking, lonely)—what the Navajo sang upon returning home. However, Ephanie's version of the song suggests that her future might be brighter than their collective one was upon returning home.

84. Silko, *Ceremony*, 126.

85. Allen, *Woman*, 189.

86. See Allen *The Sacred Hoop*, 21–22, for a discussion of the ritual meaning of war. She explains that both defeat and victory can bring the sacred knowledge that one primarily seeks in "war." On self and identity in Welch, see also Louise K. Barnett, "Alienation and Ritual in *Winter in the Blood*," *American Indian Quarterly* 4 (Fall 1978): 123–30; Jack L. Davis, "Restoration of Indian Identity in *Winter in the Blood*," in *James Welch*, ed. Ron

McFarland (Lewiston, New York: Confluence 1986), 29–43; Patricia Riley In-The-Woods, "*The Death of Jim Loney*: A Ritual of Re-Creation," *Fiction International* 20 (Fall 1991): 157–66; and Kathleen Mullen Sands, "Alienation and Broken Narrative in *Winter in the Blood*," *American Indian Quarterly* 4 (Spring 1978): 97–105; "Closing the Distance: Critic, Reader and the Works of James Welch," *MELUS* 14 (Summer 1987): 73–85; "The Death of Jim Loney: Indian or Not?" *Studies in American Indian Literatures* 7 (Spring 1980): 61–78.

87. James Welch, *The Death of Jim Loney* (New York: Penguin, 1979), 21.
88. On alienation and healing in Welch, see L. K. Barnett, "Alienation"; Davis, "Restoration"; Riley In-The-Woods, "*Death*"; and Sands, "Alienation" and "Closing."
89. "Dialog with James Welch," *Northwest Review* 20 (Summer/Fall 1982): 163–85. Other discussions of the ending of this novel include Allen, *The Sacred Hoop*, 90–95; Ron McFarland, "'The End' in James Welch's Novels," *American Indian Quarterly* 17 (Summer 1993): 319–28; Owens, *Other Destinies*, 147–56; John Purdy, "*Bha'a* and The Death of Jim Loney," *Studies in American Indian Literatures* 5 (Summer 1993): 67–71; and Sands, "The Death."
90. Welch, *Death*, 167.
91. On the "dark bird," see also Dexter Westrum, "Transcendental Survival: The Way the Bird Works in *The Death of Jim Loney*," in McFarland's *James Welch*, 139–46.
92. See Riley In-The-Woods, "*Death*."
93. Silko, *Ceremony*, 126.
94. Sebeok, *American Signatures*, 102.
95. Hodge and Kress, *Social Semiotics*, 122.

Chapter Four: They All Sang as One: Refiguring Space-Time

1. Walters, *Ghost Singer*, 120.
2. Boelhower, *Through a Glass*, 119.
3. See also Hernández-Ávila's discussion of Native American women writers' efforts to be "at home" in language—"Relocations upon Relocations," and William Bevis's analysis of the "homing" motif in Native American fiction, "Native American Novels: Homing In," in Swann and Krupat, *Recovering the Word*, 580–620.
4. On temporal structures in Welch, see also Roberta Orlandini, "Variations on a Theme: Tradition and Temporal Structure in the Novels of James Welch," *South Dakota Review* 26 (Fall 1988): 37–52.
5. Woodard, *Ancestral Voice*, 55.
6. Welch, *Winter*, 65.
7. On communion and reintegration in this novel, see also Betty Tardieu, "Communion in James Welch's *Winter in the Blood*," *Studies in American Indian Literatures* 5 (Winter 1993): 69–80.
8. Welch, *Death*, 49.
9. Hogan, *Mean Spirit*, 138.

10. Elizabeth Blair discusses the ending of the novel in the context of Hogan's feelings about Native Americans' loss of land and "home." See "The Politics of Place in Linda Hogan's *Mean Spirit.*" *Studies in American Indian Literatures* 6 (Fall 1994): 15–21.

11. Rabinowitz, in *Before Reading*, discusses the function of chapter titles in guiding the reader's response under "rules of significance" in his study of reader-expectations and reader-response.

12. As Paula Gunn Allen points out in *The Sacred Hoop*, 54–75, for Native American writers drawing on oral conventions, the so-called "traditional" linear novel form is "experimental"; the Eurocentric concept of "experimental" (or modernist and postmodernist) fiction is more "traditional" for these writers.

13. I rely here on Robert Scholes's conception (*Semiotics of Interpretation*, 60, 62) of the ways in which "events" and "narration," or "story" and "discourse," become separate parts of a text. "Narration" refers to how a story is told and includes an excess of information difficult to include in any simple time sequence. (Hence, writers use flashback, asides, etc.) "Story" refers to sequenced plot elements.

14. See my "Reading Between Worlds: Narrativity in the Fiction of Louise Erdrich," *American Literature* 62 (September 1990): 405–22.

15. See Allen, *The Sacred Hoop*, 94, 233, 238, 240, on ceremonial time.

16. On Erdrich, water, and fishing, see also M. Barnett, "Dreamstuff."

17. Silko, *Ceremony*, 69.

18. Eco's argument in *Travels in Hyperreality: Essays*, trans. William Weaver (San Diego, Calif.: Harcourt, Brace, Jovanovich, 1986), is built around this concept.

19. Silko, *Ceremony*, 154.

20. Eco in *Travels* and Baudrillard both use the term "hyperreality" to refer to particular traits of mass culture. Eco refers to theme parks, museums, zoos, etc., which are copies of original places but which somehow seem to promise a richer experience than the original offers. I use "hyperreality" more in Baudrillard's sense, to refer to the breakdown of distinctions between thing and idea. The advertisement in a consumer culture creates a world of its own—a hyperreality. This hyperreality, in turn, orchestrates consumer desire. The idea associated with the thing, and not the thing itself, is the true object of desire: "The flight from one signifier to another is no more than the surface reality of a *desire*, which is insatiable because it is founded on a lack. And this desire, which can never be satisfied, signifies itself locally in a succession of objects and need." See *Jean Baudrillard: Selected Writings*, ed. Mark Poster (Stanford, Calif.: Stanford University Press, 1988), 45.

21. Silko, *Ceremony*, 55–56.

22. In *Landmarks*, Scarberry-García discusses healing and the Southwestern Indian's relationship to land. Frederick Turner's *Spirit of Place* is also informative on this subject, as are Evers' "Words and Place," and St. Andrews' "Healing the Witchery."

23. This claim might seem to contradict an earlier discussion in Chapter Three about Silko, King, Momaday and others who insist that stasis

and rigidity characterize western forms and that fluidity and motion are Indian values. However, Silko in *Ceremony* defines Indian stillness as focused and purposive (ritualized) and Euro-American motion as random and desperate.

24. On the use of color in *Ceremony*, see Manley, "Leslie Marmon"; on sandpainting, see Beck, *The Sacred*, and Harvey, "Navajo Sandpainting."

25. Hodge and Kress, *Social Semiotics*, 3.

26. Silko, *Ceremony* 116.

27. Hodge and Kress explain how ideological complexes "constrain behaviour by structuring the versions of reality on which social action is based." The on- and off-reservation versions of Native American social reality impose a wide variety of "constraints" upon their social action, as I hope my discussion of Silko's revisionary efforts suggests.

28. Paul Ricoeur, "Life in Quest of Narrative," in *On Paul Ricoeur: Narrative and Interpretation*, ed. David Wood (London: Routledge, 1991), 31.

29. Ibid.

30. Paul Ricoeur, *Time and Narrative*, vol. 2, trans. Kathleen McLaughlin and David Pellauer (Chicago: University of Chicago Press, 1985), 101.

31. Ricoeur in Wood, *On Paul Ricoeur*, 22.

32. Walters, *Ghost Singer*, 176–77.

33. See Ricoeur's discussion of these concepts in Wood, *On Paul Ricoeur*, 27.

34. Ibid., 22.

35. Ibid., 31.

36. Willard Johnson catalogs and elucidates the various prophecies to which contemporary Native writers frequently allude. See "Contemporary Native American Prophecy in Historical Perspective," *Journal of the American Academy of Religion* 64 (September 1996): 575–612.

37. For additional remarks on the museum and conflicting epistemologies, see Erika Aigner-Alvarez, "Artifact and Written History: Freeing the Terminal Indian in Anna Lee Walters's *Ghost Singer*," *Studies in American Indian Literatures* 8 (Spring 1996): 45–59.

38. For another semiotic reading of this novel (on "virtual" and "mythopoeic" worlds), see Susan B. Brill, "When Worlds Collide: Nausea in Virtual and Mythopoeic Worlds," in *Semiotics 1993*, ed. Robert S. Covington and John Deely (New York: Peter Lang, 1995), 77–89.

39. On *Ghost Singer* as mystery, see Fiesta, "Solving Mysteries."

40. Walters, *Ghost Singer*, 177.

41. Ricoeur, *Time and Narrative*, vol. 3, trans. Kathleen Blamey and David Pellauer (Chicago: University of Chicago Press, 1988), 124.

42. Ricoeur in Wood, *On Paul Ricoeur*, 199.

43. Walters, *Ghost Singer*, 211.

44. One prominent exception to the general rule is the Heard Museum in Phoenix, Arizona, where Native people organize and preside over exhibits of tribal artifacts.

45. Ricoeur, *Time and Narrative* 2:106.

46. Ibid., 101, 107.

47. Ricoeur, *Time and Narrative* 3: 101.

48. Walters, *Ghost Singer*, 3.

49. On the nature of Tayo's illness and its relation to his half-blood status, see especially Allen, *The Sacred Hoop*, 138–47.

50. Eric J. Cassell (among a growing number of physicians who are responding to contemporary demands for more humanized medicine) explains the difference between "physiological" and "ontological" theory of disease. The former may be compared to "holistic" medicine with its "ecological" view of persons and maladies; the latter theory, which has held sway in the age of "scientific medicine" in the west, emphasizes the disease-causing "entity" (such as a microbe or a structural malfunction). It focuses therapy on the site of the problem, rather than on the patient as a whole person. See *The Nature of Suffering and the Goals of Medicine* (New York: Oxford University Press, 1991).

51. Silko, *Ceremony*, 31.

52. On healing and storytelling, see G. Frank Lawlis, "Storytelling as Therapy: Implications for Medicine," *Alternative Therapies* 1 (May 1995): 40–45; Mary Gail Nagai-Jacobson and Margaret A. Burkhardt, "Viewing Persons as Stories: A Perspective for Holistic Care," *Alternative Therapies* 2 (July 1996): 54–58; and Virginia M. Soffa, "Artistic Expressions of Illness," *Alternative Therapies* 2 (May 1996): 63–66.

53. James J. Lynch, *The Language of the Heart: The Body's Response to Human Dialogue* (New York: Basic Books, 1995), 317.

54. Arthur Kleinman, *The Illness Narratives: Suffering, Healing, and the Human Condition* (New York: Basic Books, 1988), 6.

55. Ibid., 9.

56. Wood, *On Paul Ricoeur*, 30, 33.

Chapter Five: All the Stories Fit Together: Intertextual Medicine Bundles and Twins

1. Silko, *Ceremony*, 246.

2. Theorists of postcolonialism sometimes distinguish between "recuperative" critical and cultural phenomena, which aim to restore traditional Native cultures, and "syncretic" phenomena, which reinvent. I see "recuperation" as dubious, however. The syncretic energies of cross-cultural art are constantly reinventing peoples and cultures from generation to generation. On issues of "recuperation" and "syncretism," see Ashcroft, Griffiths, and Tiffin, *The Empire*; and on strategies of invention, see Fischer, "Ethnicity," and Sollors, *The Invention*.

3. Riffaterre, *Fictional*, 86.

4. Welch, *Winter*, 68.

5. On memory in *Ceremony*, see also Scarberry-García, *Landmarks*. On Momaday's reading, see Scarberry, "Memory."

6. Joseph Bruchac, *Survival This Way: Interviews with American Indian Poets* (Tucson, Ariz.: Sun Tracks and University of Arizona Press, 1987), 315.

7. Coltelli, *Winged Words*, 81–82.

8. Erdrich mentions the works of several writers who influenced not

only her own writing, but also the sense that she makes of the world. See Coltelli, *Winged Words*, 48–49.

9. On this general subject, see also Donaldson's "Noah" on intertextual aspects of King's fiction.

10. Silverman, *The Subject*, 162.

11. Scholes, *Semiotics*, 31–32.

12. Riffaterre, *Fictional*, 99.

13. Jorge Luis Borges, *Ficciones*, ed. Anthony Kerrigan (New York: Grove Press, 1962), 50; *The Aleph and Other Stories 1933–1969* (New York: E. P. Dutton, 1978), 209, 213.

14. A fascinating "revisionary" example of captivity literature is Erdrich's poem entitled "Captivity," in *Jacklight: Poems* (New York: Henry Holt, 1984) in which the speaker assumes the voice of Mary Rowlandson, but tells Rowlandson's story from a point of view sympathetic to the captors.

15. For more details on tribal "fire" prophecies, see Johnson, "Contemporary."

16. Hogan, *Mean Spirit*, 362.

17. See Phil Lucas, *The Native Americans: The Tribal People of the Northwest*. TBS Productions, Inc (Atlanta: Turner Home Entertainment, 1994), for a good explanation of this pan-tribal concept of "time before time."

18. Riffaterre, *Fictional*, 99.

19. Silko, *Almanac*, 760.

20. Silko does not divide "Destroyers" ethnically. Some Indians are Destroyers and some whites are not.

21. See Chapman, "The Belly," on storytelling and symbolic birth in Native American literature.

22. Silko, *Almanac*, 178.

23. Silko, *Ceremony*, 226.

24. Riffaterre, *Text Production*.

25. On *Love Medicine* and *Moby-Dick*, see also Thomas Matchie, "*Love Medicine*: A Female *Moby-Dick*," *Mississippi Quarterly* 30 (Fall 1989): 478–91. On Welch's references to the grail romance, etc., see Paul Eisenstein, "Finding Lost Generations: Recovering Omitted History in *Winter in the Blood*," *MELUS* 19 (Fall 1994): 3–18; Owens, *Other Destinies*, 132; and Schubnell, *N. Scott Momaday*.

26. Erdrich, *Love Medicine*, 108.

27. Silverman, *The Subject*, 162.

28. On twins in Native American literature and culture, see Locke, *The Navajo*; Washington Matthews, "The Stricken Twins," in *The Night Chant, A Navajo Ceremonial* (New York: American Museum of Natural History 1902, 1978), 212–65; Elsie Clews Parsons, *Pueblo Indian Religion*, 2 vols. (Chicago: University of Chicago Press, 1939); Reichard, *The Navajo Religion*; Scarberry-García, *Landmarks*; Katherine Spencer, *Mythology and Values: An Analysis of Navaho Chantway Myths* (Philadelphia: Memoirs of the American Folklore Society, 1957); and Leland C. Wyman, "Navajo Ceremonial System," in *Handbook of North American Indians: Southwest*, vol. 10, ed. Alfonso Ortiz (Washington, D.C.: Smithsonian Institution Press, 1983), 536–57;

Southwest Indian Drypainting (Albuquerque: University of New Mexico Press, 1983).

29. On twins in Erdrich, see also Kristan Sarvé-Gorham, "Power Lines: The Motif of Twins and the Medicine Women of *Tracks* and *Love Medicine*," *Bucknell Review* 39 (Spring 1995): 167–90.

30. Also noting the apparent and extreme differences in ethos in Silko's two novels is Janet St. Clair, "Uneasy Ethnocentrism: Recent Works of Allen, Silko, and Hogan," *Studies in American Indian Literatures* 6 (Spring 1994): 83–98. In *The Environmental Imagination: Thoreau, Nature Writing, and the Formation of American Culture* (Cambridge, Mass.: Harvard University Press, 1995), 285–296, Lawrence Buell sees *Ceremony* and *Almanac* as, respectively, "utopian" and "dystopian" statements.

31. Riffaterre, *Fictional*, 86.

32. Silko, *Almanac*, 253.

33. See Andrew Horton, "The Bitter Humor of *Winter in the Blood*," *American Indian Quarterly* 4 (Spring 1978): 131–39.

34. See Tardieu, "Communion."

35. On the bird, see also Westrum, "Transcendental."

36. See Owens, *Other Destinies*, 130.

37. Erdrich, *Tracks*, 210.

38. Hodge and Kress, *Social Semiotics*, 40.

39. Robert Hodge, *Literature as Discourse: Textual Strategies in English and History* (Baltimore: Johns Hopkins University Press, 1990), 166.

40. Ibid.

41. See Minh-ha, "Not You/Like You," 373; and Hernández-Ávila, "Relocations."

42. See Norris, *What's Wrong*, 111. See also Rabinowitz, *Before Reading*, 5, on "formalized" and "invisible" systems of power relations in texts.

43. Hodge, *Literature*, 166.

44. *Fictional*, 95–96.

45. Turner, *The Anthropology*; and Philip Wheelwright, *The Burning Fountain: A Study in the Language of Symbolism* (Bloomington: Indiana University Press, 1968), 152.

Epilogue: All We Have Are Stories: Semiosis and Regeneration

1. Silko, *Ceremony*, 2.

2. Silko, *Ceremony*, 246. On Silko and nuclearity, see Jaskoski, "Thinking Woman's Children."

3. Woodard, *Ancestral*, 205.

4. Allen, *Studies*, 15.

5. Silko, *Ceremony*, 2.

6. See Silko's remarks throughout her interview with Coltelli in *Winged Words*, 135–54.

7. *The Sacred*, 8–9.

8. See Allen, *Studies*, 20, 34.

9. Beck, *The Sacred*, 102.
10. See Cardinal and Armstrong, *The Native*, 106,108.
11. Allen, *Studies*, 3.
12. Ibid., 4.
13. See Scott Buchanan, *The Doctrine of Signatures: A Defense of Theory in Medicine*, 2nd ed. Peter P. Maycock, Jr. (Urbana: University of Illinois Press, 1991), 164, 169; Michel Foucault, *Birth of the Clinic: An Archaeology of Medical Perception* (New York: Vintage, 1973); and Henry E. Sigerist, *A History of Medicine, Vol.1, Primitive and Archaic Medicine* (New York: Oxford University Press, 1951), 8-9.
14. Woodard, *Ancestral Voice*, 124-25.
15. Allen, *Studies*, 5-8.
16. See Jerrold E. Levy, "Traditional Navajo Health Beliefs and Practices," in Kunitz, *Disease, Change, and the Role of Medicine*, 118-45, for a discussion of cultural barriers to healing.
17. Woodard, *Ancestral Voice*, 88, 125.
18. Allen (*Studies*, 16) emphasizes the point that non-Native readers must learn to recognize the difference between metaphor and literal references in American Indian literature.
19. See Buchanan, *The Doctrine*; Lawlis, "Storytelling"; and Hammerschlag, *The Dancing Healers*.
20. See Lynch, *The Language*; and Andrew Weil, *Health and Healing* (Boston: Houghton Mifflin, 1988), on inroads of alternative or complementary medicine into conventional practice.
21. Nancy G. Moore, "A Review of Alternative Medicine Courses Taught at U.S. Medical Schools," *Alternative Therapies* 4 (May 1998): 90-101.
22. Physician-novelist Walker Percy expounds on psychotherapist Victor Frankl's notion of "logotherapy" throughout various essays in *The Message in the Bottle: How Queer Man Is, How Queer Language Is, and What One Has To Do with the Other* (New York: Farrar, Straus and Giroux, 1975). See also Victor E. Frankl, *The Doctor and the Soul: From Psychotherapy to Logotherapy* (New York: Knopf, 1955), and *The Will to Meaning: Foundations and Applications of Logotherapy* (New York: Plume, 1969). Lynch, *The Language*, Weil, *Health and Healing*, Hammerschlag, *The Dancing*, Cassell, *The Nature*, Kleinman, *The Illness Narratives*, and other physicians study what is sometimes called the "mind-body" connection in illness and health.
23. Bobette Perrone, H. Henrietta Stockel, and Victoria Krueger, *Medicine Women, "Curanderas," and Women Doctors* (Norman: University of Oklahoma Press, 1989), 199-211.
24. Lynch, *The Language*, 181.
25. Through his writings, Richard Selzer likens the doctor-patient relationship to that of the shamanic healer and subject.
26. *Taking the World in for Repairs* (New York: William Morrow, 1986), 210.
27. Richard Selzer, *Mortal Lessons: Notes on the Art of Surgery* (New York: Touchstone, 1974), 7, 15, 19, 25.
28. Stanley Burnshaw, *The Seamless Web* (New York: Braziller, 1970), 3.
29. Jane Tompkins, *Sensational Designs: The Cultural Work of American Fiction, 1790-1860* (New York: Oxford, 1985), 8.

30. For concise overviews of such contemporary developments, see Larry Dossey, "How Should Alternative Therapies Be Evaluated?" *Alternative Therapies* 1 (May 1995): 6–10, 79–85; "Running Scared: How We Hide from Who We Are," *Alternative Therapies* 3 (March 1997): 8–15; *Space, Time, and Medicine* (Boulder, Colo.: Shambala Press, 1982); "The Trickster: Medicine's Forgotten Character," *Alternative Therapies* 2 (March 1996): 6–14; "What Does Illness Mean?" *Alternative Therapies* 1 (July 1995): 6–10; "What Ever Happened To Healers?" *Alternative Therapies* 1 (November 1995): 6–13; and "When Stones Speak: Toward a Reenchantment of the World." *Alternative Therapies* 2 (July 1996): 8–13, 97–103.

31. Richard Drinnon, *Facing West: The Metaphysics of Indian Hating and Empire Building* (New York: Schocken Books, 1980), xxix.

32. Ashcroft et al., *The Empire*, 33.

Bibliography

Aigner-Alvarez, Erika. "Artifact and Written History: Freeing the Terminal Indian in Anna Lee Walters' *Ghost Singer*." *Studies in American Indian
Literatures* 8 (Spring 1996): 45–59.

Allen, Paula Gunn. "Bringing Home the Fact: Tradition and Continuity in
the Imagination." In *Recovering the Word: Essays on Native American Literature*, ed. Brian Swann and Arnold Krupat, 563–79. Berkeley: University
of California Press, 1987.

———. "The Psychological Landscape of *Ceremony*." *American Indian Quarterly* 5 (Winter 1979): 7–12.

———. *The Sacred Hoop: Recovering the Feminine in American Indian Traditions*. Boston: Beacon, 1986.

———. "A Stranger in My Own Life: Alienation in American Indian Prose
and Poetry." *MELUS* 7 (Summer 1980): 3–19.

———, ed. *Studies in American Indian Literature: Critical Essays and Course
Designs*. New York: Modern Language Association, 1983.

———. *The Woman Who Owned the Shadows*. San Francisco: Spinsters/Aunt
Lute, 1983.

Anisfield, Nancy, ed. *The Nightmare Considered: Critical Essays on Nuclear War
Literature*. Bowling Green, Oh.: Bowling Green State University Popular
Press, 1991.

Anzaldúa, Gloria, ed. *Making Face/Making Soul/Haciendo Caras: Creative and
Critical Perspectives by Women of Color*. San Francisco: Aunt Lute Foundation, 1990.

Argan, Giulio Carlo. "Ideology and Iconology." In *The Language of Images*,
ed. W. J. T. Mitchell, 15–23. Chicago: University of Chicago Press, 1980.

Ashcroft, Bill, Gareth Griffiths, and Helen Tiffin. *The Empire Writes Back:
Theory and Practice in Post-Colonial Literature*. London: Routledge, 1989.

Bakhtin, Mikhail M. *The Dialogic Imagination: Four Essays by Mikhail Bakhtin*. Ed. Michael Holquist, trans. Caryl Emerson and Michael Holquist.
Austin: University of Texas Press, 1981.

Balassi, William, ed. *This Is About Vision: Interviews with Southwestern Writers*.
Albuquerque: University of New Mexico Press, 1989.

Barnett, Louise K. "Alienation and Ritual in *Winter in the Blood.*" *American Indian Quarterly* 4 (Fall 1978): 123–30.

Barnett, Marianne. "Dreamstuff: Erdrich's *Love Medicine.*" *North Dakota Quarterly* 56 (Winter 1988): 82–96.

Barreca, Regina, ed. *New Perspectives on Women and Comedy.* Philadelphia: Gordon and Breach, 1995.

Barry, Nora. "The Bear's Son Folk Tale in *When Legends Die* and *House Made of Dawn.*" *Western American Literature* 12 (Fall 1978): 275–87.

———. "Chance and Ritual: The Gambler in the Texts of Gerald Vizenor." *Studies in American Indian Literatures* 5 (Fall 1993): 13–22.

Barthes, Roland. *The Semiotic Challenge.* Trans. Richard Howard. New York: Hill and Wang, 1988.

Baudrillard, Jean. *Jean Baudrillard: Selected Writings.* Ed. Mark Poster. Stanford, Calif.: Stanford University Press, 1988.

Beck, Peggy V., Anna Lee Walters, and Nia Francisco. *The Sacred: Ways of Knowledge, Sources of Life.* Tsaile, Ariz.: Navajo Community College Press, 1992.

Bell, Robert C. "Circular Design in *Ceremony.*" *American Indian Quarterly* 5 (Winter 1979): 47–62.

Ben-Amos, Dan and Kenneth S. Goldstein, eds. *Folklore: Performance and Communication.* The Hague: Mouton, 1975.

Benjamin, Walter. "The Storyteller: Reflections on the Works of Nikolai Leskov." In *Illuminations.* Ed. Hannah Arendt, trans. Harry Zohn, 83–109. New York: Harcourt, Brace, Jovanovich, 1968.

Berger, John. "Why Look at Animals?" In *About Looking,* 1–26. New York: Pantheon, 1980.

Berlo, Janet Catherine. "Dreaming of Double Woman: The Ambivalent Role of the Female Artist in North American Indian Myth." *American Indian Quarterly* 17 (Winter 1993): 31–43.

Berner, Robert L. "Trying To Be Round: Three American Indian Novels." *World Literature Today* 58 (August 1984): 341–44.

Bevis, Bill. "Dialog with James Welch." *Northwest Review* 20 (Summer/Fall 1982): 163–85.

Bevis, William. "Native American Novels: Homing In." In *Recovering the Word: Essays on Native American Literature,* ed. Brian Swann and Arnold Krupat, 580–620. Berkeley: University of California Press, 1987.

Bird, Gloria. "Searching for Evidence of Colonialism at Work: A Reading of Louise Erdrich's *Tracks.*" *Wicazo Sa Review* 8 (Fall 1992): 40–47.

Blair, Elizabeth. "The Politics of Place in Linda Hogan's *Mean Spirit.*" *Studies in American Indian Literatures* 6 (Fall 1994): 15–21.

Bleich, David. *Readings and Feelings: An Introduction to Subjective Criticism.* Urbana, Ill.: National Council of Teachers of English, 1975.

Blumenthal, Susan. "Spotted Cattle and Deer: Spirit Guides and Symbols of Endurance and Healing in *Ceremony.*" *American Indian Quarterly* 14 (Fall 1990): 367–77.

Boelhower, William. *Through a Glass Darkly: Ethnic Semiosis in American Literature.* New York: Oxford University Press, 1987.

Borges, Jorge Luis. "An Autobiographical Essay." In *The Aleph and Other Stories, 1933–1969*. Ed. and trans. Norman Thomas di Giovanni, 203–60. New York: E. P. Dutton, 1978.

———. "Funes the Memorious." In *Ficciones*. Ed. Anthony Kerrigan, 107–15. New York: Grove Press, 1962.

Bowers, Sharon Manybeads. "Louise Erdrich as Nanapush." In *New Perspectives on Women and Comedy*, ed. Regina Barreca, 135–41. Philadelphia: Gordon and Breach, 1995.

Bredin, Renae. "'Becoming Minor': Reading *The Woman Who Owned the Shadows*." *Studies in American Indian Literatures* 6 (Winter 1994): 36–50.

Brill, Susan B. "When Worlds Collide: Nausea in Virtual and Mythopoeic Worlds." In *Semiotics 1993*, ed. Robert S. Covington and John Deely, 77–89. New York: Peter Lang, 1995.

Bruchac, Joseph. *Survival This Way: Interviews with American Indian Poets*. Tucson: Sun Tracks and University of Arizona Press, 1987.

Buchanan, Scott. *The Doctrine of Signatures: A Defense of Theory in Medicine*. 2nd ed. Ed. Peter P. Maycock, Jr. Urbana: University of Illinois Press, 1991.

Buell, Lawrence. *The Environmental Imagination: Thoreau, Nature Writing, and the Formation of American Culture*. Cambridge, Mass.: Harvard University Press, 1995.

Burnshaw, Stanley. *The Seamless Web*. New York: Braziller, 1970.

Cardinal, Douglas and Jeanette Armstrong. *The Native Creative Process*. Penticton, British Columbia: Theytus, 1991.

Carew-Miller, Anna. "Caretaking and the Work of the Text in Linda Hogan's *Mean Spirit*." *Studies in American Indian Literatures* 6 (Fall 1994): 37–48.

Cassell, Eric. J. *The Nature of Suffering and the Goals of Medicine*. New York: Oxford University Press, 1991.

Chapman, Mary. "'The Belly of This Story': Storytelling and Symbolic Birth in Native American Fiction." *Studies in American Indian Literatures* 7 (Summer 1995): 3–16.

Chopra, Deepak. *Quantum Healing: Exploring the Frontiers of Mind/Body Medicine*. New York: Bantam, 1989.

Clark, Joni Adamson. "Why Bears Are Good to Think and Theory Doesn't Have to Be Murder: Transformation and Oral Tradition in Louise Erdrich's *Tracks*." *Studies in American Indian Literatures* 4 (Spring 1992): 28–48.

Clark, Vévé. "Developing Diaspora Literacy and *Marasa* Consciousness." In *Comparative American Identities: Race, Sex, and Nationality in the Modern Text*, ed. Hortense Spillers, 40–61. New York: Routledge, 1991.

Clifford, James and George E. Marcus, eds. *Writing Culture: The Poetics and Politics of Ethnography*. Berkeley: University of California Press, 1986.

Coltelli, Laura. *Winged Words: American Indian Writers Speak*. Lincoln: University of Nebraska Press, 1990.

Conley, Robert J. *Mountain Windsong: A Novel of the Trail of Tears*. Norman: University of Oklahoma Press, 1992.

Cornell, Daniel. "Woman Looking: Revis(ion)ing Pauline's Subject Position in Louise Erdrich's *Tracks*." *Studies in American Indian Literatures* 4 (Spring 1992): 49–64.

Covington, Robert S. and John Deely, eds. *Semiotics 1993*. New York: Peter Lang, 1995.

Crabtree, Claire. "Salvific Oneness and the Fragmented Self in Louise Erdrich's *Love Medicine*." In *Contemporary Native American Cultural Issues: Proceedings from the Native American Studies Conference at Lake Superior State University, October 16–17, 1987*, ed. Thomas E. Schirer, 49–56. Sault Ste. Marie, Mich.: Lake Superior State University Press, 1988.

Davis, Jack L. "Restoration of Indian Identity in *Winter in the Blood*." In *James Welch*, ed. Ron McFarland, 29–43. Lewiston, N.Y.: Confluence, 1986.

Debo, Angie. *A History of the Indians of the United States*. Norman: University of Oklahoma Press, 1970.

DeKoven, Marianne. *Rich and Strange: Gender, History, Modernism*. Princeton, N.J.: Princeton University Press, 1991.

Deloria, Vine. *Custer Died for Your Sins: An Indian Manifesto*. New York: Avon, 1969.

Derrida, Jacques. *Writing and Difference*. Trans. Alan Bass. London: Routledge and Kegan Paul, 1978.

Donaldson, Laura E. "Noah Meets Old Coyote, or Singing in the Rain: Intertextuality in Thomas King's *Green Grass, Running Water*." *Studies in American Indian Literatures* 7 (Summer 1995): 27–43.

Dossey, Larry. "How Should Alternative Therapies Be Evaluated?" *Alternative Therapies* 1 (May 1995): 6–10, 79–85.

———. "Running Scared: How We Hide from Who We Are." *Alternative Therapies* 3 (March 1997): 8–15.

———. *Space, Time, and Medicine*. Boulder, Colo.: Shambala Press, 1982.

———. "The Trickster: Medicine's Forgotten Character." *Alternative Therapies* 2 (March 1996): 6–14.

———. "What Does Illness Mean?" *Alternative Therapies* 1 (July 1995): 6–10.

———. "What Ever Happened To Healers?" *Alternative Therapies* 1 (November 1995): 6–13.

———. "When Stones Speak: Toward a Reenchantment of the World." *Alternative Therapies* 2 (July 1996): 8–13, 97–103.

Drinnon, Richard. *Facing West: The Metaphysics of Indian Hating and Empire Building*. New York: Schocken Books, 1980.

Eco, Umberto. *The Role of the Reader: Explorations in the Semiotics of Texts*. Bloomington: Indiana University Press, 1979.

———. *Travels in Hyperreality: Essays*. Trans. William Weaver. San Diego, Calif.: Harcourt, Brace, Jovanovich, 1986.

Eichenbaum, Boris. "The Theory of the Formal Method." In *Russian Formalist Criticism: Four Essays*, ed. and trans. Lee T. Lemon and Marion Reis, 99–139. Lincoln: University of Nebraska Press, 1965.

Eisenstein, Paul. "Finding Lost Generations: Recovering Omitted History in *Winter in the Blood*." *MELUS* 19 (Fall 1994): 3–18.

Erdrich, Louise. *The Beet Queen*. Toronto: Bantam, 1986.

———. *The Bingo Palace*. New York: HarperCollins, 1994.

————. *Jacklight: Poems.* New York: Henry Holt, 1984.

————. *Love Medicine.* Toronto: Bantam, 1984.

————. *Tracks.* New York: Henry Holt, 1988.

Evers, Larry. "Cycles of Appreciation." In *Studies in American Indian Literature: Critical Essays and Course Designs,* ed. Paula Gunn Allen, 23–32. New York: Modern Language Association, 1983.

————. "Words and Place: A Reading of *House Made of Dawn.*" *Western American Literature* 11 (Winter 1977): 297–320.

Fiesta, Melissa J. "Solving Mysteries of Culture and Self: Anita and Naspah in Anna Lee Walters' *Ghost Singer.*" *American Indian Quarterly* 17 (Summer 1993): 370–78.

Fischer, Michael J. "Ethnicity and the Post-Modern Arts of Memory." In *Writing Culture: The Poetics and Politics of Ethnography,* ed. James Clifford and George E. Marcus, 194–233. Berkeley: University of California Press, 1986.

Flavin, James. "The Novel as Performance: Communication in Louise Erdrich's *Tracks.*" *Studies in American Indian Literature* 3 (Summer 1991): 1–12.

Fleck, Richard F. *Critical Perspectives on Native American Fiction.* 2nd ed. Boulder, Colo.: Passeggieta Press, 1997.

————. "Sacred Land in the Writings of Momaday, Welch and Silko." In *Contemporary Native American Cultural Issues: Proceedings from the Native American Studies Conference at Lake Superior State University, October 16–17, 1987,* ed. Thomas E. Schirer, 125–33. Sault Ste. Marie, Mich.: Lake Superior State University Press, 1988.

Foucault, Michel. *Birth of the Clinic: An Archaeology of Medical Perception.* New York: Vintage, 1973.

————. *The Order of Things: An Archaeology of the Human Sciences.* New York: Pantheon, 1971.

————. "What Is an Author?" In *Language, Counter-Memory, Practice: Selected Essays and Interviews,* ed. Donald F. Bouchard, 113–38. Ithaca, N.Y,: Cornell University Press, 1977.

Frankl, Victor E. *The Doctor and the Soul: From Psychotherapy to Logotherapy.* New York: Knopf, 1955.

————. *The Will to Meaning: Foundations and Applications of Logotherapy.* New York: Plume, 1969.

Freeman, Walter J. *Societies of Brains: A Study in the Neuroscience of Love and Hate.* Hillsdale, N.J.: Lawrence Erlbaum, 1995.

Friedman, Susan Stanford. "Identity Politics, Syncretism, Catholicism and Anishinabe Religion in Louise Erdrich's *Tracks.*" *Religion and Literature* 26 (March 1994): 107–33.

Gallop, Jane. *Around 1981.* New York: Routledge, 1992.

García, Reyes. "Senses of Place in *Ceremony.*" *MELUS* 10 (Winter 1983): 37–48.

Gardner, Martin. *Order and Surprise.* Buffalo, N.Y.: Prometheus Books, 1983.

Giovanni, A., F. Mancini, and M. Marinaro, eds. *Problems in Theoretical Physics.* Salerno: University of Salerno Press, 1984.

Givens, Bettye. "A *MELUS* Interview: N. Scott Momaday—A Slant of Light." *MELUS* 12 (Spring 1985): 79–87.

Goffman, Erving. *Frame Analysis: An Essay on the Organization of Experience.* Cambridge, Mass.: Harvard University Press, 1974.

Gombrich, E. H. *Art and Illusion: A Study in the Psychology of Pictorial Representation.* Princeton, N.J.: Princeton University Press, 1960.

Gonzales, Irene. "Textual Stimulation: Gerald Vizenor's Use of Law in Advocacy Literature." *Studies in American Indian Literatures* 5 (Fall 1993): 31–42.

Grant, Agnes, ed. *Our Bit of Truth: An Anthology of Canadian Native Literature.* Winnipeg: Pemmican, 1990.

Hammerschlag, Carl A. *The Dancing Healers: A Doctor's Journey of Healing with Native Americans.* San Francisco: Harper and Row, 1988.

Harvey, Valerie. "Navajo Sandpainting in *Ceremony.*" In *Critical Perspectives on Native American Fiction,* ed. Richard F. Fleck, 256–59. 2nd ed. Boulder, Colo.: Passeggieta Press, 1997.

Hassrick, Royal B. *The Sioux: Life and Customs of a Warrior Society.* Norman: University of Oklahoma Press, 1964.

Hauss, Jon. "Real Stories: Memory, Violence, and Enjoyment in Gerald Vizenor's *Bearheart.*" *Literature and Psychology* 41 (Winter 1995): 1–16.

Hernández-Ávila, Inés. "Mediations of the Spirit: Native American Religious Traditions and the Ethics of Representation." *American Indian Quarterly* 20 (Summer/Fall 1996): 329–52.

———. "Relocations upon Relocations: Home, Language, and Native American Women's Writings." *American Indian Quarterly* 19 (Fall 1995): 491–507.

Hessler, Michelle R. "Catholic Nuns and Ojibwa Shamans: Pauline and Fleur in Louise Erdrich's *Tracks.*" *Wicazo Sa Review* 11 (Spring 1995): 40–45.

Hirsch, Bernard A. " 'The Telling Which Continues': Oral Tradition and the Written Word in Leslie Marmon Silko's *Storyteller.*" *American Indian Quarterly* 12 (Winter 1988): 1–26.

Hobbs, Michael. "Living In-Between: Tayo as Radical Reader in Leslie Marmon Silko's *Ceremony.*" *Western American Literature* 28 (Winter 1994): 301–12.

Hodge, Robert. *Literature as Discourse: Textual Strategies in English and History.* Baltimore: Johns Hopkins University Press, 1990.

Hodge, Robert and Gunther Kress. *Social Semiotics.* Ithaca, N.Y.: Cornell University Press, 1988.

Hogan, Linda. *Mean Spirit.* New York: Ivy Books, 1990.

———. "Who Puts Together." In *Studies in American Indian Literature: Critical Essays and Course Designs,* ed. Paula Gunn Allen, 169–77. New York: Modern Language Association, 1983.

Holford, Vanessa. "Re-Membering Ephanie: A Woman's Re-Creation of Self in Paula Gunn Allen's *The Woman Who Owned the Shadows.*" *Studies in American Indian Literatures* 6 (Spring 1994): 99–113.

Holland, Norman N. *5 Readers Reading.* New Haven, Conn.: Yale University Press, 1975.

Hollowell, A. Irving. "Bear Ceremonialism in the Northern Hemisphere." *American Anthropologist* 28 (March 1926): 1–175.

Horton, Andrew. "The Bitter Humor of *Winter in the Blood.*" *American Indian Quarterly* 4 (Spring 1978): 131–39.

Hymes, Dell. "Breakthrough into Performance." In *Folklore: Performance and Communication*, ed. Dan Ben-Amos and Kenneth S. Goldstein, 11–74. The Hague: Mouton, 1975.

———. "Discovering Oral Performance and Measured Verse in American Indian Narrative." *New Literary History* 8 (Spring 1977): 431–57.

Irwin, Lee. "Dreams, Theory, and Culture: The Plains Vision Quest Paradigm." *American Indian Quarterly* 18 (Spring 1994): 229–45.

———. "Themes in Native American Spirituality." *American Indian Quarterly* 20 (Summer/Fall 1996): 309–26.

Jahner, Elaine. "An Act of Attention: Event Structure in *Ceremony.*" *American Indian Quarterly* 5 (Winter 1979): 37–46.

———. "Allies in the Word Wars: Vizenor's Uses of Contemporary Critical Theory." *Studies in American Indian Literatures* 9 (Summer 1985): 64–69.

———. "Indian Literature and Critical Responsibility." *Studies in American Indian Literatures* 5 (Summer 1993): 7–12.

———. "Metalanguages." In *Narrative Chance: Postmodern Discourse on Native American Indian Literatures*, ed. Gerald Vizenor, 155–85. Albuquerque: University of New Mexico Press, 1989.

Jaskoski, Helen. "Thinking Woman's Children and the Bomb." In *The Nightmare Considered: Critical Essays on Nuclear War Literature*, ed. Nancy Anisfield, 159–76. Bowling Green, Oh.: Bowling Green State University Popular Press, 1991.

Johnson, Willard. "Contemporary Native American Prophecy in Historical Perspective." *Journal of the American Academy of Religion* 64 (September 1996): 575–612.

Johnston, Basil. *Ojibway Ceremonies.* Lincoln: University of Nebraska Press, 1982.

King, Thomas. *Green Grass, Running Water.* Toronto: HarperCollins, 1993.

———. *One Good Story, That One.* Toronto: HarperCollins, 1993.

Kleinman, Arthur. *The Illness Narratives: Suffering, Healing, and the Human Condition.* New York: Basic Books, 1988.

Krupat, Arnold. "An Approach to Native American Texts." *Critical Inquiry* 9 (March 1982): 323–28.

———. *Ethnocriticism: Ethnography, History, Literature.* Berkeley: University of California Press, 1990.

———. "Identity and Difference in the Criticism of Native American Literature." *Diacritics* 13 (Summer 1983): 2–13.

———. "Post-Structuralism and Oral Literature." In *Recovering the Word: Essays on Native American Literature*, ed. Brian Swann and Arnold Krupat, 113–28. Berkeley: University of California Press, 1987.

Kunitz, Stephen J. *Disease, Change, and the Role of Medicine: The Navajo Experience.* Berkeley: University of California Press, 1983.

Laga, Barry. "Gerald Vizenor and His *Heirs of Columbus.*" *American Indian Quarterly* 18 (Winter 1994): 71–86.

LaLonde, Chris. "The Ceded Landscape of Gerald Vizenor's Fiction." *Studies in American Indian Literatures* 9 (Spring 1997): 16–32.

Lame Deer, John (Fire) and Richard Erdoes. *Lame Deer: Seeker of Visions: The Life of a Sioux Medicine Man.* New York: Touchstone, 1972.

Lawlis, G. Frank. "Storytelling as Therapy: Implications for Medicine." *Alternative Therapies* 1 (May 1995): 40–45.

Lee, Benjamin and Greg Urban, eds. *Sign, Self, and Society.* Berlin: Mouton de Gruyter, 1989.

Lemon, Lee T. and Marion Reis, eds. and trans. *Russian Formalist Criticism: Four Essays.* Lincoln: University of Nebraska Press, 1965.

Levy, Jerrold E. "Traditional Navajo Health Beliefs and Practices." In *Disease, Change, and the Role of Medicine: The Navajo Experience,* ed. Stephen J. Kunitz, 118–45. Berkeley: University of California Press, 1983.

Lincoln, Kenneth. *Native American Renaissance.* Berkeley: University of California Press, 1983.

Linton, Patricia. "The 'Person' in Postmodern Fiction: Gibson, LeGuin, and Vizenor." *Studies in American Indian Literatures* 5 (Fall 1993): 3–11.

Locke, Raymond Friday. *The Book of the Navajo.* Los Angeles: Mankind, 1992.

Lucas, Phil. *The Native Americans: The Tribal People of the Northwest.* TBS Productions, Inc. Atlanta: Turner Home Entertainment, 1994.

Lutz, Hartmut. *Contemporary Challenges: Conversations with Canadian Native Authors.* Saskatoon: Fifth House, 1991.

Lynch, James J. *The Language of the Heart: The Body's Response to Human Dialogue.* New York: Basic Books, 1995.

Mails, Thomas E. *The Mystic Warriors of the Plains: The Culture, Arts, Crafts and Religion of the Plains Indians.* New York: Mallard, 1972.

Manley, Kathleen. "Leslie Marmon Silko's Use of Color in *Ceremony.*" *Southern Folklore* 46, 2 (1989): 133–46.

Martin, Wallace. *Recent Theories of Narrative.* Ithaca, N.Y.: Cornell University Press, 1986.

Matchie, Thomas. "*Love Medicine*: A Female *Moby-Dick.*" *Mississippi Quarterly* 30 (Fall 1989): 478–91.

Matthews, Washington. "The Stricken Twins." In *The Night Chant, A Navajo Ceremonial,* 212–65. New York: American Museum of Natural History 1902, 1978.

Mayhall, Mildred P. *The Kiowas.* Norman: University of Oklahoma Press, 1971.

McFarland, Ron. "'The End' in James Welch's Novels." *American Indian Quarterly* 17 (Summer 1993): 319–28.

———, ed. *James Welch.* Lewiston, N.Y.: Confluence, 1986.

McKay, Eva. "We Are Here." In *Our Bit of Truth: An Anthology of Canadian Native Literature,* ed. Agnes Grant, 345–47. Winnipeg: Pemmican, 1990.

Minh-ha, Trinh T. "Not You/Like You: Post-Colonial Women and the Interlocking Questions of Identity and Difference." In *Making Face/Making Soul/Haciendo Caras: Creative and Critical Perspectives by Women of Color,* ed. Gloria Anzaldúa, 371–75. San Francisco, Calif.: Aunt Lute Foundation, 1990.

Mitchell, Carol. "*Ceremony* as Ritual." *American Indian Quarterly* 5 (Winter 1979): 27–35.

Mitchell, W. J. T. *Iconology: Image, Text, Ideology*. Chicago: University of Chicago Press, 1986.

———. *The Language of Images*. Chicago: University of Chicago Press, 1980.

Momaday, N. Scott. *The Ancient Child*. New York: Harper, 1989.

———. *House Made of Dawn*. New York: Harper and Row, 1968.

———. "The Man Made of Words." In *Indian Voices: The First Convocation of American Indian Scholars*, 49–62. San Francisco: Indian Historian Press, 1970.

———. *The Names: A Memoir*. Tucson: University of Arizona Press, 1976.

Mooney, James. *Calendar History of the Kiowa Indians*. Washington, D.C.: Smithsonian Institution Press, 1979.

Moore, Nancy G. "A Review of Alternative Medicine Courses Taught at U.S. Medical Schools." *Alternative Therapies* 4 (May 1998): 90–101.

Murray, Laura. " 'Pray Sir, Consider a Little': Rituals of Subordination and Strategies of Resistance in the Letters of Hezekiah Calvin and David Fowler to Eleazar Wheelock, 1764–1768." *Studies in American Indian Literatures* 4 (Summer/Fall 1992): 48–74.

Musher, Andrea. "Showdown at Sorrow Cave: Bat Medicine and the Spirit of Resistance in *Mean Spirit*." *Studies in American Indian Literatures* 6 (Fall 1994): 23–36.

Nagai-Jacobson, Mary Gail and Margaret A. Burkhardt. "Viewing Persons as Stories: A Perspective for Holistic Care." *Alternative Therapies* 2 (July 1996): 54–58.

Nelson, Robert M. *Place and Vision: The Function of Landscape in Native American Fiction*. New York: Peter Lang, 1995.

———. "Snake and Eagle: Abel's Disease and the Landscape of *House Made of Dawn*." *Studies in American Indian Literatures* 1 (Summer 1989): 1–20.

Norden, Christopher. "Ecological Restoration as Post-Colonial Ritual of Community in Three Native American Novels." *Studies in American Indian Literatures* 6 (Winter 1994): 94–106.

Norris, Christopher. *Derrida*. Cambridge, Mass.: Harvard University Press, 1987.

———. *What's Wrong with Postmodernism: Critical Theory and the Ends of Philosophy*. Baltimore: Johns Hopkins University Press, 1990.

Orlandini, Roberta. "Variations on a Theme: Tradition and Temporal Structure in the Novels of James Welch." *South Dakota Review* 26 (Fall 1988): 37–52.

Ortiz, Alfonso, ed. *Handbook of North American Indians*. Vol. 10, *Southwest*. Washington, D.C.: Smithsonian Institution Press, 1983.

Owens, Louis. " 'Ecstatic Strategies': Gerald Vizenor's *Darkness in St. Louis Bearheart*." In *Narrative Chance: Postmodern Discourse on Native American Indian Literatures*, ed. Gerald Vizenor, 141–53. Albuquerque: University of New Mexico Press, 1989.

———. "Introduction." *Studies in American Indian Literatures* 9 (Spring 1997): 1–2.

———. "N. Scott Momaday." In *This Is About Vision: Interviews with South-*

western Writers, ed. William Balassi, 141–53. Albuquerque: University of New Mexico Press, 1989.

——. *Other Destinies: Understanding the American Indian Novel.* Norman: University of Oklahoma Press, 1992.

Palumbo-Liu, David, ed. *The Ethnic Canon: Histories, Institutions, and Interventions.* Minneapolis: University of Minnesota Press, 1995.

Panofsky, Erwin. *Meaning in the Visual Arts: Papers in and on Art History.* Garden City, N.Y.: Doubleday Anchor, 1955.

Parsons, Elsie Clews. *Pueblo Indian Religion.* 2 vols. Chicago: University of Chicago Press, 1939.

Percy, Walker. *The Message in the Bottle: How Queer Man Is, How Queer Language Is, and What One Has To Do With the Other.* New York: Farrar, Straus and Giroux, 1975.

Pérez-Castillo, Susan. "Postmodernism, Native American Literature and the Real: The Silko-Erdrich Controversy." *Massachusetts Review* 32 (Summer 1991): 285–94.

Perrone, Bobette, H. Henrietta Stockel, and Victoria Krueger. *Medicine Women, "Curanderas," and Women Doctors.* Norman: University of Oklahoma Press, 1989.

Peterson, Nancy J. "History, Postmodernism, and Louise Erdrich's *Tracks.*" *PMLA* 109 (October 1994): 982–94.

Pittman, Barbara L. "Cross-Cultural Reading and Generic Transformation: The Chronotope of the Road in Erdrich's *Love Medicine.*" *American Literature* 67 (December 1995): 777–92.

Purdy, John. "*Bha'a* and The Death of Jim Loney." *Studies in American Indian Literatures* 5 (Summer 1993): 67–71.

——. " 'He Was Going Along': Motion in the Novels of James Welch." *American Indian Quarterly* 14 (Spring 1990): 133–45.

Rabinowitz, Peter J. *Before Reading: Narrative Conventions and the Politics of Interpretation.* Ithaca, N.Y.: Cornell University Press, 1987.

Rainwater, Catherine. "Reading Between Worlds: Narrativity in the Fiction of Louise Erdrich." *American Literature* 62 (September 1990): 405–22.

——. "The Semiotics of Dwelling in Leslie Marmon Silko's *Ceremony.*" *American Journal of Semiotics* 9, 3 (1992): 219–40.

Reichard, Gladys A. *Navaho Religion: A Study of Symbolism.* Princeton, N.J.: Princeton University Press, 1950.

Revard, Carter. "Traditional Osage Naming Ceremonies: Entering the Circle of Being." In *Recovering the Word: Essays on Native American Literature,* ed. Brian Swann and Arnold Krupat, 446–66. Berkeley: University of California Press, 1987.

Ricoeur, Paul. "Life in Quest of Narrative." In *On Paul Ricoeur: Narrative and Interpretation,* ed. David Wood, 20–33. London: Routledge, 1991.

——. *Time and Narrative.* Vol. 1. Trans. Kathleen McLaughlin and David Pellauer. Chicago: University of Chicago Press, 1984.

——. *Time and Narrative.* Vol. 2. Trans. Kathleen McLaughlin and David Pellauer. Chicago: University of Chicago Press, 1985.

——. *Time and Narrative.* Vol. 3. Trans. Kathleen Blamey and David Pellauer. Chicago: University of Chicago Press, 1988.

Riffaterre, Michael. *Fictional Truth.* Baltimore: Johns Hopkins University Press, 1990.

———. *Text Production.* Trans. Terese Lyons. New York: Columbia University Press, 1983.

Riley In-The-Woods, Patricia. "*The Death of Jim Loney*: A Ritual of Re-Creation." *Fiction International* 20 (Fall 1991): 157–66.

Rock Point Community School. *Between Sacred Mountains: Navajo Stories and Lessons from the Land,* ed. Sam and Janet Bingham. Tucson: Sun Tracks and University of Arizona Press, 1982.

Rodríguez, Juana María. "Gerald Vizenor's Shadow Plays: Narrative Mediations and Multiplicities of Power." *Studies in American Indian Literatures* 5 (Fall 1993): 23–30.

Roemer, Kenneth M. "Contemporary American Indian Literature: The Centrality of Canons on the Margins." *American Literary History* 6 (Fall 1994): 583–99.

———. "Ancient Children at Play—Lyric, Petroglyphic, and Ceremonial." In *Critical Perspectives on Native American Fiction,* 2nd ed., ed. Richard F. Fleck, 99–113. Boulder, Colo.: Passeggieta Press, 1997.

Roscoe, Will. *The Zuni Man-Woman.* Albuquerque: University of New Mexico Press, 1991.

Ruoff, A. Lavonne Brown. "Gerald Vizenor: Compassionate Trickster." *Studies in American Indian Literatures* 5 (Summer 1993): 39–45.

Ruppert, James. *Mediation in Contemporary Native American Fiction.* Norman: University of Oklahoma Press, 1995.

Ruppert, Jim. "The Reader's Lessons in *Ceremony*." *Arizona Quarterly* 44 (Spring 1988): 78–85.

———. "Story Telling: The Fiction of Leslie Silko." *Journal of Ethnic Studies* 9 (Spring 1981): 53–58.

Sacks, Oliver. *An Anthropologist on Mars: Seven Paradoxical Tales.* New York: Knopf, 1995.

———. *Seeing Voices: A Journey into the World of the Deaf.* Berkeley: University of California Press, 1989.

St. Andrews, B. A. "Healing the Witchery: Medicine in Silko's *Ceremony*." *Arizona Quarterly* 44 (Spring 1988): 86–94.

St. Clair, Janet. "Uneasy Ethnocentrism: Recent Works of Allen, Silko, and Hogan." *Studies in American Indian Literatures* 6 (Spring 1994): 83–98.

Sands, Kathleen Mullen. "Alienation and Broken Narrative in *Winter in the Blood*." *American Indian Quarterly* 4 (Spring 1978): 97–105.

———. "Closing the Distance: Critic, Reader and the Works of James Welch." *MELUS* 14 (Summer 1987): 73–85.

———. "The Death of Jim Loney: Indian or Not?" *Studies in American Indian Literatures* 7 (Spring 1980): 61–78.

Sarvé-Gorham, Kristan. "Power Lines: The Motif of Twins and the Medicine Women of *Tracks* and *Love Medicine*." *Bucknell Review* 39 (Spring 1995): 167–90.

Scarberry, Susan J. "Memory as Medicine: The Power of Recollection in *Ceremony*." *American Indian Quarterly* 5 (Winter 1979): 19–26.

Scarberry-García, Susan. *Landmarks of Healing: A Study of House Made of Dawn.* Albuquerque: University of New Mexico Press, 1990.

Scheick, William J. "Grace and Gall." *Canadian Literature* 138 (Autumn 1993): 155–56.

———. *The Half-Blood: A Cultural Symbol in 19th Century American Fiction.* Lexington: University Press of Kentucky, 1979.

Schein, Marie M. "Alienation and Art in *The Ancient Child.*" *Studies in American Indian Literatures* 2 (Winter 1990): 11–14.

Schirer, Thomas E., ed. *Contemporary Native American Cultural Issues: Proceedings from the Native American Studies Conference at Lake Superior State University, October 16–17, 1987.* Sault Ste. Marie, Mich.: Lake Superior State University Press, 1988.

Scholes, Robert. *Protocols of Reading.* New Haven, Conn.: Yale University Press, 1989.

———. *Semiotics and Interpretation.* New Haven, Conn: Yale University Press, 1982.

Schubnell, Matthias. "Locke Setman, Emil Nolde and the Search for Expression in N. Scott Momaday's *The Ancient Child.*" *American Indian Quarterly* 18 (Fall 1994): 469–80.

———. *N. Scott Momaday: The Cultural and Literary Background.* Norman: University of Oklahoma Press, 1985.

Sebeok, Thomas A. *American Signatures: Semiotic Inquiry and Method.* Norman: University of Oklahoma Press, 1991.

———. "The Semiotic Self Revisited." In *Sign, Self, and Society,* ed. Benjamin Lee and Greg Urban, v–xiv. Berlin: Mouton de Gruyter, 1989.

———. *The Sign and Its Masters.* 2nd ed. Lanham, Md.: University Press of America, 1989.

Selzer, Richard. *Mortal Lessons: Notes on the Art of Surgery.* New York: Touchstone, 1974.

———. *Taking the World in for Repairs.* New York: William Morrow, 1986.

Sequoya-Magdaleno, Jana. "Telling the *Différance*: Representations of Identity in the Discourse of Indianness." In *The Ethnic Canon: Histories, Institutions, and Interventions,* ed. David Palumbo-Liu, 88–116. Minneapolis: University of Minnesota Press, 1995.

Sergi, Jennifer. "Storytelling: Tradition and Preservation in Louise Erdrich's *Tracks.*" *World Literature Today* 66 (May 1992): 279–82.

Sheldon, Mary F. "Reaching For a Universal Audience: The Artistry of Leslie Marmon Silko and James Welch." In *Contemporary Native American Cultural Issues: Proceedings from the Native American Studies Conference at Lake Superior State University, October 16–17, 1987,* ed. Thomas E. Schirer, 114–24. Sault Ste. Marie, Mich.: Lake Superior State University Press, 1988.

Shepard, Paul. *Thinking Animals: Animals and the Development of Human Intelligence.* New York: Viking, 1978.

Shepard, Paul and Barry Sanders. *The Sacred Paw: The Bear in Nature, Myth, and Literature.* New York: Viking, 1985.

Sigerist, Henry E. *A History of Medicine: Primitive and Archaic Medicine.* New York: Oxford University Press, 1951.

Silko, Leslie Marmon. *Almanac of the Dead.* New York: Simon and Schuster, 1991.

———. *Ceremony.* New York: Penguin, 1977.

———. "Landscape, History, and the Pueblo Imagination." *Antaeus* 57 (Autumn 1986): 83–94.

———. *Storyteller.* New York: Arcade, 1981.

———. *Yellow Woman and a Beauty of the Spirit: Essays on Native American Life Today.* New York: Touchstone, 1996.

Silverman, Kaja. *The Subject of Semiotics.* New York: Oxford University Press, 1983.

Smith, Jeanne. "Transpersonal Selfhood: The Boundaries of Identity in Louise Erdrich's *Love Medicine.*" *Studies in American Indian Literatures* 3 (Winter 1991): 13–26.

Smith, Jeanne Rosier. *Writing Tricksters: Mythic Gambols in American Ethnic Literature.* Berkeley: University of California Press, 1997.

Soffa, Virginia M. "Artistic Expressions of Illness." *Alternative Therapies* 2 (May 1996): 63–66.

Sollors, Werner. "Introduction: The Invention of Ethnicity." In *The Invention of Ethnicity,* ed. Werner Sollors, ix–xx. New York: Oxford University Press, 1989.

Spencer, Katherine. *Mythology and Values: An Analysis of Navaho Chantway Myths.* Philadelphia: Memoirs of the American Folklore Society, 1957.

Spillers, Hortense, ed. *Comparative American Identities: Race, Sex, and Nationality in the Modern Text.* New York: Routledge, 1991.

Spivak, Gayatri Chakravorty. "Imperialism and Sexual Difference." *Oxford Literary Review* 8 (1986): 225–48.

———. *In Other Worlds: Essays in Cultural Politics.* New York: Methuen, 1987.

Stevenson, Winona. "Suppressive Narrator and Multiple Narratees in Gerald Vizenor's 'Thomas White Hawk.'" *Studies in American Indian Literatures* 5 (Fall 1993): 36–42.

Swan, Edith. "Healing Via the Sunrise Cycle in Silko's *Ceremony.*" *American Indian Quarterly* 12 (Fall 1988): 313–28.

———. "Laguna Symbolic Geography and Silko's *Ceremony.*" *American Indian Quarterly* 12 (Summer 1988): 229–49.

Swann, Brian and Arnold Krupat, eds. *Recovering the Word: Essays on Native American Literature.* Berkeley: University of California Press, 1987.

Tardieu, Betty. "Communion in James Welch's *Winter in the Blood.*" *Studies in American Indian Literatures* 5 (Winter 1993): 69–80.

Tedlock, Dennis and Barbara Tedlock, eds. *Teachings from the American Earth: Indian Religion and Philosophy.* New York: Liveright, 1975.

Todorov, Tzvetan. *The Conquest of America: The Question of the Other.* Trans. Richard Howard. New York: Harper Torchbooks, 1984.

Tompkins, Jane. *Sensational Designs: The Cultural Work of American Fiction, 1790–1860.* New York: Oxford, 1985.

Turner, Frederick. *Spirit of Place: The Making of an American Literary Landscape.* San Francisco: Sierra Club, 1989.

Turner, Victor. *The Anthropology of Performance.* New York: Division of the Performing Arts Journal, Inc., 1988.

Tyler, Hamilton A. *Pueblo Animals and Myths.* Norman: University of Oklahoma Press, 1975.

Van Dyke, Annette. "Questions of the Spirit: Bloodlines in Louise Erdrich's Chippewa Landscape." *Studies in American Indian Literatures* 4 (Spring 1992): 15–27.

Velie, Alan, ed. *American Indian Literature: An Anthology.* Norman: University of Oklahoma Press, 1992.

————. *Four American Indian Literary Masters: N. Scott Momaday, James Welch, Leslie Marmon Silko, Gerald Vizenor.* Norman: University of Oklahoma Press, 1982.

Vizenor, Gerald. *Bearheart: The Heirship Chronicles.* Minneapolis: University of Minnesota Press, 1990.

————. *Darkness in St. Louis Bearheart.* Saint Paul: Truck Press, 1978.

————. "Introduction." *Native American Literature: A Brief Introduction and Anthology,* ed. Vizenor, 1–15. New York: HarperCollins, 1995.

————. *Landfill Meditation: Crossblood Stories.* Hanover, N.H.: University Press of New England, 1991.

————, ed. *Narrative Chance: Postmodern Discourse on Native American Indian Literatures.* Albuquerque: University of New Mexico Press, 1989.

————. "A Postmodern Introduction." In *Narrative Chance: Postmodern Discourse on Native American Indian Literatures,* ed.Vizenor, 3–16. Albuquerque: University of New Mexico Press, 1989.

————. "Trickster Discourse: Comic Holotropes and Language Games." In *Narrative Chance: Postmodern Discourse on Native American Indian Literatures,* ed. Vizenor, 187–211. Albuquerque: University of New Mexico Press, 1989.

Walker, Victoria. "A Note on Perspective in *Tracks." Studies in American Indian Literatures* 3 (Winter 1991): 37–40.

Walters, Anna Lee. *Ghost Singer.* Flagstaff, Ariz.: Northland Press, 1988.

Weil, Andrew. *Health and Healing.* Boston: Houghton Mifflin, 1988.

Weinstein, Arnold. *Fictions of the Self, 1550–1800.* Princeton, N.J.: Princeton University Press, 1981.

Welch, James. *The Death of Jim Loney.* New York: Penguin, 1979.

————. *Winter in the Blood.* New York: Penguin, 1974.

Westrum, Dexter. "Transcendental Survival: The Way the Bird Works in *The Death of Jim Loney."* In *James Welch,* ed. Ron McFarland, 139–46. Lewiston, New York: Confluence, 1986.

Wheeler, John Archibald. "Bits, Quanta, Meaning." In *Problems in Theoretical Physics,* ed. A. Giovanni, F. Mancini, and M. Marinaro, 121–41. Salerno: University of Salerno Press, 1984.

Wheelwright, Philip. *The Burning Fountain: A Study in the Language of Symbolism.* Bloomington: Indiana University Press, 1968.

White, Hayden. *The Content of the Form: Narrative Discourse and Historical Representation.* Baltimore: Johns Hopkins University Press, 1987.

Whyte, Launcelot. *The Unconscious Before Freud.* New York: Basic Books, 1960.

Wiget, Andrew. *"American Indian Literature: An Anthology," Studies in American Indian Literatures* 4 (Summer/Fall 1992): 215–18.

———. "Telling the Tale: A Performance Analysis of a Hopi Coyote Story." In *Recovering the Word: Essays on Native American Literature*, ed. Brian Swann and Arnold Krupat, 297–387. Berkeley: University of California Press, 1987.

Wood, David. "Introduction: Interpreting Narrative." In *On Paul Ricoeur: Narrative and Interpretation*, ed. David Wood, 1–19. London: Routledge, 1991.

Woodard, Charles L. *Ancestral Voice: Conversations with N. Scott Momaday*. Lincoln: University of Nebraska Press, 1989.

Wyman, Leland C. *The Mountainway of the Navajo*. Tucson: University of Arizona Press, 1975.

———. "Navajo Ceremonial System." In *Handbook of North American Indians*, vol. 10, *Southwest*, ed. Alfonso Ortiz, 536–57. Washington, D.C.: Smithsonian Institution Press, 1983.

———. *Red Antway of the Navajo*. Santa Fe, N.M.: Museum of Navajo Ceremonial Art, 1973.

———. *Southwest Indian Drypainting*. Albuquerque: University of New Mexico Press, 1983.

Index

Acknowledgments

I am grateful to St. Edward's University in Austin, Texas, for granting me sabbatical leave in the spring of 1997 to complete this study, as well as for supporting travel to numerous conferences, where I benefited from presenting portions of this work at meetings of the Northeastern Modern Language Association, April 4, 1997, in Philadelphia, Pennsylvania; the Southern Chapter of the Modern Language Association, November 1, 1996, in San Antonio, Texas; the American Literature Association, May 27, 1995, in Baltimore, Maryland, and October 1, 1993, in San Antonio, Texas; and the Semiotic Society of America, October 25, 1991, in College Park, Maryland.

Also encouraging in the earliest stage of my project were being invited to speak on Louise Erdrich in the Fall Humanities Series at the Johns Hopkins Medical Institutions, November 15, 1989, in Baltimore, Maryland, and receiving the Norman Foerster Prize in 1990 from the Modern Language Association for my article (cited in the next paragraph) on Erdrich in *American Literature.*

Brief portions of this study have appeared in different form in the following publications: "Reading between Worlds: Narrativity in the Fiction of Louise Erdrich," *American Literature* 62 (September 1990): 405–22; "The Semiotics of Dwelling in Leslie Marmon Silko's *Ceremony,*" *American Journal of Semiotics* 9 (1992): 219–40; and "Planes, Lines, Shapes, and Shadows: N. Scott Momaday's Iconological Imagination," *Texas Studies in Literature and Language* 37 (Winter 1995): 376–93.

Special appreciation goes to William J. Scheick (J. R. Millikan Centennial Professor of Literature, University of Texas at Austin), always my best critic, loyal supporter, and truest friend. And finally, I would like to thank Jerome E. Singerman, Humanities Editor at the University of Pennsylvania Press, for his gracious assistance with my project.